For Beth + Aidan —

Hope you enjoy the read,
especially Ch. 8!
It's been awesome being
on the Commandos together.

John Fox

The Ball

HARPER **PERENNIAL**

NEW YORK • LONDON • TORONTO • SYDNEY • NEW DELHI • AUCKLAND

The Ball

Discovering the Object
of the Game

John Fox

HARPER ● PERENNIAL

P.S.™ is a trademark of HarperCollins Publishers.

THE BALL. Copyright © 2012 by John Fox. All rights reserved. Printed in the United States of America. No part of this book may be used or reproduced in any manner whatsoever without written permission except in the case of brief quotations embodied in critical articles and reviews. For information, address HarperCollins Publishers, 10 East 53rd Street, New York, NY 10022.

HarperCollins books may be purchased for educational, business, or sales promotional use. For information, please write: Special Markets Department, HarperCollins Publishers, 10 East 53rd Street, New York, NY 10022.

FIRST EDITION

Designed by William Ruoto

Library of Congress Cataloging-in-Publication Data is available upon request.

ISBN 978-0-06-188179-4

12 13 14 15 16   OV/RRD   10 9 8 7 6 5 4 3

For Stephanie,

Amelia,

and Aidan.

For everything.

Contents

WARM-UP

There are few activities that feel as frivolous, and as deeply satisfying, as a good game of catch. There's no score to keep, no winners or losers, no rules. In its purest form catch needs no coaches, leagues, boot camps, clinics, or away games that oblige you to drive your kid for hours across state lines: catch is pre-regulation, pre-industrial, and, almost certainly, prehistoric.

On one of those early June days in the mountains of Vermont, when the grass, still wet from the snow melt, seems to thicken behind you as you run, my seven-year-old son Aidan and I were locked in a timeless, quiet rhythm—the only sound being the repeated *thwap* of ball against glove. Here, on the remote tribal boundaries of Red Sox Nation, baseball was undeniably in the air.

"Dad," asked Aidan, breaking the flow and puncturing the silence. "Why do we play ball, anyway?"

I could tell immediately that this sudden inquiry wasn't one of those random toss-off questions Aidan, like other kids his age, tended to ask on a regular basis—"What are eyebrows for?" "Is there any chance we're Navajo?" "Do we know any cannibals?"

No, it struck me that this was downright existential. The kind of reflection that arises when one detaches from a scene and looks back in, like an alien discovering a foreign world. With such an altered perspective, the things we do every day, so naturally and without so much as a fleeting thought—things as fundamental as playing ball—can suddenly seem exotic and delightfully inexplicable. Almost absurd, really.

After a weighty pause in the action, we started playing again, now awkwardly self-conscious. We'd been throwing a small sphere of cork, yarn, and cowhide back and forth for the past hour for no easily explained reason.

"Good question!" was all I could muster in response, and I meant it sincerely, though I suspect it sounded lame and dismissive. He moved on, as kids do, to more tangible concerns: what we were having for dinner and whether his friend could stay the night.

I, on the other hand, couldn't let the question go quite so easily.

Why *do* we play ball? As I turned it over in my mind in the days and weeks that followed, this basic question split into many more: How long has this love affair been going on? When and where and how did the games we play today first get started? How did something as inessential as chasing a ball around evolve into a $500 billion global industry? How,

I asked myself, did the ball come to stake an unrivaled claim on our money, our time, and our lives?

The truth is I was naturally inclined and prepared to go deep on a question that most fathers would have shrugged off or turned into a cozy aphorism: *"Well, son, playing ball teaches us how to win, but more importantly, how to lose. . . ."* You could say that I took up this particular ball and ran with it because I'd been training for the moment for years.

The son of working-class Irish immigrants, I grew up between cultures and worlds, amid the gestures, symbols, and rites that revealed my family's identity. "What are you?" was a standard question in my multiethnic neighborhood on the north shore of Manhattan Island, and every kid kept a standard answer in his back pocket. In my neighborhood, the sports you played defined who you were more than anything else. Many of my friends, whose parents were also off-the-boat Irish, took up Gaelic football and hurling—a primitive game that as far as I could tell centered on whacking your opponents' kneecaps with a heavy wooden stick. Their parents, understandably, wanted them to know what it meant to be Irish by playing the game of their own youth. For them, sports helped bridge the great distance they'd traveled to find a new life.

My father was different. Having scrimped and saved to get as far away from his dirt-poor childhood as he possibly could, he wasn't about to have his kids playing the same "backward" games he'd grown up with. He was determined to raise a son who played American sports and could hold his own some day in the neighborhood bar, talking box scores and batting averages—a pastime from which he'd always felt excluded. So I passed on hurling, protecting my young knees in the process, and declared my allegiance to both flag and father by playing baseball, that quintessentially American game.

That nearly half the kids on my Little League team were Dominican or Cuban, my dad's cheers drowned out at games by a Spanish chorus, was a delightful irony not lost on me even back then. I learned, however, that my Caribbean friends weren't playing for the same nationalistic reasons that I was, trying to assimilate. As far as they and their fathers were concerned they were playing the national game of their homelands, a game that's been evolving its own Latino flavor since U.S. sailors first brought it to Cuba in the 1860s.

About the same time I started playing baseball, my mother organized an urban youth tennis league in our neighborhood park. Like most of my friends, I regarded tennis as effete, foreign, and snobby. It was the 1970s and tennis was still mostly played by white people wearing even whiter outfits on groomed lawn or clay courts in members-only country clubs. I didn't want to play and tried to get out of it by wielding my racket like a baseball bat, hoping to wear down my mother's patience. But Arthur Ashe was winning Grand Slams and breaking new racial barriers, and my mother was determined that every neighborhood kid, including me, should play the game she'd loved since she was young. So she solicited donations for rackets from local businesses and secured sponsorship through the New York City Parks and Recreation Department, and pretty soon a ragtag mob of Irish, Hispanic, and black kids were swinging rackets like baseball bats while my mom tried to instruct us on the proper forehand stroke. The regular players weren't exactly happy that we'd decided to take up their game and take over their courts. I can remember the turf wars that erupted as kids with Afros and headbands chased stray balls.

"You kids belong over there," I recall one man scolding us, pointing to the basketball courts nearby. Part of me agreed and wished I could abandon my mother and jump the fence, but the other part of me was having too much fun participating in a social movement just by hitting a fuzzy yellow ball over a net.

Years later, it was sport that had captured my studies along with my imagination. As a young graduate student in anthropology, looking for adventure far from home, I signed onto an archaeology project in the wilds of Central America. The team was searching for the ruins of ancient Mayan houses and temples left crumbling in the jungle over a millennium ago. It seemed about as exotic and as far from the familiar as one could get.

Our first step was to scour satellite images shot from Honduran military planes looking for the orderly rectilinear patterns of ancient foundation walls and buried courtyards beneath the tropical canopy. In short order, we identified 30-plus ancient sites previously undiscovered and waiting to be explored. Next to the repeated pattern of houses grouped around patios, I spotted another unusual grouping at each site formed by two long parallel buildings separated by a narrow gap. The same pattern repeated itself in each of the satellite images.

"What are those?" I asked my professor overseeing the project.

"Ball courts," she answered matter-of-factly. "Those are definitely ball courts."

Dead center in each one of these ancient sites, long buried under farm fields or hidden away beneath a chaotic tangle of tropical vegetation, were the ruins of stone stadiums where kings and commoners once played one of the world's earliest sports.

I was hooked.

I spent the next three summers crouched with trowel in hand and swatting mosquitoes in the sweltering Honduran heat, scraping back the remnants of these ancient stadiums. Layer by layer, I revealed the sloping stone walls and hard clay playing floors where forgotten athletes once knocked a solid rubber ball back and forth to entertain their kinsmen and their gods. The game had many names in multiple languages, but it is most commonly known as *ulama*. I wanted to learn more about this game, to shed light on its meaning and importance for the Maya. All around the courts, I found piles of broken bowls and jars tossed aside by generations of feasting fans after downing venison and *chicha*, an alcoholic drink made from fermented corn—the ancient Mayan equivalent of hot dogs and beer.

Back at my university, I probed just as deeply into arcane research on the subject. I studied drawings of carved stone monuments depicting kings striking balls with their hips, the most common method of play, while wearing lavish uniforms that included feather headdresses and heavy jade jewelry. I read the decoded hieroglyphic captions that described the rulers as great ballplayers and undefeated warriors, as though the two were somehow connected. I learned that the game itself was rich with religious symbolism. Along with serving as a playing field, the ball court was also regarded as a kind of temple, and the playing of the game akin to a ritual act. And the best part of all? The losers of this ritual contest were sometimes sacrificed through ritual decapitation. This, I discovered with delight, was no ordinary game.

Ten years later, I turned in my trowel and left academia behind. I returned to Central America on assignment from *Smithsonian* magazine to cover *ulama* as a journalist. This time, however, instead of picking through pottery sherds or ancient texts I decided to seek out one of a handful of remote villages where the game was still played. In the span of several days, I learned things about the game by watching and playing it that six years of research had never brought to light.

When Aidan asked why we play ball, though, I'm quite sure he wasn't asking about dead or dying Mesoamerican traditions (though he'd enjoy the human sacrifice part!). He was wondering why we play the games he can't get enough of—baseball, soccer, basketball, football, tennis, lacrosse—the games that are still very much with us today.

However unscientific and perhaps unprovable, I deeply believe that there are seeds of meaning and values planted early on in these games that are still there, subliminally shaping how we think and play, even centuries later. That soccer began in the Dark Ages as a brutal no-holds-barred mob game played between neighboring villages is still dangerously present in the stands every time Manchester United faces archrival Liverpool. That tennis arose in medieval monasteries and the courts of French kings might explain why my friends and I weren't so welcome to pick up rackets and play the game ourselves.

But I think Aidan was also asking why playing ball matters. Why it's worth it. What it does for us that's unique and utterly irreplaceable. As I'd already learned from my time among the ballplayers of western Mexico, no game or sport can be truly understood in the abstract or explored from the quiet comfort of a library carrel. No dry history can bring to life the visceral thrill of a fast break or a perfectly executed corner kick or a bottom-of-the-ninth home run. And so I took to the road to experience the games we love firsthand. This book will toggle back and forth between past and present to explore what's changed, what's remained stubbornly the same, and what might be essential to carry forward to the future.

Now seems a particularly relevant time to explore the importance that playing ball, or playing anything for that matter, has in our lives. Recent research by psychologists and others concerned with the well-being of our kids suggests that they are playing less than their parents did, and far less than they should. This "play deficit," as it's been called, could have lasting effects on their development and on society. The decline in children's play over the past several decades has been well documented. According to a 2004 study funded by the National Institute of Child Health and Human Development, children now spend 50 percent less time playing outdoors than they did in the 1970s. The study found that children ages 10 to 16 spend an average of just 12.6 minutes per day in vigorous physical activity. As schools are pressed to boost test scores and achievement levels or lose funding, many are choosing to eliminate recess. Kids these days, many parents and researchers lament, are overscheduled, overstructured, overweight, and missing out on something fundamental to childhood. If anything, what I found in my research and travels suggests that the cost of this play deficit could have greater ramifications, socially and culturally, than research studies have accounted for.

My travels took me not to multimillion-dollar corporate-sponsored arenas and ballparks, but to small-town playing fields, gyms, and pitches from Ohio to Massachusetts. They took me to places I never would have thought to look: a French palace, an Indian reservation, a remote Scottish isle, the Amazon rain forest, and a Florida marine park, among others. Along the way, in my search for the meaning and roots of ball games, I didn't run into a single famous athlete, nor was I really expecting to. Instead I met ordinary players, coaches, die-hard fans, and keepers of the games who sew their own tennis balls, turn cowhide into footballs, craft lacrosse rackets from hickory wood—individuals whose extraordinary stories add up to as satisfying an answer to Aidan's question as I could ever hope to match.

One central character that gets kicked and batted around throughout the book is the ball itself: that deceptively simple, universally adored orb whose invention and evolution put the bounce, dribble, roll, and spin in the games we play. "Probably no other plaything is as easily recognized, easily played with and universally enjoyed by people of all cultures, skills and ages." That's what the curator of the U.S. National Toy

Hall of Fame had to say about the ball when it finally got inducted in 2009 to join such Johnny-come-lately distractions as the bicycle, kite, jump rope, and Mr. Potato Head. "High time!" I thought when I saw the announcement. The fascinating 5,000-year plus technological and social evolution of the ball, from papyrus to polymers, has never received its due—and my goal is to make up for that here.

By way of disclaimer, I should say up front what this book is not. It's not, nor did I intend it to be, an encyclopedic history of every ball game that exists or has ever existed. For that, there are some very good surveys and textbooks that can be found in the bibliography and that I turned to in my research. I chose sports that each revealed a distinct answer or added fresh perspective to the guiding question of why we play. I also chose topics that I thought best revealed key historical moments in the evolution of ball games, from the ancient world to the present, knowing I had 2 million or more years to cover. My cultural perspective, which as an anthropologist I can't pretend to shrug off, is that of a New Yorker turned Bostonian who grew up knowing that to play "football" without a helmet would be just plain foolish. I've tried, nevertheless, to take a global view and hope non-American readers will see themselves and their sporting passions (and perversions) reasonably reflected in these pages.

As I write this, our sports seem mired in controversy and the wrong kind of spectacle. When they're not covering drug abuse or collegiate impropriety, the sports pages are barely distinguishable from the business section—chock-full of labor disputes, salary negotiations, new branding deals, and stadium real estate transactions as much as actual sports reporting.

The National Football League has emerged from a four-month lockout, and the National Basketball Association has just begun what is expected to be a much longer battle. While millionaire owners and players gear up for a fight, fans, most of whom can't afford a bleacher seat anymore, wonder if they'll have a season to enjoy or not. While his labor union representatives and lawyers are busy at work, LA Lakers star Ron Artest has decided to make the world a better place by changing his name to "Metta World Peace." This from the guy who a few years back attacked a fan during a courtside brawl. Meanwhile, international soccer and the Fédération Internationale de Football Association, better known by its acronym, FIFA, are still recovering from a wave of corruption scandals after executive committee members were accused of selling their votes for the 2018 and 2022 World Cup host countries to the highest bidders. And the darkest underbelly of American college football is being exposed with a convicted Ponzi schemer admitting to lavishing money and prostitutes on more than 70 University of Miami players over an eight-year period.

With all these sideshows distracting and detracting from the sports themselves, I think we need more than ever to find an answer to Aidan's question. We need to reclaim our purest, most primal connections to the games we love and remind ourselves why they matter so much. My hope is that part of the answer might emerge from the stories to follow. The other part I think we already know.

Chapter One

PLAY BALL

Man is most nearly himself when he achieves
the seriousness of a child at play.

HERACLITUS, FIFTH CENTURY BC

lay is a funny thing to get serious about. When you
think about it, asking why we play ball or any other
game violates the most basic rule of all—what could
be called the rule of Nike: *just do it*. When a child is invited
by a friend to pretend she's a penguin or under attack by
aliens from outer space, she doesn't ask why. She happily begins to waddle and flap her wings or dives in a panic behind
the couch to avoid enemy phaser guns. We even have a term
for the kid or adult who breaks the rules of play and ruins
it for everyone else: spoilsport, which the psychologist William James famously traces back to the shah of Persia visiting
England and stuffily declining an invitation to the Epsom
Derby, reasoning, "It is already known to me that one horse
can run faster than another."

Though they exist on different ends of the play spectrum,

sport and the girl-penguin under alien
ply agree on one thing: play is silly. Or in
ing of evolutionary psychologist Gordon
of limited immediate function." Over the
play (yes, there are such people) have tried
to outdo each other in articulating the pointlessness of this
essential human activity. Carl Diem described it as "purposeless activity, for its own sake." The Dutch historian Johan
Huizinga characterized play as being "not serious" and an activity "connected with no material interest." But the hands-
down winner was Roger Caillois, a French intellectual who
defined it as "an occasion of pure waste: waste of time, energy, ingenuity, skill, and often of money," before proceeding
to waste another 200 pages writing about it.

Anthropologists, philosophers, psychologists, neuroscien-
tists, and ethologists have all taken a turn at defining play. In
The Adventures of Tom Sawyer, even Tom took a pass at it. After managing to trade the pleasure of whitewashing his Aunt
Polly's 30-yard-long front fence for an apple, a kite, a dead
rat on a string, a tin soldier, and a dozen other treasures—all
by making fence painting look like the most fun a boy could
ever have on a summer's afternoon—he mused that "work
consists of whatever a body is obliged to do, and that play
consists of whatever a body is not obliged to do."

The psychiatrist Stuart Brown, founder of the National
Institute of Play, admits that defining play is as bad as explaining a joke, but dissects the punch line nevertheless. In his
schema, play tends to be characterized by seven properties—
none of which will shock the nonscientific community:

1. It's voluntary (something you're "not obliged to do").

2. It's got what he calls "inherent attraction." In other words, it's "fun." (Try defining that!)

3. It gives us "freedom from time." When we play, we're in a state of flow and time flies.

4. We experience "diminished consciousness of self." That is, we lose ourselves in the moment.

5. It's all about improvisation, make-believe, invention.

6. It sparks a "continuation desire" in us. As every parent knows, we never want to stop playing.

7. It's "apparently purposeless."

Yet we all play. People in every culture and through all recorded time have played. It's at the core of creativity and innovation and the source of some of our greatest joy and pleasure. It's an essential part of what makes us human. But as anyone who's ever watched kittens wrestle a ball of yarn or spent time in a dog park knows well, the innate drive to play—even the attraction to playing with balls—runs deep in the animal kingdom. Animals, as Huizinga pointed out, "have not waited for man to teach them their playing."

Dogs, like most other mammals, have their own language of play that scientists have only begun to decode. My puppy will approach another dog with a ceremonial bow, crouching on his forelegs and raising his hind end in the air while barking and wagging his tail. According to Marc Bekoff, an ethologist at the University of Colorado in Boulder, who's studied dogs and their wild counterparts for 30 years, these are fixed communication signals that dogs use to establish what he calls a "play mood"—their way of saying, "Hey! I'm here to play." What follows looks an awful lot like fighting, as dogs bite each other, growl, bare teeth, and tussle on the ground in mock combat. But, says Bekoff, dogs use bows and other signals continuously throughout these bouts to reassure their playmates, as if to say, I'm sorry I just bit you hard, but it was all in good fun.

So play is on the one hand frivolous and on the other hand universal. Out in the wild, play also consumes vital energy and puts animals at seemingly pointless risk of predation or injury. Studies of young mammals have shown that they expend up to 15 percent of their calories playing—calories they might otherwise use to further their growth and development. Other research and anecdotes of animal injury and even death in the course of play give biological credence to our mothers' classic warning that as kids we all rolled our eyes at: "It's all fun and games until someone gets hurt."

One of the most dramatic recorded incidents of "death by play" involved seal pups frolicking off the coast of Peru in 1988. Robert Harcourt, a zoologist at Macquarie University in Australia, observed an attack by southern sea lions on more than 100 seal pups. As Harcourt reported, 22 of the 26 pups killed were caught up in playing in the shallow tidal pools right before the attack and didn't seem to notice they were under attack until it was too late.

What seems at first blush to be a simple question turns out to be one that has dogged biologists since Darwin. The

neuroscientist Melvin Konner has called play "a central paradox of evolutionary biology." How can humans and other
mammals have evolved, over millions of years, a set of shared
behaviors that squander valuable energy, make them vulnerable to injury or attack, and yet produce no obvious material
benefit? I decided to go straight to the source to find the
answer: the human brain . . . by way of Florida.

The main strip in Panama City Beach has seen more than
its share of "apparently purposeless behavior" leading to "diminished consciousness of self" over the years. Thankfully,
on the September afternoon when I arrived the only traces
left of spring break bacchanalia were the half-price beer
bongs in the Purple Haze Emporium. Hurricane Fred, the
sixth of the season, had just swept through, and a steady rain
was foiling the few budget travelers hoping to lounge on the
beach.

I found Gulf World Marine Park just past life-size plastic statues of Elvis and Marilyn Monroe, next to the Steak
'n Shake. Gulf World, a seaside attraction since 1969, is an
old-school marine park that features penguins, sea otters,
sharks, and a ragtag cast of performing animals, including
Russell the Crow. As the regional hub for the Marine Mammal Stranding Network, the park serves as a long-term rehab
center for dolphins and small whales that have been beached
by storms or illness. And the marine park is home to the
only group of rough-toothed dolphins under human care in
North America. Rough-toothed dolphins, or *Steno bredanen-
sis*, are smaller and have longer beaks than the more common

bottlenose dolphins. They are also more playful, which has brought scientist Stan Kuczaj back to Gulf World regularly for the past six years. Stan is a professor of psychology at the University of Southern Mississippi, where he runs the Marine Mammal Behavior and Cognition Laboratory. Specializing in both childhood development and dolphin cognition, he is one of a small but growing group of scientists working to unravel the paradox of play. Through a wide variety of studies across disciplines, from neuroscience to behavioral psychology, these researchers are finding evidence to suggest that play not only has a purpose but may serve a critical role in cognitive development and adaptation in humans and other mammals.

I figured if I was going to answer Aidan's question about ball play, I needed to start at the source, or as close to the source as I could reasonably get. I needed to understand why play exists in the first place.

I met up with Stan by the pukka necklace display in Gulf World's gift shop. Thin and tan with wire-rimmed glasses and a nervous smile, the 59-year-old self-described "dolphin nerd" presents the perfect blend of beach bum and lab scientist that you might expect from a guy who studies dolphin cognition for a living. Waving the marine park equivalent of a backstage pass, he whisked me through the employees entrance and around the back of the small stadium, where a dolphin show had just ended. The backstage pool was roiling with energy, water lapping over the sides and washing over our feet.

"I just love these guys," said Stan, clearly delighted to be back with his fun-loving subjects.

The seven dolphins chased each other full tilt around the pool. A funny way to relax after a performance, I thought. Having experienced the classic dolphin show myself, complete with hoop jumping and synchronized breaching, I had always assumed that they stopped playing the minute the spectators left the stands and the buckets of herring ran empty. I couldn't have been more wrong.

Stan zeroed in on this group of rough-toothed dolphins for his research because they play more often, longer, and with more vigor than other dolphins (and most other mammals for that matter). Kevin Walsh, the owner of Gulf World, refers to them affectionately as "Tursiops on crack" (*Tursiops* being the Latin name for the bottlenose dolphin). The young trainers who spend the most time with the animals and know each one's idiosyncrasies intimately shared their own tales of dolphin hijinks. Quite often, when they've divided the dolphins into separate pools, the trainers report, they'll return the next morning to find them all in one pool again, having leapt out and shimmied 30 feet across the pool deck to reunite with their friends.

Then there's the inexplicable behavior. "I've come by at night and seen all seven floating upright and looking up at the sky," said one trainer. "We don't know what they're doing, but we like to say they're communing with the mother ship."

Stan has been studying the animals both in the wild and in captivity for nearly 20 years. He began his career studying child language use but got hooked on dolphins while assisting a colleague's research in Hawaii. He never looked back.

Stan's unique, cross-species experience has allowed him to look at the phenomenon of play from a broad evolutionary perspective. In conversation, he toggles seamlessly between discussions of controlled experiments conducted in dolphin tanks and Piaget's theory of cognitive development, which addresses the four stages children pass through in acquiring and using knowledge.

Over the years, Stan and his fellow researchers have documented elaborate play behaviors among dolphins. As with humans, dolphin play can be solitary or social. Both in the wild and in captivity, they'll play with their own or another dolphin's bubbles. In the ocean they'll play chasing games together or one will dislodge a sponge and play with it alone for 15 or 20 minutes.

They've watched young dolphins taking turns pushing each other along the surface of the water, one on his side and the other nosing him sideways through the water, sometimes at rapid speeds. Then they'll switch places so one of the pushers gets to be the "pushee," a move that requires a high degree of social cooperation.

While snorkeling, Stan once watched two adult dolphins and one young dolphin playing together with a plastic six-pack holder. One swam toward the others with the plastic trailing from his pectoral fin. Within minutes, the three were voluntarily passing the plastic back and forth without any attempt to grab or steal it. Then the game changed. One dolphin swam ahead of the others with the plastic on his fin and let it go in the water. The second swam up, caught the plastic, and swam forward before releasing it to the third.

Stan is particularly interested in evidence such as this, which suggests cooperation and communication as well as shared "rules" of engagement, the kind of advanced behavior that dolphins depend upon for foraging and defending against predators. What his research tells him is that play is anything but trivial and purposeless, but may in fact be essential to adaptation and survival.

Research on nonhuman animals suggests that play is not only critical to our health and socialization but also affects the growth and development of our brains. In one study, rats isolated during the period of juvenile development when they play the most were far less socially adept than their nonisolated peers well into adulthood. In another study, researchers allowed 13 rats to play freely together while 14 other rats were kept in isolation. After three and a half days, the brains of the playful rats were found to contain much higher levels of brain-derived neurotrophic factor, a protein that stimulates nerve growth in the amygdala and prefrontal cortex, areas associated with emotions and decision making. Animals that play are, in other words, smarter and more socially intelligent than those that don't.

A recent study conducted by scientists at the University of Illinois at Urbana-Champaign found that playing also helps humans develop adaptive cognitive skills. They recruited 36 students, male and female, half of whom were varsity athletes across a variety of sports and half of whom were healthy nonathletes. For the experiment, each student was put on a treadmill surrounded by large video screens. Goggles gave the video images real-world dimensions and feel. They found themselves navigating a busy cityscape and were charged with walking, not running, across a busy intersection without getting mowed down by cars passing at 40 to 55 miles per hour. The athletes completed more crossings than the nonathletes by a significant margin, and not because they were quicker or more physically agile. "They didn't move faster," said the study leader. "But it looks like they thought faster." Athletes, the study suggests, have a cognitive advantage when it comes to processing visual and other information quickly enough to respond rapidly. A running back in football trying to make his way through the other team's defense needs to make lightning-quick decisions while responding in real time to the cues of every other player on the field. That not only takes physical agility; it takes mental agility as well.

Neuroscientist Sergio Pellis of the University of Lethbridge in Canada and his colleagues have found that there's a direct correlation between brain size and playfulness in mammals. They measured brain size and recorded play behaviors in 15 species of mammals and found that the species with relatively large brains played a lot more than their small-brained counterparts.

The evolutionary lines that eventually led to dolphins and humans diverged in the Mesozoic Age, more than 95 million years ago, at a time when dinosaurs still roamed Earth. Despite being virtually unrelated to humans, dolphins are by every measure among the most playful of animals, second only to humans in this department. And it's almost certainly no coincidence that they are also second only to humans when it comes to their brain-to-body size, or encephalization quotient. EQ is defined by neuroscientist and behavioral biologist Lori Marino as "a measure of observed brain size relative to the expected brain size derived from a regression of brain weight on body weight for a sample of species." The EQ value for modern humans is 7.0. Dolphins have EQ levels close to 4.5, while our closest relatives, the great apes, have levels of only 1.5 to 3. Scientists have found some correlation between EQ value and the degree to which animals are inclined to play. Dolphins and humans, Marino says, "share a psychology." You could say we're both uniquely hardwired to play hard.

At poolside, Stan made some quick introductions. Vixen, he pointed out, can be identified by the perpetual rash on her neck caused by laying her head on the edge of the pool. Astro's tail is crooked from scoliosis. Noah has pink freckles on his chest. And so on. Once I'd been told who was who, Stan walked up to a rack filled with a random array of objects—buoys of various shapes and colors, plastic pool fencing, sections of Styrofoam mats, orange traffic cones, plastic rings, and a small blue and white basketball.

"Let's give them some toys to play with," he said, grabbing a noodle. "These guys are crazy about their toys."

We began grabbing objects and throwing them in. The pool erupted with energy. Vixen darted off with the chain of pool fencing wrapped around her fin. Largo started pushing a mat through the water, then jumping on top of it to make a slapping sound, then pushing it to the pool's bottom. I threw in a blue and white ball that Ivan and Noah instantly began pushing around the pool with their noses, dodging, faking, and reversing direction to keep the ball from their opponent. They then took turns diving to the bottom and then rocketing to the surface to knock the ball high in the air, breaching behind it before slapping back down on the water.

Dolphins are extraordinary athletes. Along with having high EQs and a relentless urge to play, they are built to perform. They can achieve speeds of up to 20 miles per hour. They can dive as deep as 1,000 feet and stay down for 30 minutes at a stretch. They navigate and locate each other, along with predators and prey, through echolocation—producing sound waves that bounce off objects and bring back detailed information on distance, location, and shape. Dolphins, Stan says, can locate and retrieve an object the size of a golf ball at a football field's distance. With that lethal combination of speed, spatial prowess, and hunger to play, I thought, the Miami Dolphins would not only sail into the Super Bowl but would finally live up to the promise of their name.

After a few minutes of playing with the ball, Ivan managed to flip it out of the pool right where I was standing. I picked it up and threw it back in. Ivan chased it down and then initiated the dolphin equivalent of a game of fetch. He'd push it all the way back to me, I'd reach into the pool, pick it up, and throw it back in. After doing this repeatedly for nearly five minutes, I got distracted by another dolphin and turned away. So this time he not only brought the ball back but then smacked it out of the water with his nose, sending it whizzing past my head. Clearly he meant business.

The game had gone from just chasing, to playing fetch, to knocking the ball out of the water back to the thrower

with line drives that became more precise each time. Largo soon abandoned his mat and joined the game, adding a competitive dimension. In just ten minutes, what had begun as a frenzy of free play had evolved into a disciplined and competitive interspecies ball game with an unspoken but mutually understood set of rules.

Where I saw the rudimentary foundations of sport, Stan sees the development and maintenance of flexible problem-solving skills that dolphins depend on in the wild. His observations of Ivan, Largo, and other captive dolphins lead him to believe that they use play to continuously test and challenge themselves, constantly tweaking the "rules" to sharpen their cognitive skills. He uses Piaget's concept of "moderately discrepant events" to describe this phenomenon. Dolphins, like Piaget's child subjects, learn about their world and expand their physical and cognitive abilities by slightly modifying the rules of their play to make them incrementally more stimulating. This is how both dolphins and humans play and learn.

The evolving poolside ball game was serving as what Marc Bekoff calls "brain food" for Ivan, Largo, and their friends. The dolphins, responding to my cues and initiating variations in play themselves, were flexing their cognitive muscles, perfecting motor skills, and manipulating their watery environment in ways that could eventually be put to the test in the wild.

It's hardly a coincidence that the object at the center of all the pool action was a ball. According to Stan, balls are the hands-down favorite toy of dolphins, as they so often are for people. In a controlled study of the play behaviors of 16 captive dolphins conducted over a five-year period, he found that they were far more likely to initiate spontaneous play with balls than with other objects, with bubbles, or even with each other. Why balls?

Well, if play is brain food, then ball play is like a high-protein, calorie-packed energy bar. The ball may be one of the most animate of inanimate objects in our material world. As I watched Largo and Ivan laugh and splash and leap after their colorful ball while the other dolphins dragged mats and ropes around the pool, I coined my own term to describe balls as objects: kinetically interesting. Balls can bounce, roll, be struck, thrown and caught fairly easily at a wide range of speeds. They are highly aerodynamic and yet unpredictable in their trajectory, capable in the hands of a deft knuckleball pitcher of appearing to defy the laws of physics.

Balls are also by nature social tools. They draw animals

and humans together, inviting either cooperation or competition or, as in most sports, some dynamic combination of
the two. "I throw or kick to you, you throw or kick it back"
is very different than "you grab the ball and try to keep it
from me." But both involve tacit agreement around the rules
of fair play. Vanessa Woods, a researcher with the Hominoid
Psychology Research Group, spent time playing with bonobo
chimpanzees in the Democratic Republic of the Congo and
experienced both responses.

"We were looking at the social dimensions of bonobo tool
use," she told me. "We had this bright pink ball that the
chimps just loved. The question we asked was, were they just
going to steal it and run away? Or would they get the idea
that this is a shared experience and now we're going to play
together. So the big test was if we threw the ball to them,
would they throw it back?"

Some of the bonobos just ran off with the prized possession and didn't get the social part of it at all. "For them,
it was the equivalent of throwing a Wii to a group of kids,"
Vanessa said. "They'd fight over it and whoever got it first
would run off with it." I paused to contemplate such a scene
with Aidan and his friends and instantly got the distinction.

Two of the bonobos in the research group took to the
game right away. One chimp threw the ball back with his
hands, then with his feet, and then experimented with other
throws. He'd then clap his hands and wait for it to be thrown
back.

"When the experiment was done," Vanessa said, "he'd
throw a tantrum like a kid would do: he'd tug at your arm,

make all kinds of noise, and would try slapping the ball out of your hands even."

Animals that depend on learning for survival all play. It's how knowledge and experience are passed from parent to child, enabling a safe space where limits can be tested and new ideas and innovations can get a dry run. "In a dangerous world," wrote Diane Ackerman, "where dramas change daily, survival belongs to the agile, not the idle."

At the pool, the head trainer reluctantly interrupted our game. Vixen, Largo, and friends had a performance coming up and needed a break from the action. We gathered up all the toys and assembled them back on the rack. The dolphins got agitated, slapping the water with their fins, as though disappointed at the fun ending—"continuation desire" at work. Vixen rested her head sullenly on the side of the pool and looked instantly bored as we headed out front to find seats in the rapidly filling stadium. Ten minutes later, throbbing rock music signaled the start of the show. The dolphins swam in and were soon jumping through hoops, doing synchronized tail slaps, leaping and landing in unison, sending huge waves of water into the front row and soaking delighted audience members. Their eyes were then covered to show off their ability to use echolocation to find and retrieve several tossed rings. After each trick, the trainers shoveled a handful of herring into the dolphins' mouths. They seemed to be enjoying themselves as they hungrily devoured the fish and showed off their skills to the cheering audience. It was a great show, and exhilarating to watch. Yes, it was regimented, rehearsed, rewarded, and therefore entirely different than our backstage games. The equivalent, you might say, of a Little League championship versus a pickup game with friends.

As they did their tricks and earned their dinner, their secret was safe with me: herring or no, they'd be playing just as hard.

So when did we put it all together? Who first spoke those magical words "Play ball"? In what language were they uttered? Or were balls kicked and rolled and thrown for fun and competition long before there were even words to describe the rules or capture the play-by-play?

Since the drive to play and even to invent rudimentary games is undeniably pre-human, it is almost certain that our earliest hominid ancestors were capable of it on some level. It is also likely that it was in part through play, through testing our limits and innovating solutions, that we adapted to changing environments and evolved into our modern form. For this reason, Huizinga believed that *Homo ludens*, Man the Player, deserves his due alongside *Homo sapiens*, Man the Thinker. We play, therefore we are.

Until recently, however, the common wisdom was that play was purely an act of leisure (leisure being the opposite of work) and therefore an invention of civilization. The lives of our earliest ancestors and, by extension, of contemporary hunter-gatherer tribes were seen as an all-out grind from sunrise to sunset. Every ounce of expendable energy went into bagging the next deer, or gathering wild vegetables, or defending against predators, leaving no reserves for anything as frivolous as the playing of games (or, for that matter, arts, science, etc.). This is a compelling story that makes our great march toward civilization feel satisfyingly linear, virtuous, and inevitable. As we evolved, we not only got smarter but also had more fun. But it turns out not to be true.

In the 1960s, anthropologist Richard Lee spent time among the !Kung bushmen of Africa's Kalahari Desert and found that their hunter-gatherer lifestyle wasn't the "precarious and arduous struggle for existence" we all imagined it to be. !Kung women, who—big shocker—worked harder than the men, could gather enough food in one day to feed their families for three, spending the rest of their time resting, visiting neighbors, entertaining—enjoying some measure of leisure, in other words. Their husbands, meanwhile, had it even better. It turns out that hunters, as the anthropologist Marshall Sahlins famously put it, "keep bankers' hours."

The Australian Aborigines present the perfect example of a leisure-rich hunter-gatherer culture that historically played a wide variety of sports, including ball games. A diverse collection of groups that once spoke as many as 300 distinct languages, the Aborigines have traditionally been hunter-gatherers who traveled in small bands, had no agriculture, and employed simple stone tool technology that remained largely unchanged over their 40,000-year history. But they played ball.

The Aborigines of western Victoria played a football-like game called *marn grook* that involved upward of 50 men playing across a large open stretch of land. Accounts from the 1920s and earlier describe a contest between clans or totem groups (the "white cockatoos" versus the "black cockatoos," for example) that involved punting and catching a stuffed ball made from grass and beeswax, opossum pelt, or, in some cases, the scrotum of a kangaroo.

The rules of the game were not well understood by those white men who recorded it, but this account gives an idea:

> A ball, similar to the one used in cricket but made of grass tied up tightly with string and then covered with beeswax, is used for the game, where men of different moieties took sides as in football, and the game was started by kicking the ball into the air. Once kicked off, however, the hands could not touch the ball again, only the feet were used for this purpose, and the side who kept it in the air and away from the others were looked upon as the winners.

The winner, in some cases, earned the honor of burying the ball in the ground until it was unearthed for the next game.

On the other side of the world, the Copper Inuit are a hunting society in the Canadian Arctic that subsist on seal, fish, and, in the spring, caribou. When the ice melts in the spring and summer months they are also known to play their own variation of football, called *akraurak*. As described by the anthropologist Kendall Blanchard, the game is played with a seal-hide ball stuffed with hair, feathers, moss, or whalebone. Goals are set up on the snow and teams must kick the ball up and down the field and drive it across the opponent's goal line. This game is so important within the culture that the Inuit refer to the northern lights, or aurora borealis, as *arsarnerit*, meaning "the football players."

Where in most cultures—ancient and modern—balls have been fashioned from animal skins, in some the animal itself is the ball (or, you could say, the game is the game). In *buzkashi* ("goat grabbing"), a team sport still played on horseback among the herding people of Afghanistan, Pakistan, and neighboring parts of Central Asia, players attempt to grab the headless, disemboweled, sand-filled carcass of a goat from the ground and throw it toward a goal. This ancient game may hint at the early roots of ball games and is made all the more challenging by opponents who use all manner of force, including fists and whips, to keep a rider from successfully scoring a goal. *Buzkashi* achieved brief fame (or embarrassment) in the 1988 film *Rambo III*. In one scene, a mullet-wearing Sylvester Stallone is helping the mujahideen rebels battle their evil Soviet invaders. He is invited to join a game and prove his manhood. A profound dialogue ensues:

RAMBO: "What are the rules?"
MUJAHIDEEN: "Well, you have to take the sheep, go once around, and then throw it in the circle."
RAMBO: "Why?"
MUJAHIDEEN: "Because there is a circle there."
RAMBO: "That's it?"
MUJAHIDEEN: "That's it. Very simple."
RAMBO: "Like football."

Rambo, of course, gets the goat.

That competitive sports and ball games should be as common among hunter-gatherer and so-called primitive societies as they are in agricultural ones makes a great deal of sense. The physical dexterity, cognitive, and visual-spatial skills that ball games help develop are more elemental and essential for a hunter-gatherer than they are for a farmer or, say, a briefcase-carrying corporate attorney. Hunting was the original game, where the stakes were life or death and the competition for scarce resources fierce and relentless. For our early protein-hungry ancestors, the object was simple: chase down and kill your prey ("game") before it could run off or get nabbed by a smarter or faster competitor. If you think about it, the Paleolithic hunter's toolkit contained in its most primitive form all the basic types of equipment—stones, spears, clubs, nets—that you'd need to open a basic sporting goods store.

What if we owe our present status as walking, talking, large-brained alpha primates in part to our unique ability to throw a scorching fastball? That's what evolutionary biologist William Calvin of the University of Washington proposed in an essay from his book *The Throwing Madonna*. Calvin argues that our premodern ancestors may have accomplished more with their one-armed rock throws than simply braining small animals. The motion itself may have promoted the first lateralization of a function to the left brain, a spark that set in motion the development of language, tool use, and much more. Lateralization means that certain neural functions occur more in one side of the brain than the other. So how might this have worked? Here's how Calvin arrives at his theory.

Most animals can't throw to save their lives, especially since so few are capable of standing on two feet for more than a minute or so. Chimpanzees, our nearest relatives, are among the best, but even they don't have a good enough arm to make my son's old T-ball team. Sure, they can heave a large rock to crack open a dead monkey's skull and extract the brains. But if the monkey were alive, the chimp's only recourse would be to chase it down, which consumes a lot of energy and is pointless if the monkey's faster. Once we got bipedal, however, humans figured out that rather than go on a wild monkey chase they could pick up a small rock, throw it hard and far with one hand, and have a better chance of hitting pay dirt while conserving energy in the process. Also, if the prey was the kind that might fight back, throwing rocks offered the safety of distance. This unique ability would have conferred a tangible advantage to our ancestors, the kind that evolution might have rewarded and selected to continue and propagate.

So what? Now you've got a not-so-smart, mostly upright, well-fed primate with a killer fastball and reproductive advantage. Add a lump of chaw and you've got your average major-league baseball pitcher! (Only kidding!) But this is where Calvin's theory gets interesting. Throwing requires some pretty sophisticated rapid muscle sequencing, a function that in humans takes place in the left brain. That's why, as Calvin recounts, patients with left-hemisphere strokes have a hard time completing the sequence of activities needed to, for example, unlock and open a door. The other function that's been lateralized to our left brain is language, which is itself dependent on muscle sequencing.

Is it really possible that language, that most human of human traits, might partially owe its existence to our ability to nail a rabbit from 50 feet? Calvin thinks so. Unlike other proposed causes, such as tool use or the discovery of fire, for example, throwing offers immediate return on investment. You kill that rabbit quicker, easier, and with less energy and exposure to risk than your competitors, and you and your offspring's odds of survival start looking really good. Not in a few years or generations, but immediately.

Now, anything that might improve the speed and precision of that throw would be beneficial to survival. Such as a larger brain. With just a handful of neurons, our caveman-pitcher might find himself throwing everywhere but the strike zone. But more neurons can boost precision exponentially. Meaning a bigger brain would have drastically improved our ancestors' ERA. That larger brain would have come in handy for inventing tools, refining stone technology, and developing fire. Fire allowed food to be cooked, which meant we could extract more calories and energy from fibrous fruits and raw meat, which fed our growing brain even more—a virtuous cycle if ever there was one.

Whether rock throwing had an influence on human evolution is certainly up for debate. No one will ever fully know the answer. But it's easy to see from the picture Calvin paints how an action as seemingly trivial and mundane as playing catch with a ball might trace its evolutionary path back to something much more fundamental to our existence.

Hypothesis and speculation on the beginnings of sports don't give way to historical fact until the third millennium BC, when the first written descriptions and depictions of ball games appear in the Near East and Egypt. The Upper Paleolithic cave paintings of Europe and Africa say little about the day-to-day lives of the artists who drew them, focusing instead on their animal prey. Archaeology of this period yields little more than stone, bone, and soil.

When the ball finally enters history, it arrives as a bizarre and homoerotic form of polo played from the backs not of horses, but of humans. The account of this strange sport is found in the *Epic of Gilgamesh*, one of the first works of literature ever written. It was carved into cuneiform tablets around 2600 BC, while the Mesopotamian hero-king Gilgamesh was the ruler of Uruk, an ancient city in what is now southern Iraq. Regarded as two-thirds god and one-third man, Gilgamesh goes to impressive lengths to oppress Uruk's citizens. He exhausts, for instance, the city's young men with games of polo so he can exhaust their wives without distraction.

> [His] comrades are roused up with his ball(game),
> the young men of Uruk are continually disturbed in
> their bedrooms (with a summons to play).

Gilgamesh then takes the men out to humiliate them in the public square:

He [Gilgamesh] who had very much wanted a ball
was playing with the ball in the public square. . . . He
was mounted on the hips of a group of widow's sons.
"Alas, my neck! Alas my hips!" they lament.

Though it might be reassuring to think of this game of
people polo as just an anomalous perversion of sport—like,
say, trampoline basketball or zorbing—the game actually
seems to have had a serious fan base in the ancient world. A
similar game crops up a few hundred years later in Egypt's
Middle Kingdom, this time played girl-on-girl. In one rock-
cut tomb in the cemetery of Beni Hasan, a painted scene of
daily Egyptian life shows two pairs of girls, one girl astride
the other, throwing balls back and forth. The ancient Greeks
played it as well and gave it a name, *ephedrismos* (from the
Greek verb "to sit upon"). Scenes of both women and men
playing the game appear on painted jars, terra-cotta figurines,
and life-size statues of the Classical period. On a vase in the
collections of the Ashmolean Museum, a bearded man with
a cane prepares to throw the ball to three pairs of mounted
young men. The graffiti-like inscription that appears next to
the thrower might as well be a speech bubble. It reads, simply, "Give the word."

Inscriptions and scenes from Egyptian tombs from 2000
BC on show that sports were an important part of daily life
along the Nile. Competitions, including wrestling, boxing,
swimming, jousting, archery, and foot races, were enjoyed
by members of the aristocracy and commoners alike. The
pharaohs, like so many rulers throughout history, depicted

The game of *ephedrismos* as depicted on a Classical Greek vase.

themselves regularly as invincible warriors, hunters, and athletes—physically strong and capable of defeating enemies in sport as well as war. At the annual festival of the Sed, the pharaoh would run around the city to publicly display his stamina and power. And while ball games were mostly played by girls and children for fun, other more ritualistic games were played by the pharaoh himself.

The actual balls used in these games have turned up with

some frequency in Egyptian tombs, preserved alongside mummified cats and other personal treasures meant to accompany the deceased into the afterlife. Stitched leather balls, bearing an uncanny resemblance to modern-day hacky sacks, were stuffed with straw, reeds, hair, or yarn. Balls made of papyrus, palm leaves, and linen wound around a pottery core have turned up as well. In one case, excavations of a child's grave uncovered the first evidence of bowling, complete with stone balls and pins, still waiting to be knocked down.

Anyone who believes that the first time a bat connected with a ball was in a Cooperstown, New York, cow pasture in 1839 should see a sculpture from around 1500 BC showing King Tuthmosis III with a bent stick of olive wood batting balls away while two priests pitch and fetch. Tuthmosis was one of the greatest military leaders of ancient Egypt, reputed to have captured 350 cities in military campaigns that expanded the Egyptian empire. The hieroglyphs that accompany the image read, "Catching [of the balls] by the servants of god after he [the king] has struck them away." You can almost imagine a crowd of worshippers chanting "Tut! Tut! Tut!" as he steps to the plate to play this game, known as *seker-hemat*.

This ritual game of the pharaohs, which occurs in tomb art 19 times over a thousand-year stretch, appears to have been no ordinary game. The pharaoh is sometimes depicted playing in the presence of Hathor, a goddess associated with the afterlife. Later texts reveal that when the king ceremonially struck the ball it was believed to damage the eye of Apophis, the serpent enemy of the gods. In one image from the seventh century BC, the king runs and throws four clay balls

Tuthmosis III playing ball, Temple of Hatshepsut, Deir el-Bahri, Egypt.

toward the cardinal directions. Although the evidence is fragmented, the message seems to be that while men played other men in inconsequential earthly contests, the pharaoh battled the forces of darkness on behalf of the gods. And, according to these, his commissioned accounts, he always won.

Organized athletics and sport achieved new levels of cultural importance in ancient Greece, where the male athlete was celebrated in art and literature. The Greeks' word for athletic contests, *agon*—aptly, the root of "agony"—reflected their attitude toward the role of athletics in society. Men of worth were expected to be as combative in sport as in war, to struggle with all their strength and will to defeat their opponents. As the sports historian Allen Guttmann points out, the fit and muscular body of the athlete was the aesthetic ideal because it stood ready to defend the city-state in war. Every city had its stadiums, gymnasiums, and palaestras (wrestling academies) where athletes stripped nude and rubbed themselves down with olive oil before workouts or competitions. Athens alone had nine public gymnasia, which served not only as athletic centers but also as cultural, religious, and political centers.

Athletic festivals were held to honor the gods in cities and towns across the Peloponnesian peninsula. The oldest and most celebrated of these was, of course, the Olympic Games, which took place every four years to honor Zeus. Unlike the modern Olympics, however, which now include basketball, tennis, soccer, table tennis, handball, field hockey, and both beach and indoor volleyball, no ball game was ever played at the ancient Olympics. Ball games were still regarded as playful diversion and entertainment, not as *agon*. Never, for example, do Greek accounts of ball play ever mention the words "victory" or "defeat."

The Greeks did enjoy ball games, however, and, along with *ephedrismos*, played a wide variety. In Homer's *The Odyssey*, Odysseus is shipwrecked on the shore of Phaeacia. Nausicaa, the beautiful daughter of the king, goes with her maids to the seashore to do the laundry and, while waiting for it to dry in the sun, plays a game that sounds a bit like dodge ball: "Nausicaa hurled the ball at one of her maids. She missed the girl and threw it into a deep pool. They all shrieked to high heaven." The shrieks of the girls at play awoke Odysseus, who was dozing in the bushes nearby. He went off to the king's court, where he was honored with a feast and after-dinner entertainment that included a game played by young acrobats with "a beautiful purple ball."

Following the feast, the king calls for the athletes of his kingdom to come together for a sports contest, so "that our guest may report to his friends when he gets home how we beat the world at boxing and wrestling and jumping and running."

Odysseus resists joining in the competition, which leads the other athletes to taunt him, saying, "I do not see you as a fellow who goes in for games . . . you are not an athlete." He finally rises to the bait, grabs a discus, and throws it far beyond the other marks, yelling "Touch that if you can, young men!" Young Princess Nausicaa was impressed—she "gazed upon Odysseus with all her eyes and admired him."

Over time, though, ball games rose in popularity. Everyone who was anyone had a large room dedicated to ball play, called a *sphairisterion*. An inscription from Delphi describes the construction of one of these ball courts with its floor of smooth pounded "black earth." The most common sport played in the *sphairisterion* was *episkyros*, a team game for which the fourth-century comic playwright Antiphanes passed down what may be the earliest surviving play-by-play sports commentary:

He caught the ball and laughed as he passed it to one player at the same time as he dodged another. He knocked another player out of the way, and picked one up and set him on his feet, and all the while there were screams and shouts: "Out of bounds!" "Too far!" "Past him" "Over his head!" "Under!" "Over!" "Short!" "Back in the huddle!"

Episkyros appears to have been a rugby-like game played with a stuffed ball and two teams of 12 or so players. The ball was placed on a center line marked by white gypsum, and two other lines behind each team marked the goals. The rules of the game aren't well understood but seem to have involved passing the ball among teammates while advancing on the goal of the opposing team. A scene from a marble vase in Athens shows six nude players in the midst of a game, each in various stages of throwing, catching, or running. Other games were played with balls of different sizes. One was a child's game played with a pig's bladder inflated with air and then warmed over the ashes of a fire to help round its shape. Another game similar to basketball, called *aporrhaxis*, involved dribbling an inflated ball along the ground. A single tantalizing scene from Athens shows two men, positioned like hockey players, competing over a small ball with curved sticks, though no such game is mentioned in any surviving account.

Ball games rose to a higher level of competition in the city-state of Sparta, where all young men in their first year of manhood were generically referred to as "ballplayers." Inscriptions found there describe an annual *episkyros* tournament where the winning team was awarded a sickle as trophy.

One of the most famous ballplayers of the time was Alexander the Great. After giving up competitive athletics because his subjects always let him win, he turned to ball play for his sport of choice. He employed a professional ballplayer to train with and his endorsement of the game seems to have led to a spike in popularity and the construction of *sphairisteria* by other members of the nobility.

Following the lead of their predecessors, the Romans were enthusiastic about ball play, though the innocent games could hardly compete for public attention with the infamous spectacles of Rome's Circus Maximus, which included gladiatorial combat, lion fights, and often deadly chariot races. Ball games, by comparison, were more private affairs that emphasized exercise over spectacle and sportsmanship over violence. The first-century AD poet Martial described four different kinds of balls and the accompanying games played with them:

> No hand-ball (*pila*), no bladder-ball (*follis*), no feather-stuffed ball (*paganica*) makes you ready for the warm bath, nor the blunted sword-stroke upon the unarmed stump; nor do you stretch forth squared arms besmeared with oil, nor, darting to and fro, snatch the dusty scrimmage-ball (*harpasta*), but you run only by the clear Virgin water.

Every wealthy Roman had his own *sphaeristerium*—as the Romans called their ball courts—and they were often attached to the public baths. "Stop play," wrote Martial the poet, "the bell of the hot bath is ringing." Pliny the Younger had courts in each of his country houses, including one in Tuscany that was large enough to stage multiple games at once for his weekend guests. Another ball court in Rome was heated from underneath for winter games.

When wealthy Romans weren't gathering decadently to watch slaves fight to the death or to crucify dogs in public, they passed time playing *harpastum*, the most popular ball game of the empire. Played with a softball-sized stuffed ball, the object of the game is hinted at in its name, which means "to seize" or "to snatch." The vague descriptions available suggest an elaborate, rough-and-tumble form of monkey-in-the-middle with a player in the center of a circle attempting to snatch a ball passed back and forth between two lines of players.

One of the biggest fans of *harpastum* was Galen, a former physician to gladiators who rose through the ranks to be court doctor to the emperor Marcus Aurelius. Regarded as "first among physicians, unique among philosophers," Galen went on to pioneer the science of anatomy, dissecting pigs and apes and Barbary macaques to study their bodily systems. He was forced to draw inferences about human anatomy from these studies since, despite finding entertainment in watching people torn limb from limb, the Romans prohibited the "barbarous" practice of human autopsy. In AD 180, Galen turned his scientific eye to ball games in a treatise entitled *On Exercise with the Small Ball*, where he made the first scientific case for the benefits of ball play to exercise and physical education. Waxing philosophical as well as scientific, Galen in that early age spoke more eloquently to the boundless joys and practical merits of ball play than any writer over the next millennium and a half.

"I believe that the best of all exercises is the one which not only exercises the body, but also refreshes the spirit," he wrote. "The men who invented hunting were wise and well acquainted with the nature of man, for they mixed its exertions with pleasure, delight, and rivalry." Galen celebrated the potential of ball games to unite people across class and status lines, noting that "even the poorest man can play ball, for it requires no nets nor weapons nor horses nor hunting dogs, but only a ball. . . . And what could be more convenient than a game in which everyone, no matter his status or career, can participate."

Beyond its social leveling qualities, Galen also declared ball play to be the "best all-around exercise" because it worked out all the body parts at once.

> When the players line up on opposite sides and exert themselves to keep the one in the middle from getting the ball, then it is a violent exercise with many neck-holds mixed with wrestling holds. Thus the head and neck are exercised by the neck-holds, and the sides and chest and stomach are exercised by the hugs and shoves and tugs and the other wrestling holds.

Despite the popularity of *harpastum*, Galen apparently felt the need to defend ball games against a critique that would be heard again and again in the centuries to follow:

rather than preparing and training men for battle as archery or wrestling did, it did the opposite—distracting and diverting them in so-called frivolous play. Galen, presaging Vince Lombardi, argued that in fact "ball playing trains for the two most important maneuvers which a state entrusts to its generals: to attack at the proper time and to defend the booty already amassed. There is no other exercise so suited to the training in the guarding of gains, the retrieval of losses, and the foresight of the plan of the enemy."

Galen was way ahead of his time. He was among the first accomplished surgeons to advance scientifically substantiated theories of human anatomy, the circulation system, and even neuroscience. The systems and methods he developed held sway for centuries, dominating medical science until the 17th century. As both scientific observer and, it appears, fanatical player and lover of *harpastum*, he saw early what we now know so well: that ball games are uniquely capable of exercising and challenging both body and mind, sharpening the senses, and inspiring the human spirit.

Chapter Two

FROM SKIRMISH TO SCRUM

Bruised muscles and broken bones
Discordant strife and futile blows
Lamed in old age, then crippled withal
These are the beauties of football.

ANONYMOUS, 16TH CENTURY, TRANSLATED

FROM OLD SCOTS

I f you're searching for the remnants and roots of old ball games—or old anything for that matter—Orkney may be the best place in the world to go looking. A scattering of 70 or so barnacle-encrusted isles and skerries that extend from the northern shores of Scotland into the frigid waters of the North Sea, Orkney is a place where the present can barely hold its ground against the fierce pull of the past—a place where legend still competes with fact, passion with logic, ritual with routine.

Here, cheerfully stubborn and oblivious to the ways of

"ferryloupers" from beyond the Pentland Firth, men still gather in cobblestone streets on the coldest, darkest days of winter to play football the old-fashioned way: two large mobs, one sawdust-stuffed ball, no rules, and nearly four centuries of grudges to keep things interesting. Here they don't play games. They play the Kirkwall Ba'.

The narrow road from the ferry landing on mainland Orkney winds its way through a stark but stunning landscape of treeless hills and rocky coves, interrupted by the occasional small farmstead. Amid otherwise ordinary fields, seaweed-eating sheep rub themselves casually against megalithic standing stones and graze over the top of low burial cairns. Farther along, dominating a high plateau above two shimmering lochs, stands the mystical Ring of Brogar, a 5,000-year-old Stonehenge-like monument made up of 27 massive stones set within a deep circular ditch.

Clinging to the battered coast nearby is the Neolithic village of Skara Brae. Resembling Bedrock, home of the Flintstones, the site's remarkably preserved stone furniture, including cupboards, dressers, and pre-Posturepedic beds, has earned it the nickname "the British Pompeii." And at the heart of the island's Stone Age landscape lies the unassuming grassy knoll containing Maes Howe, a spectacular tomb formed by 30 tons of flagstone slabs stacked like Legos to form a perfect beehive-shaped tomb for Orkney's earliest chieftains. On the winter solstice, a shaft of light pierces the darkness of the chamber to illuminate the rear wall, an event that draws an annual pilgrimage of New Agers and born-again pagans from all over.

What was a sacred site for the Neolithic people of Orkney was little more than a shelter in the storm for later Viking marauders who sought refuge here in a snow squall in 1153, an incident recorded in the *Orkneyinga Saga*, an account of the conquest of Orkney and the establishment of a Norse earldom here. Out of boredom or a desire to mark their turf, the invaders scrawled runic graffiti on the walls of the ancient tomb. The 30 or so inscriptions accommodate Viking stereotypes nicely, including such literary gems as "*Thorni fucked, Helgi carved,*" and "*Ingigerth is the most beautiful of all women*" (carved, disturbingly, next to a drawing of a drooling dog).

After ruling the isles for nearly 400 years, the Norse handed Orkney over to the Scottish earls in the late 15th century. But Viking influence remains ever-present in place names and in the lilting local dialect, which the Orcadian poet Edwin Muir described as "a soft and musical inflection, slightly melancholy, but companionable, the voice of people who are accustomed to hours of talking in the long winter evenings and do not feel they have to hurry; a splendid voice for telling stories in."

One popular story still told on winter nights over peat fires, and captured by local historian John Robertson, is of how the unique and ancient ball game known as the Kirkwall Ba' came to be:

> Hundreds of years ago the people of Kirkwall, Orkney's capital town, were oppressed by a Scottish tyrant called Tusker, named for his protruding front

teeth. After years of oppression, the locals rose up in revolt and forced him to flee to the islands. With the people still living in fear of his return, a brave young man stepped forward and vowed to hunt Tusker down, cut off his head, and take it back as proof that their days of misery were over. He went off by horse and soon succeeded in his task. But while returning home with the bloody trophy swinging from the pommel of his saddle, Tusker's lifeless teeth broke the skin of the young man's leg. By the time he reached Kirkwall the leg had become infected and he was close to death. With a dying effort, the hero staggered to the Mercat Cross in the town center and threw the bloody head to the people. Grieved at the young man's untimely death, and riled by the sight of the hated Tusker's head, the people began kicking it angrily through the streets of town.

This, some say, is why twice a year a crowd of hundreds gathers at the very same town cross to knock each other senseless over a stuffed leather substitute for Tusker's head, called ba' in the local dialect. The story may well be apocryphal and revisionist, but it's as plausible as any other explanation of this unusual rite of excess. Grievances, I would soon come to learn, die slow and hard in Orkney. It's strangely satisfying to watch all these centuries later as old Tusker still pays the price for his tyranny.

The Kirkwall Ba' is a rite that for just two days each year, Christmas and New Year's Day, cleaves the friendly, picturesque port town of Kirkwall down its middle—quite literally—pitting friend against friend, neighbor against neighbor, even family members against each other. Simple to describe, but confounding to understand, the ba' is a traditional folk football game in which two "teams" of 100-plus men each compete over a homemade ball—also called the ba'—and attempt to claim it for their side, and for posterity.

The sides, known as the Uppies and the Doonies, represent an ancient, almost tribal, division of the town: the upper inland half and the lower ("doonward," as they say) portside half. Once the ball is thrown up in the town center to the pack of players, the goal of the Uppies is to move it several blocks up the street and touch it to the wall at Mackinson's Corner. The Doonies, in turn, must take the ball down-street to the port and submerge it in the bay. There are blessed few restrictions on how the ba' might reach either fate.

In all its unruly and primitive glory, this contest of wills, historians agree, is one of the only surviving remnants of the earliest form of football as it was once played across Europe—long before civilization or regulation got hold of it. As loyal Orcadians would argue, it is football as it was meant to be played. To take some measure of the distance the game has traveled, from rolling heads to aerodynamically engineered balls, and from the dirt lanes and open fields of medieval Europe to gleaming stadiums and neighborhood pitches around the globe, I decided to go to Kirkwall and experience the ba' firsthand.

When I arrived in Kirkwall on the penultimate day of 2009, a thick ice coated the cobblestone streets. Shoppers tiptoed by with caution, while the winds slicing through the narrow alleys pushed the temperature well below freezing. Scotland was suffering its coldest, snowiest winter in years. The news was filled with reports of road closings and deadly accidents, salt shortages and families stranded for days with distant relatives they'd only meant to visit for Christmas dinner.

In Kirkwall they were still recovering from the recent Christmas Ba', which had been even more damaging than usual. One ferrylouper had foolishly left his BMW parked on the street, and the pack of 200 or so burly men went right up and over the car, crushing it like an aluminum can. The Uppies and Doonies were still arguing over which side was responsible for the damages.

Most had moved on and were getting ready for Hogmanay, the Scottish New Year's celebration—and the culmination of the festivities: the New Year's Ba'. The whir of drills and rapping of hammers echoed across town as homeowners and shopkeepers erected heavy wooden barricades to protect their windows and doors from the violence of the pack.

My first stop in town was at the home of Graeme King, ba' player and 1998 champion and, at the age of 47, an emerging elder statesman of the game. A big, barrel-chested Viking of a man, Graeme's girth was nearly double my own. With a crushing handshake, he welcomed me into his sunken living room, where a fire burned next to a highly flammable-looking artificial Christmas tree. Gathered together were two other former champions—Bobby Leslie ('77) and Davie Johnston ('85), who'd been chosen to throw up this year's ba' in honor of the 25th anniversary of his win. Also in attendance was George Drever, one of a handful of craftsmen who painstakingly make the ba's each year.

All four, I quickly learned, are Doonies through and through.

"Right," asked Graeme before we'd even had a chance to sit down, "which way did you enter Kirkwall?"

"Well, let me see . . ." I recalled, tracing the route in my head. "I took the road up from the ferry landing and then came past the airport and . . ."

Davie sprung up from his chair. "Door's that way!" he shouted in mock disgust. "Now you're walking home!"

"Now hold on," said Graeme, as though arguing before a court. "He was in a car the whole time. More important is where you first set foot in Kirkwall."

"Well . . . that was at the B&B down on . . . Albert Street," I answered nervously, confused by the inquisition.

"Safely in Doonie territory!" declared Graeme with relief, slapping me hard on the back.

Once seated, Graeme explained that on ba' day everyone—players, spectators, outsiders, foreigners—is either Uppie or Doonie. It's not something you get to choose. You don't put it on or take it off like a team jersey. It's predetermined. If you're a local, affiliation is a matter of where you're born. If you're an outsider, it depends on how you enter Kirkwall for the first time in your life. Post Office Lane is the dividing line. Between that line and the shore you're a proud Doonie; between there and the head of town you're stuck being a godforsaken Uppie, forever.

"Once you've tied your colors to the mast," Graeme said,

"there's no going back. You can't say, 'Oh, I think I'll be an Uppie this year.' You are what you are for life."

I had apparently, by sheer luck of having chosen the right accommodations on the Internet, been spared a fate worse than death.

The origin of the Uppie and Doonie division is believed to date back eight centuries to the founding in the 12th century of St. Magnus Cathedral, the spectacular Romanesque structure that marks Kirkwall's town center. At that time the town was co-ruled by the Norse earls and the bishop of Orkney. Everyone who lived "down-the-gates" (*gata* being the Old Norse term for road) between the cathedral and the shore was considered a vassal of the earl. Everyone who lived "up-the-gates" above the cathedral was a vassal of the bishop. Over the centuries, a deep-seated rivalry emerged and identities hardened around which part of town you were born in. One of us—or one of them.

It's not hard to imagine that this may not have always been just a friendly rivalry. Violent clashes between the two groups, if they indeed occurred, would have threatened the order and stability of the small island community. In this scenario, the ba' may have come about as a way to settle conflict and work out differences without suffering the damages of petty wars.

In the tribal divide between Uppie and Doonie we can see the deeper roots of the greatest football rivalries: Real Madrid versus Barcelona, Celtic versus Rangers, Manchester United versus Liverpool. And that's just association football. American college football is equally famous for its annual clashes, such as Army versus Navy, Harvard versus Yale, and Texas versus Oklahoma, the "Red River Rivalry," named for the body of water that separates the two states. In fact the word "rival," which comes from the Latin *rivalis*, means "someone who uses the same stream as another." True to the name, a good rule of thumb for rivals is that the closer they are geographically, the more deep-seated the hatred. Of course, most great modern rivalries manage to exploit and exacerbate other divisions along religious, class, ethnic, or political lines. *Il Superclásico*, the epic derby in Buenos Aires between the River Plate and Boca Juniors clubs, has been cited by the London *Observer* as number one of the "50 sporting things you must do before you die." The two teams emerged in the early 1900s in the same working-class portside barrio of Boca, but River Plate moved to an affluent suburb soon after, earning the nickname *Los Milionarios* along with the eternal enmity of Boca supporters.

Now that I was a bishop's man and a Doonie, I was determined to embrace my new identity, and at least for the next couple of days I would find good reasons not to trust my Uppie enemies. But I didn't have to wait that long. As he waxed on about what it meant to be a Doonie, Graeme lamented that since he'd claimed the ba' for the Doonies back in 1998, they had managed to win just one other time—in 2006. Put in starker numerical terms, over the past decade the Doonies had a pathetic 1–20 record. My newly adopted club was, statistically speaking, a losing franchise. And we weren't happy about it.

"To be honest, it's annoying," said Bobby, a 69-year-old

retired librarian who still joins the fray every year against his wife's wishes and his doctor's counsel. "The Uppies have had the bragging rights for too long. You can't walk around with your shoulders high at this point."

Debate ensued among the men over how they'd become perpetual underdogs. One blamed the construction of the town's hospital in the late 1950s in Uppie territory. This meant more and more people since have been born Uppies—giving them unfair advantage in a contest determined as much by the size and weight of your team as anything. There have since been more than a few Doonie women who have chosen home birth over the alternative. Due in part to the arrival of the hospital, the convention for determining your affiliation began in the 1970s to shift away from your place of birth toward which side your father and grandfather had played on.

"We go around to the schools now to educate the next generation about the tradition," said Graeme. "Kids naturally want to be on the winning side. But we explain that's not how it works. We'll meet a lad who lives in Uppie territory who's sure he's Uppie, but we'll ask a few questions and find out, 'Oh, you had a granddad who won a ba' for the Doonies, did you? Well you're a Doonie then.'" Graeme and his mates were, in other words, in full recruitment mode.

Graeme ducked out of the room and returned with a shining black and brown sphere, which he ceremoniously placed in my hands. "There she is. The sacred orb herself."

Expecting to see some roughly stuffed and stitched facsimile of a ball, I gasped aloud at the obvious craftsmanship of what I held. Approximately the same size as a soccer ball but three times as heavy, the ba' is lovingly handstitched with eight-cord flax from top-quality leather donated by a German shoe company. Assembled with eight panels, painted alternately black or brown, and coated with a heavy shellac, the ba' is crafted not only to survive the punishing pressure of the pack on game day but to live on as the most cherished trophy of the man fortunate enough to take it home. At that moment, I wished Aidan could be there to hold that ball and feel with his own hands the care and artisanry that went into it. It was a thing of beauty.

George, a stocky, bearded 62-year-old whose day job is on a North Sea oil rig, estimates he's made close to 50 such balls over a 27-year span. Each ba' takes maybe 40 hours to produce. The stitching alone can take two days. The core is formed from crushed cork that came originally from the packing material in old fruit barrels and today is imported from Portugal.

"Ach, the stuffing is merciless work," he said, looking at his callused hands. "You leave a wee hole in one of the seams and keep packin' doon and doon and doon."

Rumors and accusations still fly that a Doonie ba' maker will slip a bit of seaweed in the ball or an Uppie a bit of brick from the wall to draw it magically back to its source. When asked if he'd ever attempted such sorcery himself, George pleaded the fifth. "Well, now I've heard the same stories . . ."

With a look of impatience, as though my fascination with the ball itself might distract me from the game's deeper meaning, Davie Johnston, a successful businessman in his late 50s who moved away from Orkney when he was 19 but has returned every year since to play the ba', leaned in to me and rested his hand solemnly on the ball.

"This isn't a trophy. This is heritage. This is history. This is tradition. This is what I won and my granddad and his granddad won before me and that's what it's about. It goes back that far and that deep. It's hard to understand the depth of feeling we have for it. It's huge."

Despite some recent efforts to trace the murky origins of football to the Chinese kick ball game of *cuju* or to the Roman game of *harpastum*, there's no evidence that those or any other sports of the ancient world had any direct influence on the development of football as it emerged in medieval Europe. *Cuju*, a game that may date as early as the fourth century BC, became wildly popular in the royal courts of the Han dynasty and eventually spread to Korea and Japan. The game, which resembled modern football in some ways, was described in a poem of the time:

> *A round ball and a square wall,*
> *Just like the Yin and the Yang.*
> *Moon-shaped goals are opposite each other,*
> *Each side has six in equal number.*

The stuffed ball was eventually replaced by one with an inflated pig's bladder and goalposts replaced gaps in walls as the target. Although the game played an important role in Chinese daily life and enjoyed an impressive run of more than

1,500 years, it never appears to have spread farther than the royal courts of East Asia. And while it's quite possible that Roman soldiers brought their game of *harpastum* with them when they invaded Britain, there are no accounts of Romans mixing it up with their subjects on British pitches. As one British scholar has humbly pointed out, *harpastum*, which involved assigned positions covering zones of play, was a more sophisticated game than early English football. In fact, it would take until nearly the 19th century for football to gain the level of organization and sophistication that the Roman sport—or *cuju*, for that matter—had achieved by the first century AD.

As scant as the historical record is when it comes to games and pastimes, football as it's played today can be confidently, if circuitously, traced to early medieval villages of Britain and France. One of the earliest mentions of a football-like game is from the ninth-century *Historia Brittonum*, a mythologized account of the earliest Britons. In the fifth century, according to the author, Vortigern, a Celtic king from Kent, was attempting to build a tower, but it kept mysteriously collapsing. The king's sages called upon him to sprinkle the tower's foundation with the blood of a boy born without a father, so he sent out emissaries far and wide to find such a boy. When they finally located him, he was in the middle of playing an undescribed game of ball (*pilae ludus*) with a group of boys. The fatherless child, possibly Britain's first recorded footballer, grew up to be none other than Merlin, the wizard of Arthurian legend. (Apparently, Harry Potter wasn't the first young wizard to play ball!)

Coincidentally, the first appearance of the words "ball"

and "ball play" in the English language also has an Arthurian connection. Around the year 1200, an account of the festivities surrounding King Arthur's coronation describes how the guests "drove balls far over the fields," an ambiguous reference that may or may not suggest a variation of football.

From its earliest appearance, "mob football," as the game came to be known, was played across England and France as part of festive celebrations, particularly those connected with the feast day known as Shrovetide. Celebrated elsewhere in the Christian world as Fat Tuesday or Mardi Gras, Shrovetide was traditionally the last hurrah of partying and excess before Ash Wednesday kicked in and Lenten fasting and penance began. Originally a pagan springtime celebration, Shrovetide involved a wide range of games and festivities, like bell ringing, cockfighting, cock throwing, and ball games.

What some regard as the earliest record of a football-like game in England is a description of Shrovetide games that took place in London in 1174:

> After dinner all the youth of the city proceed to a level piece of ground just outside the city for the famous game of ball. The students of every different branch of study have their own ball; and those who practice the different trades of the city have theirs too. The older men, the fathers and the men of property, come on horseback to watch the contests of their juniors . . .

Around the same time a nearly identical game, called *la soule*, was just beginning to take off in the villages of Normandy and Brittany. Played with a ball made of leather wrapped around a pig's bladder or stuffed with hemp, bran, or wool, *la soule* pitted parishes or villages against each other.

La *soule*, en Basse-Normandie.
D'après un croquis de M. J. L. de Condé.

Game of *la soule* in a village in Normandy, France, 1852.

Festive games took place at Shrovetide or at Easter, Christmas, or parish patron saint days. As with other variations of mob football, there was no limit to the number of players and no rules to speak of, with play involving huge violent scrums and chaotic melées. The goal, as in the ba', was to capture the ball and force it back to their home village, submerging it in a local pond to win the game. Some games ritualistically pitted married men against single men. One game in the town of Bellou-en-Houlme was reported to include 800 players and 6,000 spectators! After the games there would be the medieval equivalent of tailgate parties, with drinking, dancing, and carousing well into the evening. The game's early popularity in France is suggested by a deed from 1147 in which a lord specifies the settlement of a debt with the delivery of "seven balls of the largest size."

La soule and other forms of football were played not just for the sake of recreation but as magical rites to promote fertility and prosperity—thus the deep connection with Shrovetide and the arrival of spring. In his classic study of European mythology, *The Golden Bough*, J. G. Frazer interpreted early ball games as contests in which capturing the ball would ensure a good harvest or a good fishing season. In some villages in Normandy, for example, it was believed that the winning parish would secure the better apple crop that year. Another theory, put forward in 1929 by W. B. Johnson, is that the spherical ball for many early civilizations symbolized the sun. The captured ball represents the sun brought home to promote the growth of crops. The word *soule*, some linguists believe, may in fact derive from *sol*, the Latin word for sun.

In Orkney, there are similar long-standing beliefs that a win for the Uppies means a good potato harvest, whereas a win for the Doonies means the fishermen can expect a bountiful run of herring. To this day, Uppies will tell you that the potato blight that brought famine to the islands in 1846 began when the Doonies won the ba' that year and continued until 1875, when the Uppies finally broke their losing streak. That year, an old man was heard to comment, "We'll surely hae guid tatties this year, after the ba's gaen up."

It was just past noon on New Year's Day when the first spectators began to assemble on the sandstone steps of St. Magnus Cathedral. They staggered out of doorways and alleys, bundled in thick overcoats and shielding their tired eyes from the sun cresting above the glazed rooftops. The whole town, myself included, was still shaking off the dog that bit us at the previous night's Hogmanay festivities, highlights of which included the requisite bagpipe brigade and the ceremonial passing of countless bottles of Famous Grouse. I staked out a choice spot along the cathedral wall next to the Mercat Cross—the spot from which the ba's been thrown up for the past 200-plus years.

The sound of battle cries soon emerged from Albert Street as the Doonie players marched up from the waterfront—70 or so men of all ages, from 16 to 70, ready to do their part to tilt the cosmic balance back to the sea. The uniform of choice was a favorite, game-worn rugby shirt, a pair of old jeans, and steel-toed work boots. Experienced players had duct-taped their jean bottoms to their boots to deny their opponents a good handhold during the scrum. From the opposite side of town, down Victoria Street, came the Uppie contingent, prepared to push their supremacy into a new decade. Though deadly serious, the effect was pure theater—the Sharks and the Jets ready to rumble.

Reaching the cross first, the Doonies locked themselves into a tight mass, arms raised above their heads or placed around their mates' shoulders to keep them free to catch the ba'. Graeme stood up front taunting his opponents good-naturedly as they infiltrated and jostled for position like solid and striped billiard balls arranging themselves for the break.

Davie Johnston appeared from inside the cathedral with the ba' nestled safely in the crook of his arm and strode proudly to the base of the town cross. He was dressed to play, ready to jump into the fray right behind the ba'. He greeted teammates and surveyed the crowd below that had swelled to several hundred and filled in on all sides of the players. As the clock on the church tower inched toward the traditional hour of one, people began to whistle and cheer with anticipation.

"Go Uppies!" "Come on, Doonie boys!"

With the first loud clang of the church bell, Davie held the heavy ball high and lobbed it into the street below.

Arms shot up as the ba' was caught and instantly swallowed into the deep maw of the pack. The scrum surged and heaved as the two sides tried their best to gain first ground. Old codgers who in years past would have been in the eye of the storm ran around the outside where they coached and rallied their sons and grandsons.

The ba' is thrown up to the pack.

"Push now! Come on, more weight around this side!"

Players rotated in clockwork formation from the front to the back of the pack to push up- or downtown. Two-hundred-and-fifty-pound men leaned in on all sides at 45-degree angles, imposing a crushing pressure on the pack's center.

Then, either the ba'—no longer visible—moved or the weight of the pack shifted, sending the players crashing into the church wall. Spectators gasped and scurried back, some slipping on the ice that coated the grass above. As the men mashed themselves into the wall, one was lifted off his feet by the pressure and squeezed up and over the horde, feet in the air, tumbling out onto the grass. He stood up, wiping blood from his chin, and dove back into the pack, surfing the top of the mob until he sank back in. For 20 minutes, the pack moved no more than a few feet in either direction.

Several ferocious-looking wives circled the edge of the pack like wolves, riling and harassing their husbands, "Come on, Uppie men! Push harder!" It appeared to take all their restraint not to jump in themselves, which they've been known to do on occasion. A newspaper report of the 1866 Christmas Day Ba' describes a moment in the contest when the ba' was heading up-street and "an Amazon who ought to have been home with her mamma caught it and threw it down." In the 1920s an Uppie player was said to have run the ba' through the front door of his house and handed it off to his wife, who hid it under her petticoat. Once the pack of players had moved on, leaving shattered crockery in their wake, she walked unnoticed right to the goal and won the day. Despite playing a vital supporting role, though, the only time women played a ba' exclusively was toward the end of World War II, when many men were off at war and the women felt empowered to have their own game. The new variation was not well received by the traditional men of Orkney, however, and was soon shut down. One reporter expressed some relief that there were few injuries among the participating ladies and that the "casualties, for the most part, were confined to permanent waves, hats, scarves, shoes, and stockings."

I was standing about ten feet back from the pack—at a safe distance, I'd thought—fiddling with my camera when I heard, "It's going down!" The pack split open and a human stampede was coming my way. I held my arms to my sides, sucked my weight in, and did my best imitation of a lamppost while 100 or so men thundered past me on either side, knocking me back and forth. A Doonie player had made the break and gained a block before the Uppie pack caught up and tackled him. But just before his face hit the cobblestones he managed to pass the ball off to a spectator, Nigel Thomson, a veteran Doonie sprinter who'd won school medals in the 400 meter. Before anyone knew what had happened, Nigel was dashing toward the port in his winter coat and Russian fur hat with a mob of angry Uppies in hot pursuit.

As I turned and ran with all the other spectators, a Red Cross volunteer caught up to me, my notebook—now sporting a dirty shoeprint—in her hand.

"Mind yerself now," she cautioned. Nearby a disheveled young woman was hopping about on one foot searching for the shoe that had been ripped off in the frenzy.

I reached the pack several blocks away. The Uppies had caught Nigel and forced the ba' out of Albert Street into a narrow side street, or wynd, as it's known here. The move was a blow to the advancing Doonies, slowing their momentum and cutting them off from their main route to the sea. In the heat of the ba', Graeme had assured me, what appears to the observer as a random move by a mindless mob, is usually quite deliberate and strategic. Knowing every wynd, nook, and cranny between here and their goal, the Uppies would now be mapping the route that would give them the best advantage.

The pack had plugged up the ten-foot-wide wynd like a stopped-up drain. I watched as one player's back was smashed against a pipe. Arms above his head, he winced, pushed, and wriggled to create more space to breathe. Doonies ran around the back to reinforce and push the ba' back toward the main street, while the Uppies did the opposite. The effort, in either case, was useless. With occasional counts of "One, two, three . . . heave!" the pack would surge a few inches in one direction or the other but with little change in position. I spotted Graeme's bald head bobbing up in the thick of the scrum. At his age, and having won his ba' years ago, I'd have thought he might retreat to the perimeter and let younger men take the brunt of it. But there he was at ground zero.

After my last brush with near death, I planned my own escape route down a side alley strung with clotheslines should the pack break suddenly in my direction again.

Watching the gridlock in the alley, it struck me that this game is as much about moving the pack as it is about moving the actual ball, which had been out of sight since Davie first threw it in over an hour earlier. Finally, there was a ruckus and hollering up ahead. A break was on, mercifully not toward me this time. The Doonies were on the move again. They'd forced the ba' back to the corner of Albert Street and a fierce struggle was on in front of the Frozen Food Grocers. I watched fists fly and bodies hurl against the thick wooden barricade bolted into the window frames, the only thing standing between the men and freezers full of 'nips and tatties (turnips and potatoes, the national vegetables of choice). Parents with small children backed away cautiously, anticipating the worst. The pack made a turn toward the water and began to bounce its way along stone walls and shop barricades. But the Uppies managed to force the ba' off the main street once again—this time into a six-foot-wide dead-end alley between the local bank and photo store.

Fewer than half of the players could squeeze into the alley. Several young players ran around the back of the building, shimmied under a low driveway gate, propped a Dumpster against a wall, and scrambled onto a flat roof overlooking the alley.

One Doonie surveyed the scene below and reported out to his mates and supporters, "The Uppies have it wedged under a staircase."

A more seasoned player, clearly upset with this turn of events, shook his head and scuffed his boot on the ground, "Ach, it'll be in there a good long while now."

As though on cue, an icy drizzle began. Umbrellas came out and hoods went up as spectators and players alike settled in for a long "hold," as they refer to periods when the ba's movement gets shut down. Several Red Cross medics came running down the street. One of the players in the alley had passed out from lack of oxygen. A few men heaved against the gate blocking the entrance to the roof until the latch gave way. The medics rushed in and were waiting for the man to be handed over the roof when a red-haired lad ran over.

"It's okay, he's woken up!"

It was now 3:15 and, being just 50 miles of latitude south of Greenland, the midwinter darkness was already settling in. As the Christmas lights flickered on and the drizzle gave way to a lashing hail, the madness of it all came over me. I was standing outside a miserable gray alley with hundreds of other people, soaked to the bone and shivering, watching grown men risk life and limb to get a ball out from under a staircase. It was irrational, utterly pointless, and absolutely thrilling.

Did the ball first evolve from stone projectiles used by early man in the hunt? Or was it a symbolic stand-in for their prey—the object rather than the weapon of pursuit? Back in Europe's Paleolithic days—long before Maes Howe and Skara Brae were built—hunters from competing bands followed and tracked the same herds across plains and forests without reference to boundaries or territories. The band that was fastest and strongest and smartest won the day. And the hunter who led the way and outsmarted both prey and challengers was hailed as a hero. As depicted in the dramatic cave paintings of Lascaux and Altamira, magic was conjured and rituals were conducted—whatever it took to tilt the balance in favor of the home team.

The rise of agriculture roughly 10,000 years ago may

have shifted the nature of the pursuit—from a good hunt to a bountiful harvest—but it didn't change the nature of the battle. Whichever tribe or village secured and could defend the best land and most reliable water supply would have the best chance of surviving the long, cold European winter. For agricultural peoples, magic and ritual focused on attracting and capturing the sun and the rains. As populations grew and prime land became scarcer, boundaries were drawn and defended and competition grew fiercer and more violent.

It's hardly a stretch to suggest that the metaphors that still resonate most in describing football, and other competitive sports—the team "on the hunt" for the championship, "hungrier" than their opponents, "battling" and "claiming territory"—are more than mere metaphors. They're collective memories of when games also served as fertility rites and when the ball symbolized the hunter's prey or the farmer's sun—when the stakes of winning or losing were, quite literally, life or death.

The Kirkwall Ba' is a holdover from the earliest forms of football in so many respects—the near absence of rules, lack of boundaries, and large, moblike teams, to name just a few. But one element that stands out as being truly premodern is the goal of the game itself. Whereas the object of modern football, and most other ball games that have survived, is to drive the ball into enemy territory to penetrate the defended goal, the object of the ba' is quite the opposite: to capture the ball and take it home.

It's tempting to see in the ba' a survival of the primitive

magic of the hunt and the rituals of early farmers directed at claiming the prize—and the sustenance it offered—to ensure survival. The association of early football and the French *la soule* with Shrovetide fertility rites, and the ba's association with the winter solstice, supports this deep, primal connection. Over time, competition became less about survival and more about capturing territory and amassing political power. The focus of ball games shifted from capturing the prize to simply attacking and defeating the enemy—an elaborate means to an end rather than the end itself. And the "goal" became to overrun the enemy's defenses, to score against and dominate them.

However accurate a picture this may be, there's little question that the physical violence of the ba'—and the tenuous restraint of violence found in its modern variations—is fundamental to the game and its origins.

Some of the very earliest records of football are accounts of fatal accidents that occurred in the heat of the game. In 1280, a friendly Sunday afternoon game of what appears to be football in the Northumberland region of England turned deadly when one player running toward the ball impaled himself on the (supposedly sheathed) knife of his opponent and, as the witness described it, "died by misadventure." In 1321, apparently before players figured out that knives and football didn't mix, another identical "death by sheathed knife during football match" was reported that led to the acquittal of the perpetrator, a church canon, by Pope John XXII.

And just as violence and murder found their way into

otherwise innocent matches, football seems to have brought occasional inspiration to otherwise mundane acts of homicide. In the same year as the church canon's knife incident, two brothers were convicted for murdering the servant of a monastery and then playing football with the victim's head!

Like the Kirkwall Ba', medieval folk football in Britain was a consistently rowdy and violent affair played mostly by commoners in the open fields of country villages or in narrow city lanes. As with the Uppies and Doonies, everyone was invited to join the mayhem—young and old, men and women, even clergy. As an observer of the time noted, "Neyther maye there be anye looker on at this game, but all must be actours." Is it possible that the violent hooliganism that's plagued modern football in recent decades reflects a submerged desire on the part of frustrated supporters to reclaim their historic right to join the scrum? That the poor skull crackers just want their go at the ball?

Mass games played on Shrove Tuesday or other holidays—fueled by mead and beer—would wreak havoc and leave a path of destruction in their wake. By 1314, when the word "football" first appears unequivocally by name in the historical record, its reputation for inciting violence was already widespread. That first mention, in fact, is from a "Proclamation Issued for the Preservation of the Peace" on behalf of Edward II banning the game within the limits of London:

> Whereas our Lord the King is going towards the parts
> of Scotland, in his war against the enemies, and has

especially commanded us strictly to keep his peace.
. . . And whereas there is a great uproar in the City,
through certain tumults arising from great footballs
in the fields of the public, from which many evils
perchance do arise—which may God forbid—we do
command and do forbid, on the King's behalf, upon
pain of imprisonment, that such game shall be practiced henceforth within the city.

In the century following that first reference, football was
banned by English monarchs nine times. The French kings
and clerics followed suit with their equally excessive game
of *la soule*. In 1440, a French bishop called for a ban on that
"dangerous and pernicious [game] because of the ill feeling,
rancor, and enmities, which in the guise of recreative pleasure, accumulate in many hearts."

But while the violent nature of the game clearly served as
the outward rationale offered for these prohibitions, a closer
read of the records suggests something else was at work. The
sports of choice for noblemen of the times were those of the
medieval tournament—jousting, fencing, and archery—all
viewed as practical exercises that prepared men for battle.
Time spent kicking balls around fields was time taken away
from archery, which the common men were required to practice so they'd be ready to defend the kingdom. Football and
other games were seen as "useless and unlawful exercises." In
1365 Edward III insisted that "every able-bodied man" in
London "shall in his sports use bows and arrows or pellets
or bolts" and forbade them "under pain of imprisonment to

meddle in the hurling of stones, loggats and quoits, handball, football . . . or other vain games of no value."

All prohibitions, on either side of the Channel and whatever their motivation, were of course duly ignored by the fun-loving masses, and football and other "useless" games lived on. As William Baker summarized the stubborn determination that allowed football to survive into the modern era: "In the face of moral preachments and official decrees, English common folk refused to relinquish their games. Even with the passing of feudalism they had few rights, but apparently considered their freedom to play as an integral part of their birthright."

It was 4:00 PM and the residents of Kirkwall were actively exercising their birthright under a cold, lashing rain. Several more players had since passed out and been revived, but the ba' remained stubbornly tucked under the stairs in the alley behind the photo store—exactly where the Uppies had taken it nearly two hours earlier. Touched by boredom, I walked around to survey the scene from the main street. Silhouetted against a backdrop of flickering security lights, steam rose off the pack of men who plugged every crevice of the alley. It was hard to tell one player from another amid the tangle of arms and legs and rugby stripes.

I spotted a historic plaque on the wall alongside the alley. The ba', it seems, had eerily settled just a few feet from the site of St. Olaf's Church, built in the 11th century by Rögnvald Brusason, one of the first Viking earls of Orkney. A sandstone archway is all that's left of the original chapel. The plaque notes that human remains were uncovered here some years ago and reburied just beneath the alley's flagstones. It occurred to me that some of the players might be joining their ancestors in Valhalla if they didn't get out of there soon.

Just then I overheard a spectator utter the magical words, "That's it, I'm off to the pub!" Unable to feel any of my extremities at that point, I regarded the suggestion as a spark of genius. I followed my new friend to the waterfront and climbed over the barricade protecting the entrance to St. Olaf's Pub. Half the town (the smart half) seemed to be inside the jammed bar. I ordered and quickly tossed back a shot of whisky, asking the bartender if I was at risk of missing any of the action.

"Not to worry," she said. "When they get out of that alley, you'll bloody well hear about it." I ordered another shot, which she poured into a plastic cup with a wink.

Taking the cue, I climbed back over the barricade and headed up the street with my new layer of insulation in hand. From the position of the crowd, I clearly hadn't missed a thing, though there was some stirring up ahead. Minutes later a guttural roar went up as the pack shot out of the alley like a cork fired from a champagne bottle. They broke toward the harbor. The Doonies were on the go again! My heart raced as I bounded toward the water with the crowd behind the ba'. Was it going all the way?

We caught up to the pack on Harbour Street, just a hundred feet now from the water's edge. Small fishing boats bobbed in the choppy surf nearby. A fierce battle was on against the windows of St. Olaf's, where we'd just been drinking.

The chants began, "Doonies! Doonies! Doonies!" An upset was in the air and the Uppie supporters confirmed it with their silence. For another 30 minutes or so, the pack thrashed about the waterfront. A boy was thrown hard to the sidewalk and the medics stepped in. The Uppies weren't going down without a proper fight.

Then it happened. The final break, by a fellow named David Johnstone. Not, it turns out, our man Davie who threw in the ba'. And not the legendary David Johnstone who years earlier had his glass eye turned backward in the heat of a ba' contest. But yet another David Johnstone. He was on his knees in the crush of the scrum, I learned later, with the ba' in his hands when a gap appeared portside. He reached out and threw it hard. That's when I spotted it, sailing above the heads of the crowd and clearing the iron rails at the harbor wall, where it splashed into the waters of Kirkwall Bay.

A cheer went up from the crowd as four Doonie men dove into the black, icy waters after the prize. There, by the water's edge, was an ecstatic Graeme calling to his younger teammates, "If you're claiming it, get in there!" The Doonies had won the ba' and broken their long drought. Now the battle was on to see who would take home the "sacred orb." I pushed my way through the crowd and peered over the harbor railings. In the dark, I could make out traces of four or more players tussling in the water as each tried to climb up the seaweed-covered ladder with the trophy. The ba' finally made its way up to the street and through the crowd with several men grappling for it the whole time.

"Norman's ba'!" called out a young woman in the crowd. "Ronald's ba'!" cried another. Other voices joined in, offering the names of other players who they felt deserved the honor.

As Davie had explained to me two nights earlier, the winner of the ba' isn't simply the player who ends up with it, or even the one who fought the hardest that day. Just as you can't choose to be Uppie or Doonie, you can't expect to have a lucky day and walk away with the prize of a lifetime. The winner is the man who's showed up year after year in the hail and the ice, who's had more ribs broken in the thick of the scrum than he can count, who's given up his Christmas Days and New Year's Days year after year for the love of this crazy game. As Davie had enacted the real-time negotiations for me as they were playing out among the Doonies at that moment, "Did he play in other ba's? Did he help out his teammates? Did he ever miss a ba'? What was his attitude when he was losing?" Within five minutes, every part of your past will be dredged up on the spot.

Finally, after nearly an hour of heated debate and scuffling, one man was hoisted above the mob with the ba' over his head. Forty-seven-year-old veteran Rodney Spence had won the honor. After five hours of play, the ba' would go home with him, along with 300 or so players and spectators for whom he'd have to host a raucous all-night party. Rodney would, for the rest of his life, have on his fireplace mantel the greatest prize any Orkney man could ever hope for. The Doonies would hold their heads high in town once again and would enjoy bragging rights for at least another 51 weeks. And the fishing, quite possibly, would be the best it's been for years.

Chapter Three

ADVANTAGE, KING

To see Good Tennis! What diviner joy
Can fill our leisure, or our minds employ?
. . . Let other people play at other things;
The King of Games is still the Game of Kings.

J. K. STEPHEN, "PARKER'S PIECE," 1891

Sometime around AD 1220 a German monk named Caesarius wrote down a fabulous tale. It seems a few years earlier a young Parisian monk-in-training—known as something of an "idiot" by his peers—was approached by the Devil with the temptation of a magic stone. "As long as you hold this in your hand," offered the Devil, "you will know everything." Your classic Faustian bargain.

The young idiot became an instant scholar but was then quickly gripped by a mysterious illness and gave up the ghost. The young man's soul was snatched by demons and hauled off to hell. There, against a ghoulish backdrop of sulfurous vapors, the demons split into two teams and proceeded to knock the young man back and forth. "And those standing at the one end hit the poor soul after the fashion of the game at ball, and those at the other end caught it in midair with their hands," which of course had claws as sharp as iron nails.

Though it might stretch the modern imagination to connect this devils' pastime to a classic Federer-Nadal showdown, this medieval account is believed to be the first printed reference to the game we now know as tennis.

Appearing first in the north of France in the 12th century, the earliest form of tennis was known as *jeu de paume*, the "game played with the palm of the hand." Noticeably absent from the demons' bout or from other early accounts is any sign of a racket or a net, what most would consider the two hallmark features of the sport. In fact, over a period of some 300 years, most of the rules and scoring methods still used in the modern game would develop before anyone thought to string catgut through a wooden frame or stretch a net across the court.

It's no great surprise that the first account of tennis would come from a monk, given the dominant role of the Roman Catholic Church in daily medieval life. Ball games of all kinds were played on Easter and other feast days and, like most activities, were tightly controlled by the clergy to ensure that no sins were committed in the course of having fun. But unlike football, which was played by commoners among the open fields and narrow lanes of medieval villages, tennis began within the confines of cloisters, the inner courtyards of medieval monasteries. More often than not, the most avid players were the monks and abbots who lived there, as many an ecclesiastical account confirms. "On Easter Day, after dinner," a report from 13th-century France recounts, "the Canon of St. Cyr, at Nevers, joined with the Bishops in believing that their dignity would not suffer by a little volleying of a tennis ball."

What would later become known to the world as the sport of kings got its start, strangely enough, as the sport of priests.

Some 800 or so years after inventing the game of tennis, the French remain as passionate about the game as they ever were. Each May and June, thousands of fans pack themselves into Roland Garros Stadium in Paris to watch the greatest players test their mettle on its clay courts at the French Open. But I hadn't traveled all the way to France to learn about lawn tennis, a relatively recent variation devised and patented in 1874 by Major Walter Wingfield, a society Welshman looking for new ways to amuse his garden party guests.

Instead, I went to France to watch and play *jeu de paume*, an obscure, challenging, and stubbornly traditional sport that has changed little in more than 400 years.

Jeu de paume is played indoors on a large enclosed court that, even to the uninitiated, bears a striking resemblance to the medieval cloisters of its ancestors, complete with sloping penthouse roofs, open galleries, and other features with monastic origins. An intentionally sagging net divides the court in half, the net and the racket having been introduced in the 16th century.

At the game's peak there were, according to one French source, "more tennis players in Paris than drunkards in England." A Venetian ambassador of the time remarked famously that "the French are born with rackets in their hands." In 1596 there were 250 *jeu de paume* courts in Paris alone that were said to have employed some 7,000 people. Today, there are just 47 courts left in the world and only three are to be found in France. History, it seems, has been kinder to English drunks than to French *jeu de paume* players.

I began my journey on a train packed with tourists and weekenders bound for Fontainebleau, located 35 miles south of Paris. The town of 16,000 is surrounded by the Fontaine-bleau Forest, a dramatic woodland more than three times the size of Manhattan that once served as the favored hunting grounds of the French kings. My fellow travelers sported backpacks and climbing gear, no doubt on their way to enjoy a day of bouldering among the forest's famous outcrops. I stood out from the crowd in my sneakers and tennis whites, clearly bound for more civilized pursuits. I was headed for the palace grounds of the Château de Fontainebleau, site of the oldest tennis court in France and one of the oldest in the world.

A spring drizzle welcomed me. In the empty town square, an antique merry-go-round carried a lone, glum child dressed in a furry bunny suit. I could tell it was going to be an interesting day.

The chateau, together with its gardens, ornamental lakes, fountains, and endless winding pathways, is a sprawling monument to royal excess. Little more than a country cousin to the sophisticated splendor of Versailles, it nevertheless dwarfs the modern town that's grown up like a collection of caretaker cottages around it. I entered the chateau grounds through the grand Court of the White Horse and walked along the long cobbled pathway that leads to the chateau's main entrance. Straight ahead was the double-horseshoe staircase where in 1814 Napoleon bade farewell to the Old Guard and went into exile on the island of Elba.

To the left of the staircase I spotted what I'd come for. A small wooden sign, painted with a gold tennis racket, hung over an old gray door, the only indication that inside was the royal tennis court of King Henry IV.

I pushed open the creaky wooden door and walked up several monolithic stairs, my footsteps echoing in the hall. In a tiny side office that also serves as the court's pro shop, bathroom, and changing room, I encountered Matthew Ronaldson, Fontainebleau's club pro. Matty is a good-natured young Englishman of 27 with blond hair and an unabashed, near-reckless love for *jeu de paume*, or what he and his countrymen call "real tennis" (in the United States it's called court tennis and in Australia royal tennis). When I caught up with him, he was hunched over a wooden workbench with a basket of balls at his feet, a ripped-open ball in one hand, and a needle and thread in the other. "Have a seat. If you don't mind, can I keep sewing while we talk? I've got a backlog of balls to catch up on."

The sorry state of *jeu de paume* in its home country is well illustrated by the fact that the club pros at the only three courts remaining in France are English.

Matty comes from the closest thing the sport of real tennis has to a ruling dynasty. His uncle, Chris Ronaldson, was world champion from 1981 to 1987 and long-serving pro to the British royal family at Hampton Court, the oldest tennis court in the world, built between 1526 and 1529. Chris taught Prince Edward how to play and wrote the only instruction manual on the game. Matty's dad and cousin run two other clubs in England, and another cousin runs one in Washington, D.C. All told, members of the Ronaldson clan run close to one-eighth of the remaining real tennis courts in the world.

As we talked and Matty sewed balls together I soon came to learn that the difference between real tennis and what Matty and his fellow players—usually with a hint of contempt—still call "lawn tennis" begins with the balls. Your typical lawn tennis ball is factory-made in South Africa from rubber mixed with 14 to 18 chemicals and covered with felt that's steamed to make the nap fluffy, increasing wind resistance and control. All any player needs to do is purchase a can of these balls at the local sports shop and peel open the pressurized can. Ready for action.

Not so with real tennis. There's no factory in the world that makes real tennis balls, no store that sells them. Each ball is handcrafted on site by the club pro from scratch.

Matty lined up his materials to show me how a ball is made. "For starters, the core of the ball is made of crushed cork."

"Where do you get the cork?" I asked.

He looked at me in disbelief.

"Um, *wine* corks?" he answered, pointing to a couple of recently emptied bottles in the corner of the office. "The club members bring them in. And of course I do my level best to contribute to the game as well."

He pulled out a plastic shopping bag filled with corks

and fished out a couple of synthetic ones. "These might keep wine fresh all right, but they're pretty much useless for making tennis balls," he said as he tossed them in the garbage.

As we learn from Shakespeare, who mentioned tennis no fewer than six times in his plays, the most common substance used for stuffing tennis balls in 17th-century England was human hair. In *Much Ado About Nothing* there is this exchange between Don Pedro and Claudio about the bachelor Benedick:

DON PEDRO: Hath any man seen him at the Barber's?

CLAUDIO: No, but the barber's man hath been seen
with him, and the old ornament of his cheek hath
already stuffed tennis-balls.

In 1920, during renovation work at Westminster Hall in London a few old leather balls stuffed with hair were found among the rafters.

The French of that same period seem to have been less inclined to make use of human hair . . . or maybe they were just less hirsute. They used dog hair instead, stuffed into white leather covers. There was enough mystery and controversy back then around exactly what materials were being used to stuff tennis balls that one French king passed a decree requiring that the balls used on the royal court be stuffed only with wool "and not containing sand, ground chalk, metal shavings, lime, bran, sawdust, ash, moss, powder, or earth."

I mentioned this controversy to Matty as he was shredding and pounding a few corks into little bits and asked him if it continues today.

"Well, no one's stuffing balls with hair anymore—not that I know of at least." But, he added, real tennis players definitely notice the quality and craftsmanship of the balls.

"See, even after being bashed about for days, mine keep their spherical shape," he boasted, putting a worn-out old ball in my hand. "Some young pros try to cut corners or just don't take the right care and they end up with soft, lumpy balls that don't bounce properly."

Matty went back to work, pulling out a small scale and weighing out exactly 60 grams of crushed cork. He stuffed the cork into an old ball cover, tied it up, pounded it with a mallet until it formed a consistent, hard sphere, and then wrapped the core with white fabric tape.

"Now here comes the really tedious part," he announced, reaching for a spool of black thread. I admit I couldn't quite believe we hadn't yet reached the tedious part. Tying one end of the thread to the bench, he proceeded to meticulously tie the ball, first in one direction, then turning 90 degrees and tying in the other, then splitting sections to form orbits of thread at every possible angle. "Doing this right is the key to having your balls stay hard and keep their shape."

Looking at the near-finished product, with its crisscrossed layers of thread and tape, I recalled an image I'd come upon in a 1767 French encyclopedia illustrating the process of ball production and the tools involved. It struck me as remarkable that so little had changed, from the materials to the methods to the essentially medieval technology that Matty still uses to ply his craft.

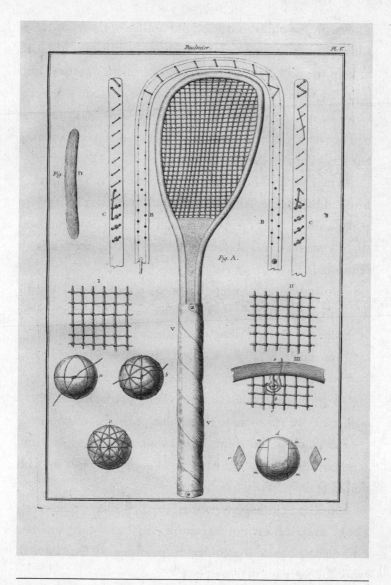

Illustration of racket and ball production, from Garsault's *Art du Palmier-Raquetier*, 1767.

Finally, he pulled out a roll of familiar optic-yellow wool felt and cut two long strips, which he tacked onto the ball to hold them in place. He then began to trim the edges into rounded forms that would neatly cover the ball's surface. Once he'd achieved the right shapes he went on to sew the ball's cover together with needle and thread, making sure the felt was tight and even all around.

"There we go!" he declared triumphantly as he tossed the finished ball to me. All told, it had taken him 45 minutes to make a single ball. The finished ball I held in my hand was slightly smaller and about 25 percent heavier than a lawn tennis ball.

"Do you mind if I keep this one as a souvenir?" I asked.

Matty's face took on a look of visible pain as he stared silently at the fruit of his hard labor in my greedy hand. "Well . . ."

"You know what, never mind," I said, immediately embarrassed.

"It's just that it takes so bloody long to make one and, to be honest, we sell these to the public for twenty euros each."

He plucked the shiny new ball out of my hand and reached into his discard basket. "Would you be okay with an old one?"

I took the gift happily, embarrassed by what would surely not be my last breach of real tennis etiquette. Matty grabbed two rackets out of the corner of his office. "That's enough work for one day. Shall we play?"

The *jeu de paume* court at Fontainebleau is a spectacular, cavernous space, the largest real tennis court in the world (there's very little standardization in the size of real tennis courts). The stone construction of the court's outer walls gives it the damp, echoing feel of a medieval castle's great hall. The original tennis court was built here by Henry IV in 1600 along with a second outdoor one of which only traces remain. When "good king Henry," one of France's most popular kings, wasn't granting religious liberties to the Protestants or guaranteeing a "chicken in the pot" for every commoner, he was known to relax with a spirited game of *paume*. In fact, he loved tennis so much that after narrowly surviving the St. Bartholomew's Day Massacre in 1572, in which thousands of Protestants perished in Paris at the hands of rioting mobs, he rose first thing the next morning to continue a tennis match he'd started the day before.

Henry's court burned down in 1701 but was rebuilt from the original walls in 1732. Napoleon restored the court in 1812. Then, during World War I it was put to use as a recovery ward for wounded soldiers and later became a concert hall before being reinaugurated as a tennis court in 1981.

As I stepped out on the court, which as recently as 1991 was still surfaced with the original Normandy limestone tiles, I could almost picture Marie Antoinette cheering on Louis XVI from the gallery. Or Cardinal Richelieu coaching Louis XIII on his forehand. A total of eight French monarchs had played on this court. Now it was my turn.

I felt honored to be learning the particulars of real tennis from a player of the Ronaldson pedigree who, by his own estimate, would be ranked around 20 in the world—that is, if the sport had a proper ranking system. Despite being among the elite players on the planet, Matty complained that it didn't mean much in a sport as obscure as his. And, worst of all for a young single guy, it didn't get him very far with the girls.

"I was with another player recently, chatting up some girls at a pub. When we told them we were among the top real tennis pros in the world and then had to explain what real tennis is, you could just see their eyes glazing over."

He handed me a racket, and for a second I thought he was having a good laugh at my expense. It looked like a relic of an earlier age, the kind of antique racket you might pick up at a country flea market and hang on your wall next to, say, your coat of armor. It was long, wooden, and incredibly heavy, with a tiny head and an unforgivably small sweet spot—what in lawn tennis would count as five excellent reasons to upgrade to a better racket.

This was no joke, however. The rules of real tennis require that rackets be made "almost entirely of wood." The heavy weight is required to handle the heavier balls and the head is kept small to allow for extremely tight strings. Most unusually, the racket head is curved slightly up from the handle like the blade of a hockey stick to make it easier to hit balls close to the floor or scoop them out of corners.

Matty held out his right hand. "If you look at the racket, it's shaped like a hand. Since the game started out with just the palm of the hand, when they got around to making rackets they modeled them after the anatomy of the hand."

The racket I held in my hand was made, like most real tennis rackets, by Grays of Cambridge, England, a five-generation family business that's had a virtual monopoly on the industry since 1885. Four long-term employees handcraft each racket from willow staves and loops of ash and, in a rare concession to modernity, strengthen and make it rigid by adding up to three layers of a vulcanized fiber. The fiber performs like graphite but is actually made from paper, which means almost the entire racket, in accordance with regulation, is made from wood or wood products.

When the racket was first introduced to the game of tennis in the 16th century, it wasn't immediately seen by all as such a great advance. In the first account to mention the racket in 1505, King Philip of Castile played a match at Windsor Castle against the marquis of Dorset while King Henry VII of England watched. The marquis used only his hand while Philip used a racket, so Philip took a one-point handicap. In another account written by the Dutch scholar Erasmus, one player suggests to the other that they employ rackets: "We shall sweat less if we play with the racket," he argued. But his opponent, either a purist or a glutton for punishment, had no time for such newfangled inventions. "Let us leave the nets to fishermen; the game is prettier if played with the hands."

We took our positions at either end of the enclosed court. Though they vary in dimensions, all real tennis courts have the same layout and are both wider (about 32 feet) and longer (about 96 feet) than a lawn tennis court. The lofty ceiling at Fontainebleau is 35 feet high, tall enough to allow all but the highest lob shots. The features of the court unmistakably resemble the medieval cloister they're based on. Three sides of the court have sloping roofs, known as penthouses, below

Jeu de paume in a royal Paris court, 1632, and at Fontainebleau, 2009.

which are netted galleries from which spectators can watch the game.

Unlike lawn tennis, there is a service end and a receiving, or hazard, end, and each has different features and means of scoring points. Having been forced to play lawn tennis by my mother as a kid, I was hopeful I could hold my own or at least keep from embarrassing myself. Matty's first serve was a slice serve that, as required by the rules, bounced off the penthouse on my end before crumpling up and dying against the back wall.

I stood there helplessly looking at the little cork-stuffed ball still wedged into the corner of the court, appreciating like never before what the introduction of rubber did for the world of sport.

"That ball didn't bounce at all!" I whined.

Matty was clearly enjoying this. "Sorry, I served it with enough backspin that it never got out of the corner."

15–love.

Unlike lawn tennis, where a hard-hit topspin kicks the ball up and out of the back court, making it hard to return, in real tennis it's the opposite. Topspin brings the ball high off the back wall and gives your opponent an easy opportunity to smash it back and score a point. Real tennis is all about the backspin, all about killing what absurdly little bounce there is in the ball in the first place.

He served again. This time the ball didn't so much bounce as roll off the side penthouse and around to the back. I readied my racket for a forehand return only to see the ball roll behind me and over to my backhand. I tied myself in knots trying to spin the heavy racket around to the other side in time, but it was too late.

30–love, and I'd yet to touch the ball.

Matty served for a third time and this time I was paying more attention to the ball's trajectory. I caught it off the back wall with a decent, if slightly shaky, backhand. He snapped the ball back to my left again. I pulled back early, ready to swing when suddenly the ball changed course, now moving sideways across the court and nowhere near my racket.

"Ha! I got the *tambour*," he declared cheerily. "You see, you thought you knew where the ball was going, and suddenly it was in a corridor of uncertainty."

From my own experience, I was quite used to dealing with base paths, alleys, sidelines, and baselines but I wasn't sure I was up for playing a sport that involved "corridors of uncertainty." Matty had quite artfully and intentionally placed the ball into an inconveniently angled buttress that protrudes into the service end of the court, just as the flying buttress would have in a medieval courtyard.

40–love.

Before going any further in describing my utter humiliation at Matty's hands, I should address one of the most obvious mysteries in this strange game of tennis. It's a question that seems to have kept etymologists busy for the past century. One has argued for the game's Arabic origins, claiming that its name refers to the ancient sunken city of Tinnis in the Nile Delta; it was famous for its fabrics, which, he guessed, could have been used to stuff balls. Good try.

Another speculated that it derived from the old German word for a threshing floor, *tenni*, which may have at times doubled as a tennis court. Yet another thought it was an English word that came from an early version of the game played with ten players. And so on.

It turns out, however, that the word "tennis," like everything else about the game, has French roots and derives from *tenez*, which means "take heed." This was what the server once called out to warn his opponent as he put the ball in play. Although French in origin, the word first appeared in Italy in 1324 in a strange account of 500 French cavaliers, "all noblemen and great barons," who arrived in Florence one day with their fancy French game (not realizing, apparently, that Italians couldn't care less about tennis and were quite content playing football for the rest of history). An Italian priest, the account states, "played all day with them at ball, and at this time was the beginning in these parts of playing at tenes."

So that's the word tennis. Now what about the bizarre scoring system that assigns 15 points instead of one and "love" instead of zero? Leave it to the French once again. Most scholars (though debate rages in esoteric tennis history circles) agree that it comes from the French *l'oeuf*, meaning "egg" (which, if you think about it, closely approximates the number zero). Over time, the English bastardized the term—as they tend to do—into "love" and we've never looked back or asked whether zero might not make more sense.

As for a scoring system that assigns 15 points for winning one measly shot, it appears that people were already scratching their heads over this one as early as 1415. Unable to find a logical explanation for the peculiar system in the here and now, one writer of the time turned to God and the afterlife: "In much the same way as a tennis player wins fifteen points for a single stroke, those who support and further righteousness and justice are also awarded fifteen times or more than normal for their good deed."

The true answer, scholars have determined, is far less noble and has to do with a practice that's been inseparable from sport since ancient times: gambling. Betting was standard practice in tennis matches for most of the game's history. As the historian Heinrich Gillmeister has documented in his study of tennis, judging by the king's own accounting book, poor Henry VII of England was about as versed in the game as I am:

> 13th June 1494: To a Spaynyard the tenes player, £4.
> For the Kinges loss at tenes, to Sir Robert 14th August 1494: At Windesor . . .
> To Sir Charles Somerset Curson, with the balls, £1. 7s. 8d.
> 8th March 1495 . . . To Hugh Denes for the Kinges losse at tenes, 14s.
> 30th August 1497: To Jakes Haute for the tennis playe, £10.

This and other similar accounts suggest that the loser, in addition to paying out cash, was often considered responsible for paying for the balls. As for the cash that changed hands, the most common coin used for such bets in medieval France was worth 15 pence. Thus, for each point lost 15 pence went with it: 15, 30, 45, for a total of four coins and 60 pence for a sweep of the game. At some point the 45 was abbreviated to 40, and voilà, we had the quirky system still used today.

At Fontainebleau's center court, I was glad no money was on the line as Matty continued to tie me in knots, now in front of a few spectators who had wandered in, no doubt at the smell of fresh meat. Matty finally took some pity on me and came around to my side to offer encouragement and some remedial instruction.

"As you've probably noticed by now, being able to swing a racket well or hit a fast serve doesn't get you all that far in this game," he said. "In lawn tennis, you can have a fellow like Ivanisevic, right? The great ape can bash a serve 135 miles an hour and can win just on his serve. He wouldn't stand a chance in real tennis, where you can't win with just a strong serve or a crashing forehand. Real tennis is often called 'chess in motion' and that's not far from the truth. It's all about positioning your opponent, thinking three shots ahead, and forcing the other guy into checkmate situations."

"Speaking of serves, why don't you give it a try?" he suggested.

Now normally—and this is where real tennis begins to make the brain hurt—as the receiver of the serve I would have to win the chance to serve by winning a "chase," as it's called. There's no automatic change of service after each game as there is in lawn tennis. If a ball I hit bounced twice on the server's end, rather than win the point outright I'd have "set a chase." The value of the chase is measured using numbered lines that divide the court—the nearer to the back wall, the better the chase. Later in the game, my opponent would have a chance to replay the same point from the receiving side and would attempt to beat my chase with a lower number. If I won the chase, I'd get to serve the next game. If not, I'd be stuck on the receiving end and at a clear disadvantage. With chases, it's possible, though not likely, for a strong player to hold onto service for an entire match. Clear? No, it wasn't to me either.

Matty stepped around to demonstrate his full arsenal of serves, each of which is designed to achieve a different effect. "You've got the 'giraffe,' a high serve that comes down hard on the penthouse usually with a bit of side- or overspin to give the ball an extra kick. Or there's the 'caterpillar,' which makes a lot of low long bounces, hits the back penthouse, balloons up in the air, and comes down flush with the back wall. Or the 'railroad,' which flies down the edge of the penthouse with a reverse spin, kicking the ball back into the sidewall. There are about seventy-five variations on serve, depending on what you're trying to do."

"Maybe I'll just try the old standard 'get the ball over the net and into the right box' serve?" I suggested.

He retreated to the receiving end while I grabbed a ball from a quaint picnic basket and settled into proper serving position.

"Tenez!" I shouted as warning for the rocket I was about to launch.

"Uh, we don't say that anymore."

"Sorry, I couldn't resist."

I sliced the ball rather nicely, I thought, enjoying the musical twang of the tightly wound strings as the ball strummed across them. It bounced off the side penthouse, bobbled sideways along the back penthouse and dropped to Matty's backhand. He punched it back low toward my forehand but this time I was ready. I drilled it down the line and smack into the tiny Plexiglas window that looks into the court's changing room.

"Brilliant!" called Matty. "You hit the grill and that's an instant point!"

The grill is one of the most indisputable connections between the modern real tennis court and its monastic origins. In the medieval monastery, the cloisters were originally restricted to the monks, who were closed off from the outside world. If relatives or visitors wanted to communicate with someone inside, they would have to do so through a barred window, called the grill.

"Be sure to tell your friends you hit the grill on your first outing!" said Matty, piling on the praise before properly dismantling me: six games . . . to one egg.

The Renaissance did wonders for tennis, and for sports in general. The same medieval church that had given over its monastic courtyards and earthly passions to the game also regarded hitting, chasing, and sweating over bouncing balls as morally suspect. In one incident from England in 1451, an illicit pickup tennis league that had started within church grounds got so out of hand that the bishop of Exeter sentenced the monks to nothing short of excommunication:

> Some members of the clergy, as well as of the laity . . .
> apparently have no scruples about playing a game, or
> rather, an evil game called "tennis" in the vernacu-
> lar, in the churchyard and the above-mentioned col-
> legiate church of St. Mary, consecrated for Christian
> burials. . . . In so doing they inveterately voice vain,
> heinous and blasphemous words and utter senseless
> curses.

As if blaspheming weren't enough, the rowdy monks were
also accused of dismantling a wooden structure on the cloister's penthouse roof because it got in the way of ball play.
Meanwhile, in the same general time frame over in Orléans,
France, a church council felt the need to pass a decree for-
bidding "priests and all others in sacred orders from playing
tennis without shame, in their undershirts, or not decently
dressed."

And so, despite (or more likely because of) the obvious
pleasure young clerics took in playing the game—in their
underwear, no less—the official stand of the church seems to
have been that tennis and other ball games led to sinful acts
unworthy of a proper Christian. They were, in other words,
far too much fun.

With the emergence of humanism in the Italian Renaissance and its emphasis on the education of *l'uomo universale*,
the "whole man," tennis and other sports came into their
own, taking their place alongside science and the arts as es-

sential character-building pursuits. The ideal Renaissance man was a scholar-athlete who was as physically capable as he was intellectually sound and morally righteous—the complete package.

In the writings of the day, tennis consistently made the short list of recommended activities befitting a gentleman of the court, alongside traditional arts of war such as archery, swordplay, and horsemanship. Baldassare Castiglione provided the most detailed how-to manual on the subject in *The Book of the Courtier*, published in 1528. Through a series of fictional conversations with the duke of Urbino and his attendants, Castiglione describes the ideal courtier as "well built and shapely of limb." Along with other forms of exercise, he recommends tennis as a game "very befitting a man at court . . . in which are well shown the disposition of the body, the quickness and suppleness of every member." The health benefits of tennis were extolled by many authors of the day, including one who went so far as to suggest it as a cure for constipation in slow-moving nobles:

> Water which stands without any movement finally transmutes into putrescence and begins to stink. . . . In order to forestall such worrisome evils, some amusing movements have been devised for such personages whose nobility and rank consist in all manner of stillness and but little motion.

Constipation aside, the game's upper-class, aristocratic associations—which linger to this day—can be traced, like so much else about the sport, to its monastic origins. In the medieval period, the children of kings and dukes were sent off to monasteries to be educated. In between Latin and theology classes, they took to the cloister courtyard with their shameless, defrocked teachers to work on their forehands. It wasn't long before these young students were heading back to their parents' castles for summer break, insisting that they simply must build a court of their own.

The royalty of Renaissance Europe took to tennis with a passion and it quickly became popular on the palace circuit. Unlike football, which involved mobs of unruly commoners strewn across village fields, tennis was a genteel sport that required fewer players, less physical exertion, and a small, delicate ball. Tennis was contained within expensive private courts, whereas football could be played almost anywhere and required nothing more than a homemade ball. Thus, early on, class lines were drawn around these games.

In England, Henry VIII had even more rackets than he had wives. He received Hampton Court as a gift from Cardinal Wolsey and is said to have heard of the execution of Anne Boleyn while in the midst of a heated game there. Across the Channel, Francis I was so passionate about the game that he had a tennis court built on his royal yacht. Henry II built his courts at the Louvre, where he was known to play daily "dressed all in white," hitting the ball "heatedly but without any pomp, except when his servants lifted the cord for him."

At Fontainebleau, Louis XIII would relax by watching matches from the window of his doctor's apartment, which looked out on the court. As a player, he was reputed to be a notoriously sore loser who "cried when he lost, because he did not like to be defeated."

With its royal endorsement, the game of tennis quickly took off among merchants, artisans, students, and others in the 16th and early 17th centuries. *Jeu de paume* halls cropped up throughout the bustling neighborhoods of Paris and other European cities and towns, operated by a growing guild of *paumiers*, master craftsmen who specialized in the making of balls and racquets and the management of courts. Along with rackets and balls, the entrepreneurial *paumiers* provided rooms where players could relax by a fire with some wine, get rubbed down with hot towels, and enjoy a side game of billiards or checkers.

But the game's meteoric rise in popularity would not last. From the late 17th century on, it began to lose its luster, particularly in its French birthplace. The colorful street signs for *paume* halls with names like the Golden Raquet or the Sphere that once dotted the narrow alleys of Paris quickly disappeared. Over time, many had become little more than betting parlors for soldiers, students, and merchants where billiards and card games became more lucrative ventures than tennis. The rise of urban property values and corresponding taxes made the huge *paume* halls an increasingly costly enterprise for their owners. Some were turned into factories, others meeting halls.

As tennis fell out of vogue in the 17th and 18th centuries and *paume* halls began to shut their doors, the theater became the biggest beneficiary of the game's demise. French comedy troupes discovered that the large, enclosed courts with their high ceilings and open viewing galleries worked well as makeshift auditoriums. The young comedic playwright

Molière and his popular Illustre-Théâtre set up their roving performances in a number of abandoned or struggling *paume* halls, many of which were eventually converted for good into theaters. Appropriately, Molière's troupe of comedians came to be known as "the children of the ball."

In France, the final blow to the game came with the French Revolution, which took aim at everything associated with the *ancien régime*. One of the defining episodes of the revolution was played out within the tennis court at the palace of Versailles. In June 1789, deputies of the newly formed National Assembly found themselves locked out of their chambers by Louis XVI's soldiers. The 600 members quickly regrouped and made their way through the rain to the nearby royal tennis court, where they signed what came to be known as the Tennis Court Oath, challenging the monarchy and claiming the right to assemble and form a constitution. The historic moment was captured in a famous sketch by Jacques-Louis David showing the deputies crowded around the court in heated debate and discussion while commoners look on with hope from the galleys and upper windows. A basket of balls and a single racket appear discarded in the corner of the great hall, suddenly frivolous, decadent, and irrelevant.

At the game's peak in 1596, there were 250 *jeu de paume* courts in Paris alone. By 1657 there were no more than 114, and by 1783 only 13.

Today, there is only one.

I emerged from the métro into a throng of spring tourists snapping their obligatory postcard shots of the Champs-

Élysées through the frame of the Arc de Triomphe. I pointed myself toward the guiding spire of the Eiffel Tower and made my way along the elegant streets of the 16th arrondissement, one of Paris's highest high-rent districts.

Walking twice past the address I was looking for, I stumbled upon 93, rue Lauriston, the infamous house where the Gestapo secretly interrogated and tortured members of the French resistance during World War II. A plaque marks the somber site. Backtracking carefully up the block in search of my happier destination, I finally spotted a sign with two crossed rackets hanging outside a stately historic structure. Above the entryway a carved lintel read JEUX DE PAUME.

The interior of the Société Sportive du Jeu de Paume et de Squash Racquets appeared frozen in time, a relic of the gilded age to which it once belonged. When it was founded more than a century ago, the club sported two *paume* courts, but in 1926 the first squash courts in France were built inside one of them. At the top of the marble staircase, the familiar squeak of tennis shoes followed by the sound of swatted balls echoed off the parquet floors and oak panels of the foyer. I had come to Paris's one remaining *paume* hall not only to pay homage to the city's last living vestige of the game it gave birth to, but to take in the competition at an annual tournament known as the French National Open.

The Open is the most prestigious *jeu de paume* tournament held in France. Any player who is a French national or resident can enter and compete. But as I perused the draw that was thumb-tacked to an antique corkboard, it became clear that what seemed like reasonable enough criteria for a national tournament were sadly far too narrow to field a proper competition. Only a dozen or so players had signed up to compete. A tidy elderly gentleman who joined me at the board assured me that there were, in fact, more than a dozen *jeu de paume* players in all of France. "It is *his* fault," he suggested with a laugh, pointing toward a player lounging casually on a nearby leather couch.

Marc Seigneur, a marginally fit 41-year-old with thinning blond hair, has been the reigning French champion for the past decade or so. The son of a French father and English mother, Seigneur is ranked in the top 20 players in the world and is the club pro at Leamington Spa, one of England's most exclusive tennis clubs, which, in 2008, opened its doors to women for the first time in 162 years. Minutes before his first-round match Seigneur looked strangely relaxed, if not downright bored, sprawled in a plush leather chair awaiting his first game. I introduced myself and asked which of his competitors he expected would give him a run for his money. He looked up at the ceiling, then at the floor, running through the players in his head, and then stated matter-of-factly, "No one should really give me any trouble, actually."

"But who might be the toughest?" I pressed on.

"Really, there is no one here in France, I'm afraid," he sighed nonchalantly.

Seigneur excused himself and headed onto the court, where he handily dispatched the first of several noncompetitors. If there was any buzz around the otherwise somnambulant affair, it involved Mathieu Sarlangue, a skinny, shy 16-year-old with a mop of black hair and a vicious forehand.

Sarlangue's family came from the Basque region, well known for birthing talented ballplayers of all kinds, and his father had been *jeu de paume* national champion during the 1970s. Sarlangue is the rare exception in France: a young man trying to break into a middle-aged man's sport that, by design, rewards age, experience, and mental acuity over speed, endurance, and gumption.

"None of my friends play," he lamented, before stepping onto the court to face Seigneur in the championship match. "It's too hard to learn quickly and takes a lot of work to be good. They just play football instead." But Sarlangue seemed wise beyond his years as, one by one, he sliced a path through his elders to face Seigneur in the final match.

I eagerly found a spot on a wooden pew with a dozen or so other spectators in the *dedans*, the netted gallery at the court's service end. A pro from another club sat nearby sewing a bagful of balls, not wasting a moment to keep up his quota.

"May I have one?" I joked, reaching out my hand.

He shook his head and shuffled further down the pew with his stash.

As the championship game began, I cheered Mathieu on, hoping he would get up in Seigneur's *grill* and take him right to the *tambour*. I was not alone, judging from the exclamations of my fellow spectators. This medieval sport of kings desperately needed a young knight from the land of its birth to lead it safely through another century.

But it was not to be—not today. Seigneur barely broke a sweat, toying with his young opponent as he dropped balls into impossible crevices and repeatedly pounded balls into the *dedans* where we sat, ringing the bell that hung from the netting like it was Sunday.

As the match moved toward its inevitable conclusion, some visiting squash players on their way to play stopped by briefly to watch. They tapped my shoulder to inquire what this peculiar game with the sloping roofs and crooked racket was called.

"Tennis," I answered. "This is *real* tennis."

Chapter Four

SUDDEN DEATH IN THE NEW WORLD

He was decapitated, Yax Xim Cabnel Ahau . . .
He played the ballgame of death
It had come to pass at the Black Hole . . .

EIGHTH-CENTURY MAYAN HIEROGLYPHIC

INSCRIPTION

D*éjamelo!*" shouted Chuy Páez. "Leave it for me!"
The nine-pound black rubber ball arced high into
the late-afternoon Mexican sky. Chuy's teammates
scattered, fanning out diagonally to defend their end zone.
With a running leap, Chuy threw his deerskin-padded hip
into the ball, connecting with a punishing thud and launching the ball fast and low across the hard-packed dirt court's
center line.

"Your turn, old man!" Chuy taunted as Fito Lizárraga, a
spry 56-year-old, prepared to return the ball. Bracing himself on the ground with one hand, Fito pivoted his hip to

strike the ball low and sent it skidding back through the dirt. Fito's teammates closed in fast behind him as players from both teams took turns flinging themselves to the ground and the ball ricocheted between hips like an oversized pinball. Then, with a dive worthy of Derek Jeter, Chuy knocked the ball past Fito and his teammates, sending it crashing into the chain-link fence at the end of the court.

On the sidelines, the 30 or so spectators of Los Llanitos erupted in cheers—a point scored in another Sunday afternoon pickup game of *ulama*, the oldest sport in the Americas.

On Christopher Columbus's second voyage to the New World in 1493, his crew brought along an air-filled ball to toss around and divert themselves in the downtime when they weren't busy enslaving local populations in their frenzied and fruitless search for gold. It's likely this was a *pelota de viento* ("wind ball"), a leather ball with an inflated bladder that was derived from the Roman *follis*. The Spanish and Italians of the era used it to play *pallone*, a handball game still played in varying forms in the Italian countryside. The game took place in a massive arena three times the size of a *paume* hall, and divided in half by a 15-foot-high net. Players wore a spiked wooden cylinder, called a *bracciale*, over their forearms, which they used to strike the ball back and forth in an attempt to score points. Back home, the conquistadors would also have been familiar with *pelota de vasca*, a game played in a court with a stuffed ball and either a glove or paddle that evolved into modern jai alai, notorious today for its rampant gambling.

Back in Europe, tennis had already spread beyond monastery walls and was fast becoming the most popular sport on the continent, the choice game of royals and merchants. Rackets were just beginning to replace the palm of the hand and nets were being strung across open courts. Not expecting to find tennis courts—or much of anything civilized—among the natives of the New World, however, Columbus's crew naturally left their rackets and beard-stuffed balls at home and made do with their inflated *pelota*.

But on the island of Hispaniola, in what is now Haiti, they found the natives—whom they regarded as savages—playing with a far superior ball. The Spaniards watched in awe as this magical ball bounced high above their heads, ricocheting and springing off the ground as if it were alive. "I don't understand how when the balls hit the ground they are sent into the air with such incredible bounce," wrote Pedro Mártir d'Angleria, the royal historian to the Spanish court of Charles V, a century later. The Dominican friar, Fray Diego Durán, was equally entranced. "Jumping and bouncing are its qualities, upward and downward, to and fro. It can exhaust the pursuer running after it before he can catch up with it." Columbus himself was so impressed with the properties of the ball that he took one back with him when he returned to Seville.

It was the Europeans' first encounter with the material we know as rubber, and the sports world would never be the same again.

For 3,500 years or so, the people of Mexico and the northern reaches of Central America—a cultural region known as

Mesoamerica—have been coming together to play a variety of competitive games with balls made of indigenous, natural rubber. There are 2,000 known plant species that produce latex containing rubber particles, and most can be found in the hot, humid, low-altitude tropical regions of the world. In Mexico and Central America, the most common variety of rubber plant is *Castilla elastica,* which is indigenous to the coastal lowlands of the Gulf of Mexico and the Pacific.

In its natural state, the latex produced by rubber plants is a white, sticky liquid that gets deformed when heated and hard and brittle when cold. Chemically, the latex is made of polymer chains that move independently of each other, easily losing shape. Not the best material to work or play with. To turn latex into usable rubber, the polymer chains need to be linked up so the rubber, once formed, can retain its strength, shape, and elasticity.

The West wouldn't discover the industrial process of vulcanization that connected these polymer chains and made rubber commercially viable until 1839, when Charles Goodyear, after having been imprisoned for debt and nearly suffocated by toxic gases in his lab, finally made his breakthrough discovery that the addition of sulfur at high heat cured the rubber and made it durable and lasting. But by 1500 BC, the ancient inhabitants of coastal Mexico had not only determined how to extract and naturally cure and stabilize rubber but figured out that they could shape it into spheres and have a whole lot of fun playing with it—more than three millennia before Goodyear's name ever appeared on a tire.

For decades, archaeologists and historians were mystified

as to how ancient Mesoamerican cultures managed to turn raw latex into serviceable rubber without access to sulfur and the high temperatures produced by industrial heat sources. So they turned to the 16th-century Spanish chroniclers, who had obsessively documented the strange and exotic culture of the Aztecs, even as they systematically dismantled and destroyed as much of it as they could. Fray Toribio de Benavente Motolinia, one of the first 12 Franciscans to arrive in the New World in the early 16th century, provided a clue in an early description of the ball and the process the Aztecs used to fabricate it:

> Rubber is the gum of a tree that grows in the hot lands, when [this tree is] punctured it gives white drops, and they run into each other, this is quickly coagulated and turns black, almost soft like a fish; and of this they make the balls that the Indians play with, and these balls bounce higher than the wind balls used in Spain, they are about the same size and darker; the balls of this land are very heavy, they run and jump so much that it is if they have quicksilver within.

But it was an account by Mártir d'Angleria that led researchers to the discovery of the missing ingredient in ancient rubber production:

> The balls are made from the juice of a certain vine that climbs the trees like the hops climb the fences;

this juice when boiled becomes hardened and turned into a mass and is able to be shaped into the desired form . . .

In the 1940s, Paul Stanley, a botanist at the Field Museum of Natural History in Chicago, identified the vine as *Ipomoea alba*, a kind of night-blooming morning glory commonly known as moon vine or moonflower. Recent studies show that when latex from *Castilla elastica* is boiled with the juice of moon vine, sulfonic acids that occur naturally in the vine increase the plasticity and elasticity of the rubber and produce a degree of vulcanization—enough for the ancient Mesoamericans to make sandals for ruling elites, tips for drumsticks, armor to protect against obsidian arrows, and extraordinary bouncing balls.

Rubber balls and the Mesoamerican game that put them into play got their debut with the Olmec, one of the earliest civilizations in the Americas that emerged along the tropical coast of the Gulf of Mexico. The Olmec, whose name translates as "Rubber People," not only invented the process for making rubber and devised a game to capitalize on its wondrous properties. They also built cities with monumental, psychedelically colorful pyramids; carved mysterious colossal 15-ton heads depicting semidivine rulers; developed the earliest writing system in the New World; and may have been the first to invent a sophisticated calendar that introduced the concept of zero to the world of mathematics. No slackers, this bunch.

Discoveries by archaeologists give a surprisingly complete

picture of the ancient ball game as it was played by the Olmec as far back as 1500 BC. At El Manatí, a waterlogged bog
on the coast of Veracruz, archaeologists dredged from the
ancient muck a dozen rubber balls that had been ceremonially deposited there alongside statues of deities and other
ritual offerings.

Found nearby was a belt made of exotic greenstone that a
ballplayer may have worn around his waist and used to strike
the ball. Farther west, in Michoacán, a group of eight clay
figurines found in a tomb show a scene of five men playing
ball while three women sit and lie around as if watching the
game. And to the south, on the coast of Chiapas, the remains
of the Americas' first ball game stadium were uncovered at a
place called Paso de la Amada.

To date, more than 1,500 ancient ball courts like the
one in Chiapas have been found in archaeological sites from
Flagstaff, Arizona, in the north to central Honduras in the
south, though only a fraction have been studied or excavated.
Hundreds more lie buried beneath city streets and sprawling
highways or await discovery in remote jungles.

With a unique architectural form that persists across
centuries, the ancient Mesoamerican ball court is as easily
identified and as iconic as our modern baseball diamonds.
Although the size and features of these courts vary widely
according to their age and location, their basic form stayed
remarkably consistent: two long, low parallel buildings bordering a narrow playing alley with sloped interior walls ex-
tending from the top of the structures to the playing field.
The alley, where the action took place, was usually paved

The ancient Maya ball court at Cobá, Mexico.

with stone and covered with limestone plaster. End zones closed in by temples or other buildings were typically wider than the playing alley, giving many courts a distinctive I shape if viewed from high above.

As with sports stadiums today, almost every midsized town or city in Mesoamerica could boast at least one ball court, usually located right downtown alongside the most sacred temples and elaborate royal palaces. One early archaeologist, bushwhacking his way through Mexico's densest jungles in the 1920s to record ancient ruins, stumbled upon so many of these courts that he described them as an "epidemic." Not surprisingly, many larger towns and cities had multiple ball courts, with one presumably fanatical Gulf Coast city containing as many as 24.

When it comes to figuring out what the game was like that took place in these courts, archaeologists have had to patch together scraps of evidence found among the crumbling ruins of ancient courts, a handful of descriptions from 16th-century Spanish chroniclers, and depictions of ballplayers in early pre-Hispanic art.

It's clear from the diverse representations of players, and variation in the features of the courts themselves, that the game took different forms in different regions and time periods. Most commonly, two teams of up to seven players would face off against each other, separated by a dividing line of some kind. Players would strike the ball with their arms, their shoulders, or, most often, their hips. Players wore a range of protective leather belts, gloves, and padding. Much as in tennis, points were scored when a ball was not returned or was knocked out of bounds or touched the wrong part of the body.

Against all imaginable odds, the ancient game of *ulama* has survived the rise and fall of the Olmec, Maya, and Aztec civilizations, the devastation and near genocide wrought by the Spanish conquest, and a string of modern revolutions, migrations, and social upheavals. Played today in just a handful of tiny, isolated villages in west Mexico, *ulama* is hanging on by a thread to a richer legacy than any other living sport can claim. But having made it this far, the game may now be facing extinction for the first time in its 3,500-year history.

The remaining players' relative poverty and geographic isolation, a lack of available natural rubber, and fierce competition from "newcomer" sports like baseball and volleyball have driven *ulama* to the brink. In Mexico, the threat has brought together an odd coalition of academics, athletes, and local businessmen trying to preserve and study it for clues to how the ancient Mesoamericans once lived and played.

A battered, sun-bleached sign announced our arrival in the village of Los Llanitos, population 151. In the car with me were James Brady, an archaeologist from the California State University at Los Angeles, and his graduate student, Sergio Garza, from the University of California, Riverside. The hour-and-a-half drive from the beach resort of Mazatlán to our destination had brought us from a jammed coastal highway lined with fast-food joints and high-rise hotels to a bone-jarring dirt road that wound its way through withered cornfields.

At first blush, Brady and Garza appear to be the unlikeliest of sports fans. Brady, a red-haired midcareer academic steeped in the esoterica of ancient Maya ritual, and Garza, a young up-and-coming Mexican archaeologist of Huichol Indian descent, have spent most of their careers doing archaeological investigations of Maya caves. Even by day they sport flashlights on their belts, as if a dark, unexplored crevice might present itself at any moment.

Back in 2003, on their way home to California from a spelunking expedition in the Yucatán, Brady and Garza decided to take a detour through the coastal towns of Sinaloa, having heard that *ulama* was still being played nearby.

"For years," said Brady, "we archaeologists were stuck in a major rut. We'd go out, dig up an ancient ball court, date it, and publish an article about it. But we rarely learned anything interesting or new about the game that was played there." For him, *ulama* presented a live opportunity to conduct what's known in the field as ethnoarchaeology: by studying the modern game, he and his colleagues hope to better understand its past. "For so long, archaeology had ball courts without people in them. By recording the game as it's played today, we're putting the sport, the enjoyment, and the competition back into the ball court."

Just past a church and a corral packed with cattle, Brady, Garza, and I pulled up to the tin-roofed home of 28-year-old farmer Chuy Páez. Tan, trim, and wearing buffed cowboy boots and a large silver belt buckle, Chuy (pronounced "Chewy") stepped over a dog sleeping in the shade of the porch and extended a hearty welcome.

Inside his concrete-floor bedroom we encountered Chuy's personal Wall of Fame. In one photograph, he's captured in midair, arms out and hip thrust forward, just seconds after striking the ball. In another, Chuy's 11-year-old son, Chuyito, posed proudly in his deerskin loincloth, holding a ball that looked to be nearly half his size. As we toured the gallery, Chuy reached up into the rafters of his house and untied a rubber ball, his prized possession, from a hanging neckerchief.

Leading us back outside, Chuy positioned me in one corner of the porch and walked 10 feet to the opposite corner.

"*¿Listo?*" he asked with a grin. "Ready?"

I nodded tentatively. He bounced the black ball—a little smaller than a bowling ball—across the patio floor. As I reached out to catch it, the ball's nine-pound solid mass smashed through my hands and into my chest, almost knocking me to the ground.

Brady laughed, having warned me earlier of the ball's punishing weight and superball-like action. "See what I mean?"

For me, absorbing the ball's impact for the first time was

A player holds an *ulama* ball.

a moment of utter revelation. I'd written a 300-page doctoral dissertation and several academic articles on the ancient game and had lectured on the topic at conferences. I'd dissected the game's ritual meaning and political symbolism and diligently pieced together and cataloged thousands of pottery fragments excavated from the ruins of courts. But I'd never before felt the blow of a ball against my body.

"It's one of those things you can read about all you want," said Brady, "but until you feel it for yourself and have the bruise to show for it, it's meaningless."

With virtually no real-world experience playing a game in which hands, feet, and sticks are all considered off-limits, it had always struck me as odd that the ancient Maya and Aztecs played ball with, of all body parts, their hips. But in that moment I finally understood why. The hip is one of the only parts of the body that can safely withstand the force of a solid, heavy rubber ball without risk of serious injury or death. At the time of the conquest, Diego Durán had described games where Aztec players were killed when the ball "hit them in the mouth or the stomach or the intestines." And even when they struck the ball properly, the players still "got their haunches so mangled that they had those places cut with a small knife and extracted blood which the blows of the game had gathered."

After sharing a huge midafternoon lunch of *pozole*, a traditional Mexican hominy stew, with Chuy's extended family, we followed him across town to the playing field, or *taste* (pronounced TAS-tay). The word *taste* is thought to derive from *tlachtli* (TLASH-tli), the Aztec word for ball court, much as the name *ulama* derives from the Aztec word for rubber, *ulli*, and the ancestral game, *ullamalitzli*.

The Los Llanitos *taste* hardly suggests the grandeur of the ancient stadiums that were its precursors; it is a long, narrow alley of hard-packed clay, about 12 feet wide and the length of roughly half a football field, lined with palm trees and ringed by a chain-link fence. At two o'clock on a Sunday, the first of eight players arrived. He was soon joined by others in a corner of the court that seemed to serve as a makeshift locker room. They stripped to their underwear and put on four-piece leather-and-cloth girdles that protect the stomach, hips, and buttocks.

As the players took to the field to warm up, spectators staked out the best, and safest, spots—mostly in the end zones, the better to avoid a hurtling ball, which travels up-

ward of 30 miles per hour. Young boys, wearing smaller girdles and the occasional LA Dodgers baseball cap, imitated
the adult players on the sidelines, while toddlers played safely
outside the fence.

The game traditionally begins when a team of three to
five players throws the ball high or rolls it low across a chalk-
marked center line. Play continues back and forth, with

contestants using only their hips to strike the ball. A point is scored when a team fails to return the ball, as in tennis, or when the ball is driven past the opponent's end zone, as in football. Faults are called if a player hits the ball with a part of the body other than the hip or crosses the center line, among other reasons I failed to understand.

The first team to achieve eight points wins, though owing to a complex and utterly confounding scoring system that not only rewards points but also strips them away, games can go on for hours, or even days. One match on record from 1930, between the nearby villages of La Palma and Puerto de Las Canoas, is said to have lasted a week before La Palma claimed victory.

On November 8, 1519, the forces of Hernán Cortés first entered the Aztec capital of Tenochtitlán, the ruins of which lie beneath the busy streets of Mexico City. The conquistadors were awestruck by the city's magnificent scale and grandeur. With an estimated population of more than 200,000, this city, built on a lake, was five times the size of Madrid and nearly three times the size of London at that time. While crossing one of the many causeways that connected the lakeshore to the city center, Bernal Diaz del Castillo, Cortés's personal chronicler, found himself at a rare loss for words: "I do not know how to describe it, seeing things as we did that had never been heard of or seen before, not even dreamed about."

Along with their accounts of monumental pyramids, lively marketplaces, and lavishly appointed royal palaces, the Spanish described with great interest the presence of ball courts in the heart of the city's ceremonial precinct, and were captivated by the games that took place there:

> The playing of the ball game began. And the spectators sat above the ball court on both sides; all the noblemen, or lords, or seasoned warriors sat divided into two sections. And on each side above the ball court, each on his own side, sat the contenders to whom the ball game pertained. And to each side of the court was attached a [circular stone] called tlachtemalacatl, which had a hole [in the center]. And he who put [the ball] through it, won the game.
>
> The man who sent the ball through the stone ring was surrounded by all. They honored him, sang songs of praise to him, and joined him in dancing. He was given a very special award of feathers or mantles and breechcloths, something very highly prized. But what he most prized was the honor involved: that was his great wealth. For he was honored as a man who had vanquished many and had won a battle.

Not surprisingly, some chroniclers of the time compared *ulama* to the games they were familiar with back home, particularly tennis. Antonio Herrera y Tordesillas, described *ulama* as "being like our tennis" and repeatedly referred to the Aztec ball courts as simply "tennis-courts." Cortés was himself so delighted by the game that he brought a team of players back to Spain in 1528 to perform in the royal court of Charles V.

When my son Aidan was 8 we spent a family vacation in Mexico's Yucatán Peninsula. After days baking on the beach in the hot Caribbean sun, we packed into a jeep and drove to Cobá, an ancient trading center that at its peak had a population of more than 50,000. Entering the welcome tropical shade of the ruins, we rented bicycles and wound our way along ancient raised limestone roads, called *sacbe* by the Maya, that once connected Cobá to a network of other cities hundreds of miles away. Climbing 120 vertigo-inducing steps to the top of the site's highest pyramid, we gazed out across 50 square miles of jungle canopy, imagining the scene as it might have appeared 1,000 years earlier: colorful temples, children chasing each other through streets and courtyards, bustling markets filled with goods from distant ports—and somewhere down there, a game of *ulama* under way in the site's ball game stadium.

We descended carefully, got back on our bikes, and found our way to the ball court, a spectacular stone structure meticulously reconstructed by archaeologists. Facing each other across the 12-foot-wide alley, Aidan and I imagined ourselves as ancient Mayan athletes. I explained how we would have knocked the rubber ball back and forth, banking it off the sloped playing walls to make it bounce and spin and ricochet off the hard playing surfaces. I pointed out the small vertical hoops—the *tlachtemalacatl*, as the Aztecs referred to them— protruding from either side at a height of 10 feet or so off the alley floor.

"They had to get the ball through those?" asked Aidan. "With their hips?!"

That was the game clincher, I explained. There were other ways to score points and win, like field goals and safeties in American football. The court was divided by a marker and further separated into zones by chalk lines that marked the alley, as in a tennis court. Aidan nodded, struggling to picture it. Aidan then shifted his gaze downward to examine the stone marker embedded in the center floor of the playing alley.

"Dad, why is there a skull in the middle of the court?"

The Spanish were asking the same question 500 years earlier when they first learned about the Aztec beliefs surrounding this game. That was when their delight at the game gave way to dismay. They noticed that prominent ball courts were often decorated with sculptures depicting skulls along with sinister-looking Aztec gods, which for these fanatical Catholics might as well have been images of the Devil himself. They soon learned that when important games were played, they were accompanied by elaborate pagan rituals. Herrera described in great detail how some "tennis-courts" were ritually consecrated before use:

> On a lucky day, at midnight, they perform'd certain ceremonies and enchantments on the two inner walls, and on the midst of the floor, singing certain songs or ballads; after which a priest of the great temple went with some of the religious men to bless it; he uttered some words, threw the ball about the tennis-court four times and then it was consecrated, and might be play'd in, but not before.

And right next to the city's central *teotlachtli*, the "ball court of the gods," the Spanish encountered a grisly sight: a small structure, known as the *tzompantli*, lined with wooden racks that held the skewered skulls of thousands of slain war captives and sacrificial victims. *Ulama*, the Spanish discovered, was for the Aztecs as much a religious rite as it was an athletic contest—and it had a dark side unlike any sport that has been played before or since.

More than 1,000 years before the Spanish landed on the shores of Mexico's Yucatán Peninsula and began their con-

quest of the Aztecs, the Maya were playing ball in cities like Cobá scattered throughout the jungles, mountains, and lowlands of southern Mexico, Guatemala, Belize, and Guatemala. For the Maya, like the Aztecs, the ball game contest had profound symbolic meaning, featuring prominently in their most sacred creation story—the Maya equivalent of Genesis—known as the *Popol Vuh*.

Though it was first recorded in the mid-16th century in highland Guatemala, archaeologists have found scenes from the *Popol Vuh* depicted on painted pottery and ancient sculptures dating to the earliest periods of Maya history. The

Ancient Maya ballplayers compete as musicians sing and dance on a grandstand, from a polychrome vase, ca. AD 600–900.

creation story traces the many failed attempts by the gods to create humans. It centers on the exploits of two brothers, Hun Hunahpu and Vucub Hunahpu, and two hero twins who were born to one of the brothers.

The story begins with the first pair of brothers playing ball just above the entrance to the Maya underworld, called Xibalba. The lords of the underworld become annoyed by the incessant pounding of the rubber ball on the earth above, so they lure the brothers down to the ball court of Xibalba, where they are soon sacrificed. The gods decapitate Hun Hunahpu and hang his head in a calabash tree. One day, while a goddess is passing the tree, the brother's head spits into her hands, miraculously impregnating her. She gives birth to hero twins, who soon discover their father's ball game gear hidden in his house and start playing ball, again angering the lords of Xibalba.

History repeats itself as the twins are called down to the underworld to face a series of trials and to play ball against the gods. At one point, one of the twins is decapitated and his head is put into play as the ball, but the twins retrieve and reattach it, ultimately winning the contest against the lords of the underworld. In the process, they also defeat the forces of darkness and ascend into the heavens and bring light to the world as the sun and the planet Venus.

As art historian Mary Miller interprets the symbolic role of the ball game and ball court in the Maya creation, "Life is both taken and renewed in the ball court. The ball court is the place where fortunes are reversed, and then reversed again. It is the ultimate place of transition." This idea of transition, death, and renewal of life and fertility is a theme that crops up again and again in association with the Mesoamerican ball game. In the sacred books, or codices, of the Aztecs the bouncing ball was compared to the cosmic journey of the sun into and out of the underworld. Ritual ball games were played during key religious festivals to magically enact and maintain the cycles of nature and the cosmos.

The *Popol Vuh*, and a host of other accounts and visual depictions, leaves little doubt that the violent sacrifice of defeated players, or unlucky stand-ins captured in battle, was a postgame rite performed at some, though certainly not all, ball games. These sacrificial games were most likely part of elaborate ceremonies that took place after important battles, where war captives were forced to play against each other in life-or-death gladiatorial contests. The winners would presumably have had their lives spared, whereas the losers were decapitated, their hearts ripped out and offered up to the gods.

In one particularly gruesome depiction found on the walls of the monumental ninth-century Maya ball court at Chichén Itzá, in the Yucatán, serpents and squash plants sprout from the neck of a kneeling, decapitated ballplayer, bestowing fertility on the land and the living. The winning rival stands to the side, wielding a stone knife and the freshly severed head as his bloody trophy. Similar scenes connecting ball play and human sacrifice are repeated on sculptures, pottery, and paintings across Mesoamerica.

Scholars believe that these agonistic rites were played out again and again as reenactments of the creation story. Maya kings, often identified as great ballplayers in hieroglyphic inscriptions, may even have dressed as the hero twins for important ceremonial games. In ball courts that served as symbolic portals to the underworld, these kings appeared before their subjects as the ultimate sports heroes—semidivine warriors and athletes capable not only of defeating their enemies but of vanquishing death and darkness and bringing life and light to the world. Whereas ordinary men played ordinary games with ordinary outcomes, went the message, kings played games of cosmic significance.

Of course, the nuances of the Mesoamerican belief system were of little interest to the Spanish friars who were intent on eradicating all traces of this diabolical pastime. In 1585 the Spanish authorities banned all ball games, citing their corrupting influences on native populations. But on the outer fringes of what was then New Spain, in the remote frontier villages of Sinaloa and Nayarit, the game managed to slip just below the radar of the centralized Spanish bureaucracy.

A handful of missionary and travelers' accounts of *ulama* from the 17th through the 19th centuries give a glimpse of a game still steeped in ceremony, though heads no longer rolled and hearts stayed safely in chests. According to a 17th-century account of a mountain tribe called the Acaxee, competitive ball games between villages involved the entire community and were accompanied by mock battles, singing, dancing, and elaborate feasts. Accounts of the same games from the early 20th century, however, reveal a tradition gradually stripped of most of its ceremony and cultural meaning—one in slow but steady decline.

Manuel Aguilar, an art historian working on the Ulama Project, has been investigating the modern game of *ulama* for traces of its ancient symbolism. "When the Spanish friars drove the game underground," said Aguilar, "it almost certainly lost most of its religious overtones." But some intriguing practices might be holdovers from the days when the game was more than a game. According to Spanish accounts, for example, the Aztecs played primarily on religious feast days; today in Los Llanitos, the game is played mostly on Christian holidays. And just as ancient ball courts were often associated with death and the underworld, as the *Popol Vuh* story makes clear, today's *tastes* tend to be located next to village cemeteries.

Not that *ulama* was ever an entirely spiritual affair. Even when players weren't risking their heads and hearts to the game, there were some pretty high stakes involved. Elite sponsors provided housing and food for the best ballplayers, trained them rigorously and then challenged other teams to competition, wagering significant sums on the outcome. Durán describes how some players "gambled their homes, their fields, their corn granaries, their maguey plants. They sold their children in order to bet and even staked themselves and became slaves to be sacrificed later if they were not ransomed."

After a day in Los Llanitos, I hopped back into our jeep with Chuy and the archaeologists and drove 12 windy miles to the rival village of El Quelite to track down local *ulama* legend Rafael Lizárraga y Barra. El Huilo, "the skinny one," as he's known to his friends and fans, is the oldest living *ulama* player. At 95, he still has the cockiness and competitive streak of a revered athlete, despite the fact that it's been 30 or so years since he last put hip to ball.

Within minutes of pulling up at his modest roadside house, El Huilo, without provocation or the benefit of teeth, began teasing and baiting Chuy, strutting like a cock in a hen house. "Ha! You players today! You're just sissies compared to how we were!" Chuy unwrapped his ball from the folds of his neckerchief and bounced it over to the old man. El Huilo caught the ball expertly, turned it in his bony hands, clearly assessing its quality. Bouncing it up and down like a kid, he recalled the days when sponsors would take him and other players "into the hills" for intensive periods of training. "The man who used to organize the games really watched the players. He wouldn't let them have any women or drink. And since we couldn't work while they were training, he'd take care of us, like good horses."

"And the women," he broke into a wide, toothless grin and swiveled his hips. "The women *loved* us ballplayers because we knew how to move our hips, if you know what I mean . . ."

Back in his youth, when *ulama* was literally the only game in town, money was always on the line when the players stepped on the court—just as in the days of the Aztecs and the Maya.

"What was your most memorable game?" I asked.

He described point for point an epic two-day battle with a neighboring village. "They said I hit the ball so hard that day it looked like I wanted to kill someone!" He wasn't just playing, but was betting his opponents 20 pesos a point. "Boy, I made a lot of money that day!" he laughed, rubbing his hands together, still pleased with his performance—which, I came to learn, took place in 1934.

Back then, *ulama* dominated the western Mexican sports annals, and being a top player could win you fortune, fame, and women. But today, few local youths are interested in taking up a sport as obscure, difficult, and physically punishing as *ulama*. The day I watched Chuy and his teammates face off on the *taste*, 20 or so teenagers packed the nearby volleyball court. I couldn't resist asking Chuy which was harder, volleyball or *ulama*.

He looked at me and scoffed. "*Ulama*, of course! It takes years of practice and most players don't have what it takes. You can't have fear. You need to be strong." The implication was clear: volleyball, unlike *ulama*, is no sport for real men.

There are no opportunities for scholarships or professional contracts for *ulama* players. Although Chuy and other players have been invited to faraway Cancún to perform for tourists in faux-Maya extravaganzas—complete with drums, feather headdresses, and face paint—most decline, regarding the displays as exploitative and inaccurate. On the website of Xcaret, a beach resort south of Cancún on the Mayan Riviera, ballplayers are shown prancing about in campy costumes that would be perfectly at home in the Broadway production of *The Lion King*. The accompanying copy claims that "Xcaret has rescued and disseminated a millenary tradition. What was once only imagined from the archaeological remains of ball courts throughout Mesoamerica has come spectacularly to life at Xcaret." Of course, given the choice, some things may be better off left to the imagination. For Chuy and his teammates, *ulama* is an aggressive blood sport, not a curiosity to be exploited for tourist theater—especially if there are feathers involved.

But as challenging as it might be to keep the *ulama* tradition intact and alive among the younger generation in the face of competition from modern alternatives, the game's survival may ultimately hinge on something far more basic: the availability of rubber to make balls.

At one time, Los Llanitos and the surrounding lowlands was a booming center of rubber production. The Codex Mendoza, a 16th-century Aztec document, records that a nearby area of coastal Mexico paid an annual tribute of some 50 tons of rubber to the Aztec ruler, to be used for medicinal, utilitarian, and ritual purposes—including the production of balls. Brady's team calculated it would have taken about 1,300 acres of land and 427 full-time rubber tappers to meet this annual levy.

But since then, the rubber trees that once grew here have been wiped out by the spread of beach resorts and other coastal developments, and the people of Los Llanitos now have to travel hundreds of miles into neighboring Durango, a region increasingly under the control of local drug lords, to find rubber trees to tap. A recent chilling news story underscores the challenge presented by the drug trade in this region. The body of a member of the Juarez drug cartel was left in seven pieces on the streets of a town to the north of Mazatlán. In what almost seemed a sadistic homage to the region's ancient sacrificial rites, the victim's face was stitched onto a soccer ball and left in a plastic bag in front of the town hall!

As a result of rubber's scarcity and the dangers involved in acquiring it in Mexico's wild west, the price of a single *ulama* ball has soared to a staggering $1,000—about $250 more than the annual income of the average player. Remarkably, Chuy's prize ball is one of only three balls in Los Llanitos and the only one in good enough shape for competition. Being made of natural rubber, the more the ball is used, the more it shrinks and deforms over time.

Which leads to the question: How can you keep a ball game alive if you don't have balls to play with?

A Mazatlán businessman and longtime supporter of the game, Jesús Gómez, has taken the lead in the search for an answer, and the Ulama Project's researchers have teamed up with members of the Mazatlán Historical Society to experiment with commercial latex imported from as far away as New York City. "If we can't get natural rubber," said Gómez, "we need to find another way. Otherwise, *ulama* will not survive. It's that simple."

So far, though, artificial rubber has failed to replicate the look or feel and, most important, the remarkable bouncing properties of traditional balls. "Look at this," said Chuy after the game at Los Llanitos. He dropped a lumpy white blob of low-grade latex, the result of Gómez's latest experiments, and watched it bounce erratically off his patio.

"This doesn't work," he exclaimed with visible disgust. "It's not natural rubber!"

As the owner of the town's lone regulation ball, Gómez suggested, Chuy may have a vested interest in making sure no substitute is found. "Unfortunately, the ball has come to symbolize control of the game." And for Chuy and his teammates, debates about the ball and the game seem to feed their sense of competition: Who's going to decide the future of *ulama*—the players who remain or some well-meaning but meddlesome academics and outsiders?

As I expressed my thanks to the players and their families who had hosted me in Los Llanitos and got ready to head back to Mazatlán, Chuy pulled me away from the other visitors and project members and cornered me with his prized ball in hand, determined to have the final word.

"This ball is special. It's made from a process that's thousands of years old."

He dropped the smooth, heavy mass into my hands. "This ball," he said, as if holding it were the only way to really understand, "is not of these times."

Chapter Five

THE CREATOR'S GAME

There are two times of the year that stir the
  blood:
In the fall, for the hunt, and now for lacrosse.

OREN LYONS JR., FAITHKEEPER OF THE

ONONDAGA NATION

t's May 22, 2009, at the New England Patriots' stadium in Foxborough, Massachusetts, and another, much older contest has taken over the gridiron: the NCAA lacrosse championship. Two powerhouses, Syracuse and Cornell, have been pushed to "sudden victory" overtime by an improbable fusillade of goals by the Orange in the final minutes of regulation. Cornell wins the face-off and gets it to one of their top scorers. Syracuse defenseman Sid Smith checks him hard, strips him of the ball, and works it quickly down field to his best friend, attack man Cody Jamieson. Jamieson winds up with a left-hand shot so perfect, so routine, that he never had to look back to know it went in.

Having just clinched the championship, Jamieson, a Mohawk Indian, turns and charges 80 yards upfield, stick over his head and a trail of white-and-orange jerseys in jubilant pursuit, to embrace Sid, a Cayuga Indian whom he'd grown up with on the Six Nations of the Grand River Reserve in Ontario.

It was a moment that, by all reasonable odds, should never have taken place. That Syracuse should pull off its 10th NCAA championship win was historic but not surprising. What defied the odds was that an American Indian game banned by early missionaries as "sorcery" should have hung on through four centuries of disease, genocide, and warfare. Lacrosse, which had patiently infiltrated the white culture that nearly extinguished it, had now arrived at the point where it could be played live on ESPN in front of 68,000 fans: this was truly remarkable. Decades after their great-grandfathers had been barred from playing their game, two young men of the Wolf Clan of the Iroquois League shared a victory that, save the efforts of their determined ancestors, could quite easily never have occurred.

But lacrosse is a survivor.

By AD 800 *ulama* had worked its way across the Rio Grande, influencing the development of a short-lived rubber ball game in ancient towns throughout Arizona and New Mexico. The long-distance running Tarahumara people played a kick-ball game, called *rarajipari*, across the deserts and canyons of northern Mexico. Shinny, a popular stick-and-ball game similar to women's field hockey, brought women and men out to play in villages from California to Virginia. And many Indian tribes, from the Inuit of Alaska to those encountered by the first Pilgrims, had their own versions of football. The game of *pasuckuakohowog*, played by 17th-century New England tribes, for example, involved hundreds of villagers kicking an inflated bladder across a narrow, mile-long field. It was not all that different, the Pilgrims noted, from their own football.

Few of these games are still played, and some are remembered only by archaeologists and museum curators. Some live on in tribal legend or tradition—preserved and reenacted but long divorced from their vitality and cultural relevance. Then there's lacrosse, one of the fastest-growing sports in the world.

At the time of European colonization, lacrosse was played in one form or another from the western Great Plains to the eastern woodlands and as far south as Georgia and Florida. Despite variation from one region to the next the game was everywhere essentially the same. Teams of up to several hundred men would face off across an open field, often oriented to the cardinal directions, which could stretch for a mile or more in any direction. The only boundaries recognized were natural ones—a rocky outcrop, a stream, a dense stand of trees. Using carved wooden sticks terminating in a pocket made from either wood or woven strips of leather or animal gut, players competed over a stuffed animal-skin ball or one carved from the charred knot of a tree. Through a run-and-pass game they would attempt to score points by hitting a single large post or passing it through a goal formed by two upright posts. Games were known to last for hours or days depending on their purpose and importance.

Three types of sticks were used, representing three different regional traditions, each with its own rules and techniques. The Ojibwe, the Menominee, and other tribes of the Great Lakes and upper Mississippi played with a three-foot stick that had a small, enclosed wooden pocket. In the southeast, the Cherokee, Choctaw, Creek, and Chickasaw played a variation of the game using a pair of small sticks with enclosed webbed pockets with which they trapped the ball. In the Northeast, the tribes of New England and the Iroquois Confederacy played with a four-foot stick whose crook-shaped head formed a large webbed pocket.

This crook-shaped stick was first encountered in the early 17th century by French Jesuit missionaries living and spreading the Gospel among the Huron Indians, who lived in palisaded villages just 100 miles or so north of where Cody and Sid grew up. The "Black Robes," as the clerics were known to the Indians, called the stick *la crosse*, using a term that the French of the time seem to have associated with any game played with a curved stick. As early as 1374, in fact, a document refers to a stick-and-ball game played in the French countryside called *shouler à la crosse*. In *The Jesuit Relations*, a series of field reports the priests sent back to their superiors, Father Jean de Brébeuf provides the first written account of the game, describing with obvious displeasure the association of this stickball game with ritual healing: "There is a poor sick man, fevered of body and almost dying, and a miserable Sorcerer will order for him, as a cooling remedy, a game of crosse."

A more detailed description of early Indian lacrosse comes from Baron de Lahontan, a French explorer who in the 1680s was given command of Fort Joseph, a military outpost on the south shore of Lake Huron. Like many other tennis-crazed European explorers of the time, he couldn't help but compare this very different team racket game with the one he had quite likely played back in Paris:

> They have a third play with a ball not unlike our tennis, but the balls are very large, and the rackets resemble ours save that the handle is at least 3 feet long. The savages, who commonly play it in large companies of three or four hundred at a time, fix two sticks at 500 or 600 paces distant from each other. They divide into two equal parties, and toss up the ball about halfway between the two sticks. Each party endeavors to toss the ball to their side; some run to the ball, and the rest keep at a little distance on both sides to assist on all quarters. In fine, this game is so violent that they tear their skins and break their legs very often in striving to raise the ball.

Brébeuf and his fellow clerics sought to understand the Indian culture, games included, so they could spread a native form of Catholicism. Although they shared with their earlier Spanish counterparts in Mexico an unwavering mission to convert the "heathen" Indians, the French had a kinder, gentler, and more laissez-faire approach to colonization. As the 19th-century historian Francis Parkman characterized the difference, "Spanish civilization crushed the Indian; English civilization scorned and neglected him; French civilization embraced and cherished him." The French, whose interests in the New World were largely commercial and centered on the lucrative fur trade, were more likely than the English or Spanish to establish cooperative trade relations and military alliances with the Indians and to recognize tribal rights.

For the Iroquois, Creek, Cherokee, and other tribes, lacrosse was a surrogate for war—"little brother of war" as some Indians called it—and shared much of the same symbolism. Lacrosse sticks and even players' bodies were sometimes painted with red war paint before important games. In a Creek legend uncovered by historian Thomas Vennum, a father hands his son a war club and sends him into battle, saying, "Now you must play a ball game with your two elder brothers." Ball games not only served as an important proving ground for young warriors training for battle, but, as lacrosse historian Donald Fisher points out, also provided a diplomatic means of building alliances and avoiding war with neighbors. Ceremonial games brought tribes together to mend political bonds and settle disputes, shoring up tribal confederacies that might otherwise have fallen apart over time. In this way, the Iroquois Confederacy used lacrosse to help establish itself as a dominant military power in the eastern United States and Canada in the late 17th and early 18th centuries.

Ball play of the Choctaw—Ball Up, 1846–50, George Catlin.

In 1763, a group of Ojibwe and Sauk Indians staged a game for the British troops at Fort Michilimackinac in what is now the state of Michigan and succeeded in merging the sport almost seamlessly with war. With the defeat of the French in 1761, the outpost and trading depot had been handed over to the English, whose poor treatment of the Indians provoked the movement known as Pontiac's Rebellion. In honor of the king's birthday, the Indians offered to entertain the English with a game just outside the walls of the fort. The English were kicking back and enjoying the "savage" game, different as it was from their football or tennis, when one of the players fired the ball through the gates of the fort.

The warriors rushed into the fort after the ball, traded their lacrosse sticks for weapons that their women had hidden under blankets, and proceeded to massacre the British troops inside. They seized the fort and held it for a year, using their position to extract demands from their new overseers.

As bad as English occupation was for the Iroquois and other eastern Indians, the American Revolution proved to be even worse. The Americans, intent on controlling and expanding their young republic, drove many Iroquois off their lands and into Canada, dividing the Confederacy and initiating a long period of rapid cultural decline. But lacrosse, stripped of some of its religious meaning and importance, hung on and gathered new fans among Canadians and Americans alike. In the years following the revolution, games of lacrosse were recorded in Ontario, played between relocated Mohawk and Seneca groups in an effort to build new alliances. In the 1830s, George Catlin exhibited his romanticized paintings of the "vanishing" Indian, which included depictions of Choctaw Indians playing lacrosse in Oklahoma. In 1844, the first game recorded between Indians and whites took place in Montreal. And just 25 years later, a mere century after the massacre at Michilimackinac, it had been reinvented as the national game of Canada.

Onondaga is *the* place, I was told. I'd called tribal representatives and the heads of lacrosse programs at several of the other Iroquois nations. If I wanted to learn about the roots of lacrosse, they all told me, the Onondaga Nation is the place to go. "Lacrosse is practically a religion up there," according to one Oneida Indian I spoke with.

Located just seven miles south of the Carrier Dome, home to the Syracuse Orange, 10-time NCAA Division One champions, Onondaga is a kind of spiritual center and pilgrimage site for anyone looking to worship at the altar of lacrosse. With a population of just 2,000 or so people, the nation has over the years contributed five players to the Canadian Hall of Fame and one to the U.S. Hall of Fame and has fielded more All-Americans per capita than any other community in North America.

For a month or so I'd traded phone calls and emails with Freeman Bucktooth, coach of the Onondaga Redhawks, the nation's team that competes in the Canadian-American box lacrosse association. Freeman played for Syracuse and was captain and lead scorer for the Redhawks for more than a decade. He's also raised and trained four lacrosse-playing sons, including two-time Syracuse All-American Brett Bucktooth. When we spoke, he was gearing up for a trip to Manchester, England, to assistant coach the Iroquois Nationals at the World Lacrosse Championships. The Nationals, an all-Iroquois field lacrosse team that includes seven Onondaga players, was ranked fourth in the world. This, said Freeman, was their year to challenge the U.S. and Canadian national teams for the world title. I wished him luck and told him I'd help him celebrate in a few weeks once they'd returned to Onondaga.

A week later, seated in an airport lounge, I looked up at the TV and there was Freeman being interviewed on CNN. The caption scrolled across the set, "We're lacrosse players, not terrorists." The team had been prevented from board-

ing a plane at JFK bound for England because their Iroquois
League–issued passports did not meet post-9/11 security and
technology requirements. They'd been traveling on these
passports without trouble since 1977. Times had changed.

I shot an email to Freeman to show support. The response
came back within minutes: "Thanks. It's not looking good."

In the days that followed, the team made international
headlines as they holed up in a Comfort Inn and played
scrimmages with local New York City teams. Federation officials met behind closed doors with U.S. immigration officers.
Film director James Cameron offered to donate $50,000 to
help pay for extra travel expenses. Opposing teams already
competing in Manchester expressed disappointment and
outrage. "We're playing their game," commented the American coach of Team Germany in an interview. "And our politics denied them the ability to participate in their game. Just
terrible."

At the 11th hour, Secretary of State Hillary Clinton inter-
vened to give the team a one-time travel waiver. But the British government refused entry. They missed the tournament
and the United States went home with the gold.

If you get distracted driving south on I-81 out of Syracuse,
you can easily miss the exit for the 11-square-mile patch of
land that constitutes the Onondaga Nation. One green-and-
white exit sign hardly seems to do justice to an entire sovereign nation, but that's what's left after 200-plus years of
failed or broken treaties and what the Onondaga describe
as a history of "illegal takings" of land by New York State.

Small as it is, however, the Onondaga Nation remains sovereign, independent, and proud. The "People of the Hills," as their name translates, pay no state or federal income taxes, receive no subsidies or oversight from the federal Bureau of Indian Affairs, and recognize traditional Iroquois law, which predates and some say influenced the U.S. Constitution. One of the Six Nations along with the Cayuga, Mohawk, Oneida, Seneca, and Tuscarora that make up the Iroquois League, the Onondaga are considered the "Keepers of the Fire" and the traditional center of the League.

When I made the long drive to Onondaga, Aidan had just begun playing lacrosse for the first time. To me, it was still a foreign game and I was hungry to learn more about it. No one I grew up with ever played it, and only my friends who went to prep schools and elite northeastern colleges had any connection to the game. But watching Aidan and his team play was riveting and made me realize what I'd been missing out on. The tribal roots of the game were unmistakable as sticks clashed, helmets connected, and kids piled up in heaps on the ground: this was a warrior's game.

Just off the exit, the Onondaga lacrosse stadium looms large, by far the biggest structure on the nation. I slowed down in an attempt to scan the mouthful of a name that emblazons half the width of the building: Tsha'Hon'nonyen'dakhwa'. It means "where they play games" in the Onondagan language. Literal, but fitting, I thought, for the site where they play the game they call *deyhontsigwa'ehs*, "they bump hips." No ambiguity there, though I've watched enough lacrosse to know there's a lot more than hips getting bumped. The

$7 million, 2,000-seat stadium, built in 2001, is decorated in purple with two wampum belts: one represents the five original Iroquois nations, the other their peaceful coexistence with the non-Indian society around them. As I got up to the stadium, I found myself stuck in a traffic jam. Was there an afternoon game, I wondered?

The cars, it turned out, were filled with smokers dismally lined up to get their nicotine fix tax-free at the nation's smoke shop—a necessary economic evil, perhaps, for a nation that has rejected casinos and gambling as sources of revenue. The stadium, on the other hand, is a symbol of unmistakable pride, part cultural center and part shrine to the Creator's game (as they call lacrosse). Glass cases are lined with trophies, mementos, and photos dating back to the 1890s of Onondaga Athletic Club players grasping old-style wooden sticks and sporting striped jerseys with distinctive *O*s on their chests. Lacrosse moms were picking up their kids from practice, checking gear bags to be sure all the equipment they had come with was going home with them.

Freeman was sitting patiently at a table in the arena's Fast Break Café working on his roster for upcoming games. He's widely known as "Boss," a nickname he got pegged with as a kid because he was big for his age and had a reputation for throwing his weight around. He's still a big guy, with shoulder-length black hair and a hoop earring. As he smiled and said hello in a gentle voice that didn't seem to match his frame, all I could think was how devastating his hip check must have been back in the day.

He went to the counter, ordered a couple of sandwiches

Onondaga lacrosse team, ca. 1902

for us and then sat down. I told him again how sorry I was that his team had missed out on the World Championships. "How are your guys taking it now that they're back?" I asked.

"I've been really impressed by how well they handled it all along, even some of the younger guys," he answered without pause. "They worked hard for that chance. But you know what? We're stronger as a team because of it."

His proudest moment, he recalled, was when a CNN reporter asked for a show of hands of players who would be willing to travel on U.S. passports to England in order to make the game. "Not one hand was raised. No one even flinched or looked around. Why would we travel on another nation's passport? Not just any nation, but the one we were planning to face in the finals?!"

After lunch and a quick tour of the stadium, we jumped in Freeman's car and headed toward his house. A mile down the road we passed a kid walking along with a lacrosse stick in hand, practicing his cradling. "See that?" he laughed. "Everyone plays lacrosse here. When a boy's born, he has a stick put in his crib. When he dies as an old man, his favorite stick gets buried with him. It's the circle of life."

"What if you don't like lacrosse?" I asked, half kidding.

He looked at me as if there might be something seriously wrong with me. "Mostly you learn to like it. But hey, we got kids who play basketball and do pretty well. Baseball too. We invented that too you know."

"Baseball?" I responded skeptically.

"Yeah, we call it longball but it's pretty much the same game. Only we were playing it long before the whites came along."

Farther down the road he spotted a guy on a building site scraping and cleaning up a 40-foot iron girder. He pulled up and the man leaned into the car. "Hey, Boss, what's up?"

"That for the new place?" Freeman inquired. The two began to discuss the plans for the home he was helping his son build. Freeman offered some muscle and equipment to help haul free timbers that he'd heard were available. One of the downsides—or not, given the recent national epidemic of foreclosures—of being a sovereign nation is that banks won't underwrite mortgages for homeowners, because if they don't pay, the bank can't come onto the nation to seize their property. As a result, people chip in to help each other build their own homes.

"You be sure to give those Braves a beating tonight!" the man called as we drove off.

The Braves were the Tonawanda Braves, a Seneca Indian team from near Buffalo that was coming down to play Onondaga in a three-game playoff series.

Freeman took me up to his home, a stately log cabin built on a couple of hundred acres of hillside forest. "No spikes, no nails," he pointed out, proudly running his hands along the huge timbers. "The guys on my team and my own boys helped cut them down and drag them here." He chuckled and cupped his hand over his mouth like he was sharing a secret, "I just told them it was part of preseason training!"

No one, Indian or white, has ever gotten rich from lacrosse. But when the sport first spread beyond the reservation, there was money to be made with traveling Indian shows. In 1878, a group of Mohawk and Onondaga Indians—faces streaked with war paint for full effect—arrived in New York City with a brass band in a four-horse wagon covered with advertisements for a lacrosse tournament to be held in what would later become Madison Square Garden. Custer had made his last stand just two years earlier, Buffalo Bill's Wild West Show was just getting going, and elites in eastern cities were enthralled with the romantic image of the "vanishing" Indian.

Accompanying the Indians was promoter and Montreal-born dentist William George Beers, the man often called "the father of modern lacrosse." As a young member of the Montreal Lacrosse Club, which provided opportunities for middle-class residents to play games with nearby Mohawks, Beers became passionate about the game and determined to expand its popularity. At the age of 17, while working as a dental apprentice, Beers published the first pamphlet of rules, defining the length of sticks, field of play, size of goals, and so on. He was determined to bring "science" to the game and tame its more primitive elements. Though he admired the Indians' athletic prowess, he argued that "the fact that they may beat the pale-face, is more a proof of their superior physical nature, than any evidence of their superior science." Shorter fields, as historian Donald Fisher has put it, helped advance a game "in which 'civilized' team play and finesse replaced 'savage' mass play and brute force."

Ironically, just as Beers and other early supporters brought lacrosse to the forefront and saved it from obscurity or worse, they also systematically excluded Indians from participating in the revival. Take this excerpt from Beers's first full set of rules published in 1869, which were adopted widely as the holy scripture of organized lacrosse for years to come:

> Sec. 5.—Either side may claim at least five minutes' rest, and not more than ten, between games.
> Sec. 6.—No Indian must play in a match for a white club, unless previously agreed upon.
> Sec. 7—After each game, the players must change sides.

There, nestled innocuously between other how-tos, was one of many rules—some written, some just understood—

that would be used to effectively bar Indians from competing internationally for decades. Indians were barred from play, at first, because they were better and stronger players than their white counterparts. When white teams played Indian teams the Indians would field fewer players to allow for an even match. Indian "ringers" would be hired and paid to play on amateur teams filled with middle-class whites, who regarded the game as recreation. This gave Indians from poor reservations a source of income but led them to be labeled "professionals" and therefore barred from all national and international amateur competitions.

A nationalist with a grand vision, Beers began to spread the gospel of lacrosse as the new national game of Canada. By invigorating Canadians with his newly conceived sport that "employs the greatest combination of physical and mental activity white men can sustain in recreation," lacrosse could forge a unique national character and identity distinct from England and the United States. In Beers's view, the noble "sons of the forest," as he often referred to the Indians, would be remembered through lacrosse "long after their sun sinks in the west to rise no more."

"We don't give up easily," said Freeman's brother, Chief Shannon Booth. He had just returned from a meeting of the Grand Council, the traditional 50-seat governing body of the Iroquois League, which had been called to address the recent passport issues. "We felt the pain of 9/11. We understand and respect security needs as much as anyone," complained Shannon. "But security doesn't trump sovereignty."

If I had even a vague stereotype in mind of what a mod-

ern Iroquois chief would look like, Shannon quickly shattered it. A boyish 35-year-old with a wispy mustache, faded
trucker cap, T-shirt, and sneakers, Shannon is a chief of the
Eel Clan, one of 14 chiefs representing the Onondaga in the
Grand Council. Naively, I asked him how someone as young
as he managed to get elected.

"No such thing as elections in our government," he responded. "You can't campaign your way into this job. The clan
mothers watch all of us closely as kids, and when a chief dies
and it's time to appoint a new one, they get together and decide
who has the right qualities. You're chosen to play your part."

The topic shifted back to lacrosse as we pulled up to "the
box," the outdoor rink that has been the heart of the game
on the reservation for decades. A group of teens was applying
a fresh coat of paint to the poke-checked and weather-beaten
boards. "Be sure to paint the Visitors bench pink!" called out
Shannon, laughing. On the other end of the patchy grass-
and-dirt rink, three boys took turns practicing their 2-on-1
offense in the crease.

Box lacrosse is a faster, rougher, and, as most Iroquois
will tell you, just plain better version of the game. Popular
in Canada, and typically played on a cement surface in a
defrosted hockey rink, "box" is a six-person game that lacks
the verdant setting, loping grace, and exciting breakaways
of field lacrosse but makes up for it with bullet-fast action,
tight stick work, hot dog moves, and a 30-second-shot clock
that keeps the pace frenetic. It's been called the fastest game
played on two feet, though its field-loving detractors call it a
degraded, "hack-and-whack" version of the sport.

Box got its start in Canada during the Great Depression when the owners of the NHL hockey team the Montreal Canadiens were looking for a way to make money from their rinks during the off-season. While Iroquois teams continued to play field lacrosse right up to the 1950s, they consistently found themselves shut out from competitive play as the sport became the domain of middle-class "amateurs" in eastern prep schools and elite eastern universities. Exhibition games played between the Onondaga and college teams during this time were often marred by racism. As documented by Fisher, before one 1930 game between Onondaga and Syracuse University, local papers described the Indians as "a fighting band of Redskins" who were "out to scalp the Hillmen."

So the Iroquois turned to box lacrosse. It was a more physical, high-contact game that appealed to their traditional style of play, with looser rules around checking and more opportunities for every player to run the whole field, shoot, and score. As field lacrosse got coopted and remade into the sport of choice for upwardly mobile Easterners, box was a game the Indians could make their own.

"Every Onondagan player gets his start here," said Freeman, leaning against the splintered boards of the box.

Shannon agreed, reminiscing. "As soon as you're old enough to hold a stick and get here on foot or bicycle, you show up for pickup games. If you're the first, you start shooting around. Soon, another kid will be there to toss the ball with. Then, a third will arrive, and a fourth. In no time, you've got enough for a game."

Freeman trained his four sons here. He took them up I-81 to the Carrier Dome, where they studied the field lacrosse game that their great-grandfathers had been excluded from.

"I'd teach them how to apply what they learned in the box to the field. I'd quiz them on plays as they happened. 'Would you have made that pass?' 'What other options did he have?'"

Two of his boys went on to play for the Orange—Brett becoming captain and All-American—following in the footsteps of pioneering Onondagan Orangemen like Hall of Famer Oren Lyons Jr., Barry Powless, Travis Cook, and more recently, Marshall Abrams.

Now Freeman's two young granddaughters have picked up sticks, a novel and even radical concept in Onondaga. Despite the explosion of popularity of women's lacrosse elsewhere in the United States, Iroquois women are by tradition barred from playing the game. This may not always have been the case, however. There are accounts dating to the late 18th and early 19th centuries of women of several tribes playing the game, sometimes alongside or opposite men.

As Shannon explained the prohibition, "There's medicine in the stick and the ball that's not good for women. If your stick is lying in the middle of the living room, your mother or wife or sister can't pick that stick up. That's the way it's always been with the Creator's game."

But Freeman's granddaughters weren't content to just watch and cheer from the sidelines, so they begged their father and grandfather to be allowed to join a girls' league that had formed off the nation.

"Those girls worked on me real hard!" said Freeman. "So I went and asked two of our clan mothers for their permission, and they granted it." He then proceeded to tell me how many goals they've scored this season, clearly proud that the Bucktooth touch had successfully jumped the gender divide.

Here in Onondaga, it's not unusual for people to speak of lacrosse, even in casual conversation, as "the Creator's game." For all Indian tribes that have played it, lacrosse is, like everything on this Earth, a gift from the Creator and therefore bestowed with supernatural power, or "medicine." One Ojibwe legend, as retold by Thomas Vennum, explains how the way of playing lacrosse first came in a dream to a boy adrift in a canoe:

> In his dream, the boy saw a large open valley and a crowd of Indians approaching him. A younger member of the group invited him to join them at a feast. He entered a wigwam "where a medicine man was preparing medicine for a great game." The lacrosse sticks were held over the smoking medicine to "doctor" them and ensure success in the game. After the players had formed into two teams and erected the goal-posts, the medicine man gave the signal to start, and the ball was tossed in the air amid much shouting and beating of drums. In his dream, the boy scored a goal. When he awakened, he related the details of his experiences to his elders, who interpreted it as a dictate from the Thunderbirds. This is how the game of lacrosse began.

Traditionally, the outcomes of games were believed to be controlled by spirits that could be manipulated only by powerful medicine men, or shamans, who were hired by teams to help ensure victory. One anthropologist who studied the Iroquois game in the late 19th century described how "shamans were hired by individual players to exert their supernatural powers in their own behalf and for their side." Cherokee conjurers made the equivalent of voodoo dolls from the roots of a plant and used them to cast spells to make opponents sick. Mirrors were used by Choctaw medicine men during games to transfer the power of the sun to their players.

Balls were often made under the direction of the medicine man and imbued with magic in the process. Cherokee balls had to be made from the skin of a squirrel that hadn't been shot. Parts of animals or birds would be secretly sewn into the ball to help it fly or roll fast or to otherwise invest it with magical properties. Among the Creek, Vennum relates, a team that had scored three goals could substitute a special "chief ball" that contained an inchworm and was believed to make the ball hard for the other team to see. Other objects placed inside balls included herbs, snake nests, fleas, and—much like the early tennis balls of the French—human hair.

Just down the road from the lacrosse box in Onondaga is a large open field where men still gather on occasion to play ceremonial games, which they refer to as medicine games. There's no season schedule or roster for medicine games. They're played only when they're needed, for example, when there's a serious illness or a social problem affecting the community.

"If I called a game now," said Shannon, holding out his cell phone as though about to dial, "within a half hour I'd have thirty or forty men of all ages here with their sticks ready to play."

The very first European accounts of lacrosse dating to the early 17th century describe remarkably similar ceremonial games being called by the medicine men. Father Brébeuf described such a game in 1637, referring to the game's organizer as a "juggler":

> Sometimes, also, one of these Jugglers will say that the whole Country is sick, and he asks a game of crosse to heal it; no more needs to be said, it is published immediately everywhere; and all the Captains of each Village give orders that all the young men do their duty in this respect, otherwise some great misfortune would befall the whole Country.

Medicine games are still played the traditional way, with wooden sticks and a stuffed deerskin ball instead of a rubber one. Sides are chosen symbolically, often pitting married men again single men, or old against young. The number of goals to be reached is decided in advance. The emphasis is not on winning but, as Shannon put it, "playing the Creator's game with a pure mind and heart."

Alf Jacques handcrafts all the wooden sticks used in Onondaga medicine games in a small workshed down the hill from his mother's house. The day I paid a visit he was also in the middle of washing all the Redhawks team jerseys in preparation for that night's game.

How, I asked him, did the greatest living stick maker get stuck with such an onerous duty?

"Well, who else is gonna do it?" he shot back gruffly. "If I don't do it, they show up to a game without their jerseys or they stink and look like hell."

As the general manager of the Redhawks for the season, he was so busy with practices and road trips and laundry, he complained, that he was getting backed up on stick orders. He grabbed a beat-up notebook off his workbench to show me how he records the more than 200 orders a year he receives from all over the world. He has no website or email address.

"All word of mouth," he said. "No one else in the world can make a stick like I do."

Alf, 61, has a bushy mustache and wears his frizzy gray hair in a long ponytail down his back. He's been making sticks in the same workshop since 1962. That year, he was 13 and a promising and tenacious young goalie who'd come up under the tutelage of his father, Louis Jacques, a Canadian Hall of Famer. As for so many on the reservation at the time, jobs and money were scarce, and when his stick broke the family couldn't afford the $5 it cost to buy a new one. So, his father decided, they'd just make their own.

"We went in the woods, cut down a tree, and made the ugliest stick you ever saw. Then we made another that was a little less ugly."

Alf Jacques crafting a lacrosse stick in his workshop.

Within six years the father and son had hired a team of workers and were producing 12,000 sticks a year. But they and the other Iroquois stick makers still couldn't come close to matching the rising demand of a growing sport. In those years, even as the Lacrosse Hall of Fame was being enshrined at Johns Hopkins University and new programs were cropping up at colleges and prep schools up and down the East Coast, any player who needed a high-quality stick had to make the long road trip to the reservations of New York and neighboring Canada to buy one straight from the source. Efforts to mechanize the careful twisting and bending required to shape a stick failed repeatedly. The traditional technology of wooden sticks, which took up to a year each to produce, had become a major obstacle to the growth of the sport.

Even though it was forty years ago, Alf still sounds wounded when he talks about what happened next. In the early 1970s, after years of experimentation by entrepreneurs, the Brine Company in Boston and STX, a subsidiary of DuPont, began introducing plastic heads that were durable, flexible, and interchangeable with different sticks.

"Our production," recalled Alf, "went from twelve thousand to twelve hundred almost overnight."

Alf's shed is one part museum and one part wood shop. On the wall behind his bench, in no apparent order, can be found a shiny new regulation stick ready to be shipped to Europe, a 19th-century replica of a Great Lakes stick with its signature small round pocket, and a prized stick he made for himself in 1978. Several metal sticks with purple and orange plastic heads propped in the corner look like children's toys next to Alf's originals, which are made from hickory.

The wood is split with a club and axe, carved into the right lengths, and then set aside to dry over a stove. He then steams the wood in a wood-fired oven to soften it for bending. Using a metal plate as a vise, he bends the head into the traditional crook form, ties it with wire, and leaves it for eight months until it's dried and permanently bent. He then hand-carves and finishes the stick, using deer gut for the netting.

He pulled his own stick off the wall and handed it to me. The wood was worn and patinaed from 32 years of play. The handle is noticeably darker than the head, cured over years by the oils and sweat of countless games. Carved along its length are the Iroquois tree of peace, a turtle representing his clan, a fish (Fish being his nickname), and an image of male genitalia pierced by an arrow. "Dead nuts," he said, referring to an old expression used in the building and machinery trades. "Means it's perfect."

I turned the stick in my hand, feeling the perfect balance of its weight, tracing the grain running lengthwise for strength. Alf grabbed it from my hand suddenly.

"You don't want this stick!" he declared sarcastically, throwing it aside with practiced flare. "It's old and worn out. You want the latest model, a 2010 titanium stick with an aerodynamic ultra-light molded head that comes in five different colors. Right?"

Once he'd gotten through his rant (which included the declaration that "there are a lot of things about plastic that truly bother me") Alf acknowledged that nothing could stand in the way of progress and that if sticks were still made of wood there would be no forests left. For the game to take off and be accessible to millions of people all over the world, the technology needed to change and adapt. He knew that.

But, he added, something has been irretrievably lost in the process. He picked up the first stick he ever made with his father in 1966. "The spirit of the tree is alive in that stick, and the life of that tree came straight from the Creator." He gripped the stick and began to dodge and roll around me as though advancing on an opponent. "When you're playing, the life of that tree, that energy is transferred to you. That stick is talking to you, and if you listen you can learn."

"With this"—he held up a titanium and plastic version—
"you're on your own."

It was Friday night and the first semifinal game against the
Braves was the big-ticket event of the weekend. The Redhawks were coming into the playoffs as the clear favorite,
having lost just one regular season game. Families were piling into the metal bleachers, sporting team T-shirts and
caps. Visitors from the Tonawanda Reservation had driven
six hours for this event, and everyone would be making the
journey to Tonawanda the next day for the second game of
the series. For hundreds of years, games between villages or
between nations have been major social events, providing a
welcome excuse to visit old friends and renew ties. Thomas
Vennum described such a game played in 1797 between the
Seneca and the Mohawk: "On one side of the green the Senecas had collected in a sort of irregular encampment—men,
women, and children—to the number of more than a thousand. On the other side the Mohawk were actively assem-
bling in yet greater numbers."

In earlier times, before the Onondaga decided to reject
gambling and casinos altogether, a game like tonight's would
have involved widespread betting. Money, blankets, food,
land, sometimes even human services were staked in collective bets intended to inspire players to give it their all. But
even with thousands of dollars of bets on the line, winning
has never been of much concern to Indian players and spectators. As the lacrosse great and spiritual Faithkeeper of the
Onondaga, Oren Lyons Jr., once explained, winning and los-

ing "didn't seem to be so much a point of the game as the celebration, the sense of community, the being together with pride."

A pregame announcement was made over the PA: "Women and girls attending tomorrow night's game in Tonawanda are kindly asked to respect their nation's ways by staying clear of and not touching the lacrosse box."

Freeman spotted me and called me down to the box to watch his team warm up. Players were practicing power plays, setting up the pick-and-roll to free up the shooter. Eighty-mile-an-hour shots pounded off the enormously oversized pads of goalie Ross Bucktooth, a nephew of Freeman's, who deflected every attack with one of Alf Jacques's wooden goalie sticks. Freeman introduced me to assistant coach "Meat" Powless.

"How'd he get that name?" I made the mistake of asking.

Freeman leaned over, elbowing his friend and laughing, "Because he was blessed by the Creator!"

He walked me into the locker room and introduced his sons Brett, Drew, Grant, and the other players. Several, I noticed, wore Indian-themed tattoos and mohawks or long braids that trailed out of their helmets. After more than a century fighting stereotypes and caricature—especially in the world of sports, where tomahawk-wielding Indian mascots have been a sore point for years—these young Iroquois were comfortably reclaiming and reinventing symbols of their Indianness as if to say, "Still here, still warriors."

The game was about to begin so I found my way to a safe seat behind the glass. The rubber ball was placed in the center rink for the face-off. In the 18th century, by contrast, games were often initiated by a young maiden throwing the deerskin ball down the field toward two facing lines of players. Jeremy Thompson, the Redhawks' face-off master who had just finished his first season at Syracuse, won the battle and snapped the ball to a runner who quickly worked the ball into the crease, opening up a shot and scoring the game's first goal.

The action was riveting and chaotic. The hard rubber ball ricocheted off the boards and glass, bouncing high off the cement. With no limit on substitutions, Alf worked one of the two doors to the Redhawks' bench, opening and slamming it as players got sent on and off the rink. Penalties called for illegal checks or the occasional sucker punch or fistfight set up tense power plays.

The Braves hardly lived up to their name that night, giving up nine goals before scoring their first. Every play called by the announcer seemed to involve a Bucktooth: "It's A. J. Bucktooth to Drew Bucktooth who takes a shot. Miss! Scooped up by Wade Bucktooth and fired hard. Goal!" They won 26–3, and in the days and weeks ahead would sweep the series and win the Can-Am League championship, earning them a trip to British Columbia to play against the best indoor Canadian teams in the Presidents' Cup. They went all the way to claim the gold medal for Onondaga, a first in league history.

"They couldn't handle us," Alf boasted later. "We took care of everybody."

Lacrosse, slow out of the gate, continues to pick up steam as one of the fastest-growing sports in the United States. According to the Sporting Goods Manufacturers Association's annual participation study on team sports, it's one of seven "niche" sports that saw increased participation in 2009 (up 6.2 percent). That's all the more striking when you learn that basketball, baseball, soccer, and football all saw declines in participation in the same year. An early beneficiary of Title IX, women's lacrosse has exploded, with the number of U.S. high school teams growing 127 percent between 2001 and 2009. The surprising departure at the end of the 2009 season of Princeton's fabled winning coach, Bill Tierney, for the University of Denver—the edge of the known lacrosse universe—signaled that the era of eastern dominance and provincialism might finally be on the wane. And yet, even as the sport grows up and broadens its reach, it still can't quite shake its reputation as an affluent white sport, more than ironic given its humble and diverse roots. In 2010, lacrosse in the United States had the highest percentage of participants (48 percent) from families with household incomes more than $100,000.

The recent swirl of international publicity surrounding the Lacrosse World Championships and the Iroquois passport issue served as a needed reminder, or first-time education, to many that this rising sport of lacrosse is an Indian creation, the ancient inheritance of a league of sovereign nations. Cody Jamieson and Sid Smith's triumphant moment on the field in Foxborough had signaled for some commentators the arrival of a "new wave" of Native players who would define not just the past of the sport but its future.

Wondering about what that future might hold, I sought out Jeremy Thompson, as shining an example of that new wave as you can find. After a few challenging years, which included struggles with alcohol, he had just been named Most Valued Player of the Presidents' Cup tournament and had finished his first season as All-America, second team, with the Orange. He and his three brothers—all rising lacrosse stars—had just graced the cover of *Inside Lacrosse* magazine armed with Alf Jacques originals and wearing moccasins and the bad-ass-don't-fuck-with-me grimaces that lacrosse magazines love to feature. "The New Familiar Face of Lacrosse," the headline reads.

When I mentioned it, Jeremy seemed somewhat embarrassed by all that attention focused on him. "Uh, no, haven't read that yet."

He also sounded conflicted about having achieved his dream of playing for the Orange. I asked him to compare the experience of playing in the box for the Redhawks with being on the field for Syracuse.

"On the nation, you know, I'm playing with my brothers. I know they're most likely thinking the same thing I'm thinking. We're there to play together, be with each other. Now at Syracuse, I don't feel that way. I feel I'm in two different worlds."

Until Jeremy was 12 or so he was in fact deep in another world, attending a Mohawk language immersion school on the Akwesasne reservation in upstate New York. The family's decision to move back to Onondaga and enroll him and his brothers in public school was, he lamented, the worst thing for him at that time.

"I feel like I was just starting to learn where I came from, who I was, and then I got plunged into this other society. I've been trying to find my way ever since."

Jeremy's enthusiasm picked up while talking about an Iroquois cultural program he and a friend had just started in Onondaga for 12- to 14-year-olds. The kids learn about Iroquois language, crafts, and traditions, and elders and clan mothers come in to speak and share stories.

"Going through what I went through," he said, "I just want to help make it easier and better for the young ones coming up now. If they learn who they are first and get grounded, then they can go out and handle American culture."

When Jeremy's lost his way in the past, he said, the medicine games have always brought him back to who he is and reminded him why he plays. "When we play our medicine games, you know, the ball is made out of the skin of the deer, stuffed with tobacco that grows from our Mother Earth. By playing, we're giving thanks for the life in that ball and in the stick and all around."

Chapter Six

HOME, WITH JOY

Baseball is continuous, like nothing else among
American things, an endless game of repeated
summers, joining the long generations of all
the fathers and all the sons.

DONALD HALL

The year was 1859. About the time the Indian game
of lacrosse was getting polished up and "civilized" in
Montreal, another game played with ball and stick
was spreading like wildfire along the eastern seaboard. On
the eve of the Civil War, extra ferries were needed to shuttle
24,000 spectators from Manhattan to New Jersey to watch
an eagerly anticipated match at Hoboken's now-famous Elysian Fields. Commentators heralded it as "the favorite game
of the country village and the country town, as well as the
larger commercial cities." From its early epicenter in New
York and Philadelphia the game had swept westward, "with
the advance of civilization," as one sports weekly put it. In
a short time, it had picked up players and fans in 22 states.

In antebellum Savannah, New Orleans, and other southern towns, a dozen active clubs had cropped up and were signing on new members monthly. One enthusiastic promoter went so far as to suggest that the sport had "every prospect of becoming [America's] national game."

The game was cricket. And within a decade it would be little more than an also-ran, a quaint—and for too many, unwelcome—reminder of the nation's colonial past.

America, it turned out, needed its own game—not some Old World hand-me-down. We needed baseball, just as we needed the telegraph and the automobile and the electric lightbulb. And so we got it, invented it, brought it to life fully formed like Athena from Zeus's forehead onto a cow pasture in Cooperstown, New York. Or so the story goes.

Before America had a president or a Constitution, it had baseball. In the winter of 1778 at Valley Forge, the cold, jaundiced, undernourished troops played baseball for exercise and to boost their spirits. Even General George Washington was known to take to the field. According to a French visitor at camp, "he sometimes throws and catches a ball for hours with his aides-de-camp." By 1791, baseball was a common enough occurrence in the small towns and villages of New England for it to be a public nuisance, contributing to broken windows and other damage. That year, the word "base-ball" made its first U.S. appearance in a Pittsfield, Massachusetts, bylaw prohibiting its play within 80 yards of the town's new meetinghouse windows.

The law conjures a kind of Currier and Ives nostalgia for the joys of youth and for "the old ball game," as the refrain from the ritual seventh-inning song goes ("Take Me Out to the Ballgame," written in 1908 by a vaudeville star who had never actually been out to a ball game). The image is one we all know: a merry band of marauding youth playing a pickup game on a small-town green on a lazy summer afternoon. A deep, arcing fly ball connects with a small window. The sound of shattered glass scatters the boys over hedges and fields, nervous laughter trailing behind them.

Baseball was off to a great start.

Let's be clear up front. Exploring baseball's roots is more like joining a mass pilgrimage than it is setting off on a solitary journey into uncharted terrain. No other sport is as concerned, or as obsessed, with its founding. Tennis fans seem content knowing its roots are sufficiently old and aristocratic (and for the French, French). That one Scottish clan or another had something to do with golf's founding somewhere near the holy links of St. Andrews satisfies most golf enthusiasts. Soccer's only real historical debate in recent years has been whether, being the global game and all, FIFA should give an official nod to the fact that the Chinese emperor may have kicked a ball before English peasants thought of it. (In 2004, when FIFA president Sepp Blatter called China the "cradle of the earliest forms of football," he set off a flurry of debate across Europe.) Yet over the past century, the subject of baseball's origins has earned the attention of commissions, public hearings, press conferences, editorials, books, conferences, and more. The Society for the Advancement of Baseball Research (SABR), a 7,000-member organization formed to advance the research, preservation, and dissemination of baseball history, even has a separate "origins committee," currently chaired by MIT political scientist Lawrence McCray.

To join the baseball pilgrimage I could have visited the Lourdes of sports shrines—Cooperstown, New York, birthplace of James Fenimore Cooper and a certain Civil War hero named Abner Doubleday, baseball's mythological founder. Here, a young Doubleday supposedly interrupted a group of kids playing marbles in Elihu Phinney's pasture on a summer's afternoon, drew out a diamond-shaped field in the dirt with a stick, and proceeded to educate them on the rules of his new game. The town's Baseball Hall of Fame and Museum today draws 350,000 devotees a year from around the world to view a collection of 130,000 baseball cards, 33,000 bats, balls, and other equipment, and 12,000 hours of recorded film clips. As French philosopher Bernard-Henri Lévy described the place after his own visit:

> This is not a museum, it's a church. These are not rooms, they're chapels. The visitors themselves aren't really visitors but devotees, meditative and fervent. I hear one of them asking, in a low voice, if it's true that the greatest champions are buried here—beneath our feet, as if we were at Westminster Abbey, or in the Imperial Crypt beneath the Kapuziner Church in Vienna. And every effort is made to sanctify Cooperstown itself, this cradle of the national religion, this new Nazareth, this simple little town.

I could have gone to the far less well known but no less sacred Baseball Reliquary, a traveling museum based in Monrovia, California, and assorted nearby storage units that houses such memorabilia as a piece of skin from Doubleday's thigh, one of Babe Ruth's half-eaten hot dogs, and the jock strap of Eddie Gaedel, the three-foot, seven-inch player who in 1951, wearing the number "1/8th," got to base on a walk in his one and only time at bat for the St. Louis Browns. The Reliquary even has its own alternative hall of fame, the Shrine of the Eternals, celebrating such unsung heroes as Dock Ellis Jr., the curler-wearing Pittsburgh Pirates pitcher who in 1970 threw a no-hitter while tripping on LSD.

Even before Ken Burns captured the notion so eloquently in his 18-hour Emmy Award–winning documentary series, it was widely understood—a cultural given, in fact—that, as the historian Jacques Barzun declared, "Whoever wants to know the heart and mind of America had better learn baseball." Walt Whitman, who as early as 1846 wrote lovingly of observing youngsters playing a game of "base" in "the outer parts" of Brooklyn, later in life reflected on the emerging national sentiment toward the game:

> Well—it's our game; that's the chief fact in connection with it; America's game; it has the snap, go, fling of the American atmosphere; it belongs as much to our institutions; fits into them as significantly as our Constitution's laws; is just as important in the sum total of our historic life.

Other nations and cultures have long delighted at making their own claims to baseball's genesis. A letter sent to the Hall of Fame in 1975 by a Polish researcher, for example, reads, "For your information and records, I am pleased to inform you that after much research I have discovered that baseball was introduced to America by the Poles who arrived in Jamestown in 1609." He cited an obscure but since verified account of Zbigniew Stefanski, one of many Polish settlers brought over to the Jamestown colony to help with glassmaking and working with pitch and tar. The workers had taken with them a popular game called *pilka palantowa*, or "bat ball," to fill their few hours of recreation:

> Soon after the new year, I, Sadowski, Mata, Mientus, Stoika, and Zrenic initiated a ball game played with bat. . . . Most often we played this game on Sundays. We rolled rags to make the balls. . . . Our games attracted the savages who sat around the field, delighted with this Polish sport.

Not to be outdone, in 1990 the former president of the Romanian Oina Federation suggested that baseball was inspired by his country's national game, which involves pitching a ball stuffed with horsehair to a batter who must run a circuit of nine bases across a rectangular field. Oina is said to date to the early 14th century when it was first played by Transylvanian shepherds. The federation president has made the unverified claim that Romanian immigrants serving with Doubleday in the Civil War clued him into the secrets of that great eastern European pastime before he scratched his rules into New York soil.

Then there is the tantalizing account of the fascist Italian demographer Corrado Gini, who in 1937 encountered Berber tribesmen playing a game remarkably like baseball in a desert village in Libya. The tribesmen called the game *ta kurt om el mahag*, which translates as "the ball of the pilgrim mother." As described by IBM engineer-turned-baseball-historian David Block, the pitcher stood just a few feet from the batter and tossed the ball in a gentle arc. The batter could then be retired by having the ball caught on a fly or by being hit by the thrown ball while running between two bases. Gini suggested that the game was left behind by migrating blond Europeans who visited the region during the Stone Age. That he was the author of *The Scientific Basis of Fascism* surely didn't influence his interpretation at all.

When Gini first proposed his outlandish theory at a conference in Copenhagen in 1938, Danish researcher Per Maigard was in the audience. Maigard, who was conducting his own research on bat and ball games, came to his own conclusion a few years later that—surprise, surprise—the Scandinavian game of longball had influenced the development of baseball, cricket, and every other game worth playing. The mysterious Berbers, Maigard declared, must have picked up the game from Germanic Vandals who had brought it with them when they invaded North Africa in the fifth century AD.

So who threw the first pitch? Polish glassblowers, Berber tribesmen, Transylvanian shepherds, Egyptian pharaohs, and marauding Vikings have all had their backers. As, of course, has Abner Doubleday. The answer, it turns out, is none of the above.

If we're content with locating the origins of the game with the first time bat-struck ball, then we should accept that we'll never find that first box score, unless it's exposed someday in the dark recesses of a Paleolithic cave. Going back to my rock-throwing theory for ball game origins, it wouldn't have overly taxed our early hominid neurons to figure out that the club they used to brain small mammals might also launch a projectile farther than they could throw it. Stripped of baseball's esoteric rules and historical context, the fundamental act of hitting a ball with a bat is, as George Vecsey has pointed out, a "rather basic human pleasure, easily im-

Medieval bat-and-ball game, Flanders, 1301, from the *Calendar of the Ghistelles Hours.*

provised by a couple of bored sentries or monks or schoolgirls with access to a thin stick and something round. The rules sort of fall into place." The amateur historians of the Society for American Baseball Research have in fact exhaustively documented this basic pleasure, recording nearly 300 references to bat-and-ball games before the year 1800.

Among these references is an image dating to 1301 from a French medieval manuscript, the *Calendar of the Ghistelles Hours*, which clearly shows one young man hitting a line drive to another player who appears ready to snag it for the out. Another, from a 1555 poem by an English vicar condoning youthful recreation (at a time when many games were being banned), seems to indicate that base running was already a feature of some games:

> To shote, to bowle, or caste the barre
> To play tenise, or tosse the ball,
> Or to rene base, like men of war,
> Shal hurt thy study nought at al.

But the first mention by name of the sport that Ruth and Mantle and Mays built is from a popular English children's book, *A Little Pretty Pocket-Book*, published in London in 1744. A woodcut image entitled "Base-Ball" shows three boys Aidan's age wearing tricornered hats arranged on a field marked with three high posts for bases. One player looks ready to pitch a ball. The "batter" stands out for having no bat, preparing instead to strike the ball with the flat of his hand. A short child's verse below the image reads:

Woodcut of game of "Base-Ball," from John Newbery, *A Little Pretty Pocket-Book*, 1744.

The ball once struck off,
Away flies the boy
To the next destined post.
And then home with joy.

The book, with the fantastic subtitle "Intended for the Amusement of Little Master Tommy and Pretty Miss Polly with Two Letters from Jack the Giant Killer," was written by the early children's author John Newbery of the Newbery Medal. Copies of the popular book were at the time sold together with a ball for boys and a pincushion for girls, the use of which, according to the marketing copy that accompanied it, "will infallibly make Tommy a good boy and Polly a good girl."

In all its innocence and simplicity, this first reference captures the essence of baseball as it's still played today. A ball is pitched by a fielder and struck by a player "at bat" who runs a circuit of bases in some set order in an attempt to get safely "home." Throw in some peanuts and Cracker Jacks and we've almost got the full package!

This first reference also captures an important feature of baseball as it was played right up until the first modern rules were written down. It was, at its core, a game for boys and girls, though adults seem to have indulged as well—less for competition than for diversion and the desire to re-create the carefree days of their youth. Underscoring this childhood connection is the second historical reference to the game, which appears in a 1748 letter written about the activities enjoyed by the family of the Prince of Wales: "In the winter, in a large room, they divert themselves at base-ball, a play all who are, or have ever been, schoolboys are well acquainted with." The inference that the royal adults would have remembered the game from their childhoods suggests that "base-ball" must have been played from at least the early 1700s.

During the game's infancy, baseball was just one of a collection of similar games enjoyed and improvised upon by English boys and girls. These included trap-ball—a game in which a batter would attempt to strike a small wooden ball released from a mechanical trap. Also played were tip-cat and a host of other "cat" games in which the player would hit a lever to catapult a small piece of wood, known as the "cat," into the air and then hit it with a stick to score runs. But baseball most likely owes its greatest debt to a medieval game known as stool-ball, played in England as early as 1450. Stool-ball featured many of the elements that we now associate with baseball. Batters would run a circuit of wooden stools without being put out by being struck, or "soaked," by the ball.

Like early baseball, stool-ball was a pastime enjoyed by both sexes. Young men and women took to the fields together in the springtime, exploiting the game's innocent childhood associations to spend time together at play. The "play," however, seems to have occasionally stretched the standard rules. Shakespeare used the expression "play at stoole ball" as a thinly veiled euphemism for sex. And this exchange from a contemporary play takes the association further still, working trap-ball into the saucy mix:

WARD: Can you play at shuttlecock forsooth?
ISABELLA: Ay, and stool-ball too, sir; I have great luck
    at it.
WARD: Why, can you catch a ball well?
ISABELLA: I have catched two in my lap at one game.
WARD: What, have you, woman? I must have you learn
    to play at trap too, then y'are full and whole.

So "America's pastime," history confesses, actually emerged in England from a collection of children's sandlot games (including one that served as adult foreplay as much as it did child's play). What about cricket, then, that quintessentially English game that once vied for the hearts and minds of Americans? Many (particularly the English, of course) assume that it must have formed the trunk of baseball's evolutionary tree. Both games, after all, involve a ball and bat, scoring "runs" in "innings" with a set number of "outs" in games officiated by "umpires." But as Block points out, cricket is more like an elder cousin than a parent to baseball. In an evolutionary flowchart of baseball's evolution that Block developed, cricket breaks off early on its own proud branch, the Neanderthal line that lived on and still thrives wherever the Union Jack once flew.

Cricket first appeared in the southeast of England in the 16th century where it was played among Flemish immigrants. English researcher David Terry has offered the treasonous theory that the name "cricket" may derive from the continental hockey game *met de krik ketsen*, which the Flemish brought with them to English shores. There, according to Terry, they blended it with stool-ball and other local bat-and-ball games to form cricket. As an American, I must admit, I take some comfort in knowing that while we clearly owe the English for birthing baseball, the English may also need to look east for the inspiration of their own national game.

As a child's game, baseball had the tug and yearn of nostalgia from the start, part of the original playbook. As early as 1870, just 25 years after the sport's rules were first written down, the Brooklyn Excelsiors were already pining for the good old days. That powerhouse of early baseball made a Fourth of July trip that year upriver to Peekskill "to avail themselves of passing the Fourth pleasantly in the country, and on a ball field where the surroundings would remind them of the good old times when games were played for the pleasure and excitement incident to the sport."

In order to experience baseball's "good old times" for myself, I decided to forego Cooperstown, Monrovia, and every other well-revered shrine. Instead, I chose to visit the past itself—or at least a faithful reenactment of it. I spun the clock back to the early 1860s, back to the halcyon days before multimillion-dollar contracts, steroids . . . and gloves.

I kicked off my time travel in Washington, D.C., in the summer of 2009. Baseball had hit yet another low point. The sports channels were all abuzz with news about "The List." Word had been leaked that David Ortiz and Manny Ramirez, the two powerhouse hitters for the Red Sox at the time, had in 2003 tested positive for performance-enhancing drugs (PEDs). Players and coaches were calling on the league to release the entire list of offenders and move on. PEDs were old news for the sport by this point. Jose Canseco, Mark McGwire, and other players had been called before Congress to testify four years earlier. Everyone had long forgotten that way back in 1889 "Pud" Galvin, baseball's first 300-game winner, openly injected himself with testosterone derived from the testicles of a guinea pig and a dog.

When I stepped off the metro in Anacostia on the gritty southeast side of town and asked the station attendant for walking directions to Anacostia Park, he looked me up and down and said, "There's no easy way for *you* to walk there."

I only understood his caution later upon learning that Anacostia had one of the highest homicide rates in the country. Marion Barry, the city's former crack-smoking mayor, had been referencing Anacostia and other east-side neighborhoods when he famously remarked that, "Outside the killings, D.C. has one of the lowest crime rates in the country." I made a call and 10 minutes later a blue minivan pulled up outside the station. Out stepped Jeff "Bucket" Turner sporting white knickers, high blue-and-yellow argyle socks, a flat-topped cap, and a bib shirt with the letter *P* embroidered on it. Jeff, a 40-year-old Baltimore accountant, is the manager of the Chesapeake and Potomac Base Ball Club, one of nearly 200 vintage ball clubs across the United States that play the game by 19th-century rules using replicas of Civil War–era equipment and uniforms.

"Sorry for the hassle getting out here," Jeff apologized. "We were supposed to be playing down on the Mall but got bumped by a big soccer tournament." Nineteenth-century baseball, it seems, doesn't rank the way it used to. I asked "Bucket" about his nickname.

"Oh, all our players have nicknames just like they did in the early days. I got mine 'cause when I first started with the team I had my 'foot in the bucket' with a major hitting slump."

We drove down to the park, which runs alongside the Potomac River, where the DC Classic was under way—an annual matchup of a dozen or so vintage teams from as far away as Minnesota and Ohio. The setting was no field of dreams. The grass was pocked with brown patches from the August sun. There were no diamonds or dugouts in sight and the base paths sprouted weeds. But families, oblivious to the urban blight, lined the field on blankets and in lawn chairs

to cheer on their players, who sported a range of period outfits, many based on uniforms worn 150 years ago. Jeff's team
was in the middle of the fifth inning against the Minnesota
Quicksteps. On the field were men of every age, from 18 to
60, as well as a couple of young women.

"If you can swing a bat and run the bases without hurting
yourself, we'll take you," said Bob "Slow Trot" Tholkes, the
Minnesota manager.

Jeff started his club four years ago and quickly gathered
players via Craigslist. "I wanted to get out and be active, but
I wasn't into softball and I wasn't up for sixty-mile-an-hour
overhand pitching." Mid-19th-century ball fit the bill. Long
before the era of fastballs and curveballs, the pitcher was
called a "feeder" and was expected to toss the ball underhand
so that the batter could easily strike it. As Henry Chadwick,
the Englishman credited with developing the box score and
earned run average, among other innovations, described the
rule in 1868, "When the batsman takes his position at the
home base, the umpire asks him where he wants a ball, and
the batsman responds by saying 'knee high,' or 'waist high,'
or by naming the character of the ball he wants, and the
pitcher is required by the rules to deliver the batsman a ball
within a legitimate reach of his bat and as near the place indicated as he can."

Jeff and his fellow time travelers have a weekend mission
to reclaim the innocence and civility of the "gentleman's
game" that was baseball in the mid-1800s.

"It's about getting back to where it started," said Jeff as
he selected a heavy antique wooden bat from a pile and got

ready to take his turn. "It was a more casual game with fewer rules before the 1860s, when it started to get regulated and competitive."

Jeff stepped up to bat. The pitcher, gloveless as all but a handful of players were until the 1880s, lobbed the slowest pitch I'd seen since I coached my son's second-grade Little League team. Jeff swung and missed. Strike one. Another pitch floated squarely over the plate, but Jeff gave it a look and let it go.

"Warning, striker!" called the umpire. According to the 1866 rules, the next time Jeff avoided hitting a ball the arbiter deemed playable he'd be called for the strike. Having been warned, Jeff connected solidly with the next pitch, sending the ball toward the shortstop, who barehanded it off the bounce and tossed it back to the pitcher.

"One hand!" called the arbiter, using the old term for an out.

I was ready to leap onto the field to protest when "Sparks," a young electrical engineer on Jeff's team, pulled me back and explained that by the rules of the day a ball caught off the first bounce was as much an out as one caught on the fly.

More precisely, Jeff was out because of rule 12 of the very first 1845 set: "If a ball be struck, tipped, and caught, either flying or on the first bound, it is a hand out." The man behind those first rules was a Manhattan bank clerk, bookseller, and volunteer fireman named Alexander Joy Cartwright, one of what seems to be an ever-growing list of "fathers" of baseball. For a few years, Cartwright and a group of merchants, bankers, and other solidly middle-class men had been breaking from work at 3:00 PM to play a standing game in a vacant lot at 27th Street and Park Avenue near what would later become the first Madison Square Garden. They called themselves the Knickerbocker Base Ball Club, using a Dutch name made famous years earlier by Washington Irving, who used it as a pen name. Though Cartwright and his Knickerbockers have been given a special spot in baseball history, historian John Thorn points out that they were by no means the only game in town. Several named clubs—Gotham, Washington, Eagle, Olympic, and New York—preceded them with teams competing as early as 1823.

The term "club" is still used quaintly to describe today's bloated corporate franchises, but in the 1840s baseball clubs like the Knickerbockers were real social fraternities that brought men of similar professions and social status together. The Industrial Revolution had transformed the leisure lives of city dwellers, subjecting them to what historian George Kirsch calls "the tyranny of the clock." Where the lines between work and leisure were once fluid and blurred, they were now sharply drawn. White-collar merchants, shopkeepers, bookkeepers, and other city dwellers found themselves working ever-longer hours to keep up with the demands of business. Free time was in short supply in a six-day workweek, with Sundays still regarded in many places as the "Lord's day," inappropriate for frivolous games and play. At the same time, restrictive Victorian attitudes toward sport and recreation were giving way to acceptance of the healthful benefits of respectable, "manly" pastimes like baseball. And so, after a long day hunched over desks in factories these new urbanites happily escaped to nearby ball fields for recreation, exercise, and socializing. The old "child's game" of their youth, they found, was the perfect antidote to the pressures of modern life.

The Knickerbockers and other baseball clubs of the time were governed by constitutions, bylaws, and annual dues. The 40 members were divided into a "first nine," which was their best players, a "second nine" bench squad, and a "muffin nine" last resort. The final category was gently defined by Henry Chadwick as "a class of players who are both practically and theoretically unacquainted with the game. Some 'muffins,' however, know something about how the game should be played, but cannot practically exemplify their theory."

Matches between clubs were arranged by written challenge. The clubs would agree upon an umpire, a place, and a time. The prize in interclub matches was typically the game ball, which was inscribed with the date and score and put in a trophy case in the club room. The ball was a fitting prize given the difficulty and cost of making one before the era of mass production of sporting goods. While the average life of a ball in today's major-league games is just six pitches, in the early days one baseball was used for the entire game unless it was lost or completely demolished. A ripped ball was cause for a break in the action as needle and thread were brought to the field for repairs. A ball that got whacked out of shape would be remolded to a usable form. A lost ball could cause a serious delay to an already long game as players and fans set off to scour bushes and high grasses. It became enough of a problem that in 1877 a five-minute limit was put on such searches before a second ball was introduced.

As reported in the *San Francisco Examiner* in 1888, one of the first matches ever played in that city was nearly canceled owing to the lack of a suitable ball. With both clubs and spectators gathered and the threat of postponement looming, one industrious club member approached "a German immigrant who was the possessor of a pair of rubber overshoes. These he bought, after much dickering, for $10, and with the yarn unraveled from a woolen stocking and a piece of a rubber overshoe the first ball ever used in this city was made."

Until the 1860s most balls were homemade from rubber, yarn, and leather, though players were known to get creative with whatever materials were available. In the lake regions of the Midwest, where fish were more plentiful than rubber, baseballs were reputedly made from sturgeon eyes! As baseball historian Peter Morris recounts, the eyes of that fish were rubbery in texture and the size of walnuts. Players wrapped the eyeballs with yarn and covered them with leather or cloth to make for what was said to be a "lively ball."

Daniel "Doc" Adams, a lesser-known father of baseball and early president of the Knickerbockers in 1846, reminisced a half-century later about the challenge of securing suitable balls for play:

> We had a great deal of trouble in getting balls made, and for six or seven years I made all the balls myself, not only for our club but also for other clubs when they were organized. I went all over New York to find

someone who would undertake this work, but no one could be induced to try it for love or money. Finally I found a Scotch saddler who was able to show me a good way to cover the balls with horsehide, such as was used for whip lashes. I used to make the stuffing out of three or four ounces of rubber cuttings, wound with yarn and then covered with the leather. Those balls were, of course, a great deal softer than the balls now in use.

So soft and lightweight was the ball that even the strongest arm couldn't get it from the outfield all the way to the pitcher. Doc Adams's solution in 1849–1850 was a new non-base-tending position called the shortstop designed originally to intercept and relay weak throws from the outfield. Adams, one of baseball's unsung heroes, also deserves credit for setting the base paths at 90 feet.

For the Knickerbockers and other clubs in the mid-1800s, the awarding of the game ball was just the beginning of the festivities. No matter who won or lost, the visiting club was invited to a sumptuous meal hosted by the home club at a local tavern. Kegs of lager fueled toasts, speeches, and songs well into the night. The farther a club traveled for the game, the more lavish the treatment. In 1860, the Brooklyn Excelsiors traveled to Baltimore, where they were met by their hosts and "escorted in carriages to the various places of interest throughout the city, every attention being given them by the gentlemanly members of the Baltimore Excelsiors." When it was game time, a streetcar decked with flags and drawn by four horses was arranged to take them to the playing field.

By all accounts, however, the Knickerbockers were "more expert with the knife and fork at post-game banquets than with bat and ball on the diamond," as the great baseball historian Harold Seymour put it. Their skills were put to the test on June 19, 1846, in what is often heralded as the first true interclub baseball game in American history (though scholars have since discovered reports of possible games played in New York a few years prior). With green space becoming scarce in Manhattan, and their old spot on Park Avenue and 27th Street under development as a railroad terminal, the Knickerbockers took their games across the river to Hoboken's Elysian Fields (named, fittingly, after the mythological resting place of ancient Greek heroes). That June Friday they boarded the ferry in their freshly pressed blue woolen pantaloons, white flannel shirts, and straw hats to face a scrappy team known as the New York Nine. They were crushed, 23–1.

A team called a "nine" or "picked nine," as opposed to a club, usually meant they were made up of tradesmen who worked together, drank in saloons together, and played ball together. The most common baseball nines of the period were drawn from volunteer fire companies and from pressmen and typographers in the print trade. In 1840s New York, these were among the tightest social fraternities and unions, with their own activities and rituals. As Warren Goldstein points out in his compelling social history of early baseball, *Playing for Keeps*, the names of early baseball teams and fire companies were nearly identical. The New York Mutuals, which became one of the leading clubs of the 1870s, was started in 1857 by the Mutual Hook and Ladder Company No. 1. Even the earliest baseball uniforms, like those sported by Jeff and his teammates, were derived from firefighter uniforms, with their distinctive shield-shaped shirt panels embroidered with the insignia of the team or company.

After being throttled, the Knickerbockers retreated with their coattails between their legs and didn't play another interclub match for the next five years. No sooner had the rules for baseball been set forth than a struggle for the game's soul had begun that, in a sense, continues to this day. Would baseball be a respectable game of gentlemen, played "just for enjoyment and exercise," as Doc Adams fondly recalled from his Knickerbocker days? Or would it be a game of scrappy upstarts, played hard, played for money, and played to win?

When I next dipped my toe into the embattled past of baseball, it was five years earlier—1861—and I'd chosen a more idyllic and period-appropriate setting. It was a blustery fall day at the Spencer-Pierce-Little Farm in the picturesque New England town of Newbury, Massachusetts. The main farmhouse, which sits on 230 acres bordering the Merrimack River, is the only 17th-century stone house in New England with its outside walls still intact. Beyond a stately row of maples, Big Dave and Little Romeo, the farm's resident pigs, rooted around behind home plate for hot dog scraps. An old-timey cheer—"Huzzah!"—was raised without a hint of irony to signal the end of a successful inning of vintage ball. The crisp white uniforms of the Essex Base Ball Club and Lynn

Live Oaks stood out against the arboreal wash of reds and golds.

Jeff Peart, the bespectacled, gray-bearded umpire, stepped forward to make a request of the fleece-wrapped spectators—known in the lingo of the times as cranks, bugs, or rooters—"Please do not stretch in the seventh inning. That hasn't been invented yet. Please do not sing 'Take Me Out to the Ballgame.' That has not been written yet."

Jeff, a 53-year-old pharmaceutical company manager, played master of ceremonies, with black top hat, tails, and a gold-tipped cane that belonged to his great-grandfather, an itinerant preacher.

"Kids are always asking me why I'm dressed as an undertaker," he said, brushing dirt off his coat.

A longtime Civil War history buff, Jeff was looking for ways to immerse himself in his favorite period. But, he says, "I'm too much of a pacifist to run around with a gun, even a fake one. So vintage baseball seemed like a better fit."

I joked that I'd recently come from 1866 and was happy to report that, postwar, the game was still very much in vogue.

"More in vogue is the truth, and more of a national game," said Jeff. "In 1861, baseball was still mostly played in New England and New York. After the Civil War, soldiers took the game back to their hometowns with them and it spread like wildfire."

On the eve of the War Between the States, baseball was often promoted in the press as useful preparation for battle, with its physical demands, sharpening of skills, and promotion of the values of teamwork and fraternity. A newspaper editorial that year remarked that "Baseball clubs . . . are now enlisted in a different sort of exercise, the rifle or gun taking the place of the bat, while the play ball gives place to the leaden messenger of death."

Jeff introduced me to Brian "Cappy" Sheehy, a cheerful, barrel-chested 28-year-old high school history teacher and club captain. Brian started the club in 2002, naming it after a club that had played in his hometown back in 1859.

As the eighth inning was kicking off, he asked me if I wanted to play.

"I'm afraid I left my knickers at home," I replied.

"Don't worry," he assured me. "We'll take you as is."

A vintage baseball game underway in Washington, D.C.

Taking to the field with my teammates, I felt like Kevin Costner in the closing scene of *Field of Dreams* (without the 1980s mullet). I assessed the familiar geometry of the diamond (falsely named since the 1830s: diamonds have two acute and two obtuse angles). I manned second base as the lead-off batter took the plate, wondering whether the second base force-out had been instituted yet (it hadn't). And whether batters were allowed to overrun first base yet (they weren't). The batter drove the first pitch well into center field, rounded first, and headed for second. The center fielder chased down the ball and fired it hard to me. As the ball burned a hole through my fingers and kept going I thought to myself how remarkably helpful a glove would have been at that very moment.

"Muffin!" yelled a player on the other team.

With little help from me, we eventually managed to retire the side. Soon it was my turn at bat. I selected a caveman club from the pile and headed to home plate, which was literally a heavy round iron plate stuck into the ground.

The catcher pointed to the outfield. "If you hit the goat, it's an automatic home run." I looked and there was indeed a rather large white goat browsing in left field. I felt suddenly lucky, thinking of the curse of the angry goat brought on the Chicago Cubs in the 1945 World Series when the club's owner ejected a local tavern owner's goat from the ball park. Truth is, goat or no goat, a home run would have been a rare occurrence in 1861 owing to the combination of large unbounded fields and soft homemade balls. Baseball was still a "small ball" game. In the absence of gloves, it was best to attempt a line drive or a hard grounder, forcing one player to barehand the ball and throw it to another player who had to barehand it to make the out.

I let the first pitch pass, knowing there were no called balls or strikes to worry about. It bounced past the catcher and into Big Dave's mud pit.

"It's okay, he's sleeping," called out a crank as the catcher bounded over the electric fence to pluck the ball from a pile of rotten vegetables.

The second pitch came right down the middle. I swung my club and tipped it back and foul—or so I thought.

"One hand!" called the umpire.

I opened my mouth to protest but checked myself.

I stomped back to the bench, wishing I had a helmet to throw. Brian explained that I was out because the catcher had caught the ball after it bounced once in fair territory. The notion of foul versus fair territory was a welcome contribution of the Knickerbockers to the game of baseball. Before the Knickerbockers imposed order on chaos, players would commonly reverse-hit the ball behind the catcher or chip it far wide of the baselines to give themselves extra time to reach first base. Nevertheless, the rules around "tipped" balls took time to evolve and, much to my chagrin, in 1861 a ball was called fair as long as it bounced once in fair territory.

Strange as the rule was, I could live with it. But rule 12 was another story. The fly ball rule I got. A ball caught on the fly is an out. It's the first rule any Little Leaguer learns and, as David Block points out, is probably the oldest rule in the game, forming the basis for stool-ball, trap-ball, and most other early bat-and-ball games. But being called out on a ball caught on the bounce?

"What kind of lame rule is that?" I muttered to myself.

In the 1860s, it turns out, there were plenty of other like-minded players muttering to themselves. The "bound rule," as it was known, was a Knickerbocker innovation, and it quickly became the lightning rod in a struggle over what Goldstein calls the "two ethics of the game."

Considering the great historic rivalries of baseball—Yankees versus Red Sox and Giants versus Dodgers to name just two of the longest lasting—and the passions they stir in players and fans alike, it's nearly impossible to conceive of a time when excessive competition was regarded as a problem for the sport. But for its first two decades, baseball was a game of gentlemen played not for money or even victory but for fun and fraternity. Sportswriters of the time were as likely to applaud how players cheered each other at the end of the game and left the field "arm and arm" as they were to provide a blow by blow of the game itself. Players who swore or otherwise got carried away in the heat of the competition were fined on the spot—anywhere from 10 to 50 cents—the money put to good use to pay for after-game festivities. And cranks were the worst offenders of all, as they are today. As one club's officers lamented, "What . . . can any club do? Can we restrain a burst of applause or indignation from an assemblage of more than 15,000 excited spectators, whose feelings are enlisted as the game proceeds, by the efforts of this or that player or players?"

As spirited competition became more broadly accepted

as good for the sport, the bound rule came under attack as an "unmanly" remnant of baseball's childish roots. In 1858, the newly formed National Association of Base Ball Players (NABBP), attempting to distance their manly sport from its boyish associations, voted to exclude any members under the age of 21. Younger players protested. One correspondent to a sports weekly who signed his name "Infant Ball Player," argued, "The *boys* have a say in regard to this game, which they have *always* played, and which most of you have only just now taken out of their hands."

The Knickerbockers had already taken concrete steps to remove the game from the domain of youth. In rule 13 they made it clear that "in no instance is a ball to be thrown" at a runner. Reasonable as that sounds in this age of 80 mph missiles fired to first base, players before this rule were put out by being "soaked" or "plugged" with the ball. Abandoning what was widely regarded as a childish practice made for a more advanced level of play by fielders and base runners. It also allowed for balls to get harder, which in turn made the thrilling crack of a Hank Aaron or "Big Papi" home run possible.

Likewise, many argued through the 1850s and 1860s, catching a ball on one bounce was, as Henry Chadwick stated at the time, "a feat a boy of ten years of age would scarcely be proud of." He called on fielders to do their best to catch the ball on the fly, arguing that "nothing disappoints the spectator, or dissatisfies the batsman so much, as to see a fine hit to the long field caught on the bound in this simple, childish manner."

The dwindling defenders of the old bound rule, who

Chadwick chided as a "muffin fraternity," suggested that eliminating the bound rule would make baseball too much like cricket or cause more injury to hands. Most traditionalists, however, were just trying in vain to hang on to the spirit of the game as a social outlet for fun, exercise, and friendship—a game all comers were welcome to play.

But the press and spectators favored excitement and skill over fraternity and tradition. The fly rule, codified at last in 1864, made for faster, more riveting play that pushed fielding skills to a new level. It gave outfielders a reason to make graceful, diving catches that brought fans to their feet, and it gave batters a reason to push the ball high and deep to test the pluck and athleticism of fielders. It also brought out the crowds.

By the summer of 1858 baseball fever had officially swept New York. The Brooklyn clubs, the best in the nation, issued a challenge to the New York clubs (Brooklyn then being a separate city). In what would become the very first All-Star game and New York's first (pre-subway) subway series, each city was to pick their best "nine" from among various clubs to compete. The neutral ground chosen was the Fashion Race Course in Queens. To accommodate the crowds, which swelled to 10,000, the *New York Tribune* announced that steamer ships would leave the Fulton Market in Manhattan and horse-drawn carriages would take fans from the Queens slip to the ball field. Having assembled the best players in the game, the series promoters had the novel idea of charging spectators a steep admission price of 50 cents to attend the contest. The series was a wild success. Brooklyn edged New York in the third game and, after expenses, $71.09 in profits was donated to the two cities' fire departments.

No one had imagined that there was money to be made from baseball. But as club competition became more intense and the first stars began to emerge in the game, the age of professional sport was just around the corner. By 1860, Jim Creighton, who threw the first fastball, completed the first triple play, and threw a wicked underhand change-up he called the "dew drop," was being paid under the table by the Brooklyn Excelsiors. Under the table, because the NABBP at the time prohibited player salaries. To get around the prohibition while retaining the appearance of upholding the amateur spirit of the game, teams commonly laundered salaries through local city businesses.

One of the first to decry the hypocrisy of such arrangements was Albert G. Spalding, a rising pitching star with a club called the Forest Citys in Rockford, Illinois. When he was approached by the Chicago Excelsiors to join the team, the offer came with no salary but with a $40 a week grocery clerk job. He leapt at the chance to play big city ball but, as he wrote later in his autobiographical account, *America's National Game*, "I was not able to understand how it could be right to pay an actor, or a singer, or an instrumentalist for entertaining the public, and wrong to pay a ball player for doing exactly the same thing in his way." Spalding's stint with the Excelsiors was brief. The team folded in his first season in uniform, and he returned to his old team in Rockford to plan his next move.

As documented by his biographer, Peter Levine, back home the 17-year-old Spalding filled his scrapbook with news clippings on subjects ranging from baseball to banking and other business stories. Highlighted in black ink were stories about the Cincinnati Red Stockings and their celebrated manager, English-born cricket pro Harry Wright, who openly recruited and paid salaries to the best players around. Also marked off was an announcement that Wright and his brother George had opened a store in New York "for the sale of bats, balls, bases and all the paraphernalia needed for outdoor games."

Spalding's "cannon ball" underhand caught Wright's attention after it laid waste to the Red Stockings in a 12–5 upset in the fall of 1870. The next year, after moving the Red Stockings to Boston—where they would eventually become the Red Sox—and organizing baseball's first professional league, the National Association of Professional Base Ball Players, Wright signed "Big Al" as a pitcher with an annual salary of $1,500.

But Spalding had bigger plans in baseball than being a star pitcher. Under Wright's tutelage, he learned the business of managing a club. When Wright decided in 1874 to fulfill a personal dream and stage a barnstorming tour of his homeland with his Boston Red Stockings, he sent Spalding ahead as his agent to make arrangements for the visit. Although the curiosity factor of Yanks in brightly colored socks brought out spectators, the tour, intended to spread the new American gospel of baseball to English cricket lovers, lost money and did little to convince the English to forsake their wickets for bases. "Few of the youth of Great Britain," one English commentator noted, "will desert cricket with its dignity, manliness, and system for a rushing, helter-skelter game." But Spalding learned firsthand the power of marketing and public relations for generating buzz, skills he'd make good use of in the years ahead.

By 1876, Spalding had taken his free agency and business acumen to the Chicago White Stockings, leaving Boston in the dust and in mourning. It was a straight-up business deal, and a sweet one at that, having negotiated with team president William Hulbert a $2,000 annual contract, 25 percent of gate receipts, and a role as player-manager. Over the next 16 years, as player, manager, and later as president, he helped turn the White Stockings into the most dominant team in baseball. Over 10 seasons between 1880 and 1890 they boasted a winning percentage of .676, and in 1880 set the still unbroken record of .798, winning 67 out of 84 games.

But as anyone knows who's ever owned a baseball or a glove, or who has grown up in the city playing stickball with that wondrous pink sphere known as a Spaldeen, Al Spalding wasn't content with having his name inscribed only on his jersey. Baseball was finally becoming the business he'd envisioned it could be, and he was determined to lead the charge. In 1878, the *New York Clipper* sports weekly noted that "bats are being made by the 500,000, balls by the thousand gross." The same year Spalding moved back to Chicago, he and his brother Walter opened their own "baseball and sporting-good emporium" at 118 Randolph Street. Walter, a bank teller, ran the business at first while Spalding played the star pitcher, bringing in publicity and sales.

In the years that followed, Spalding more or less invented sports marketing, blurring the lines between play and business long before the days of Michael Jordan or Tiger Woods. In his first year in business he launched *Spalding's Official Baseball Guide*, a publication that included his full-page autographed picture on the cover. For more than a half-century, the guide was the favorite reading choice of young boys eager to get the latest how-tos from the pros.

By 1884 the publication had a circulation of 50,000 and was serving as a marketing platform for selling the firm's sporting goods to a growing nation of baseball fanatics. Spalding quickly cornered the market after his "Spalding League Ball" scored exclusive designation as the official ball of the National League. Then there were his "wagon tongue baseball bats" made of "the finest straight grained, well seasoned, second growth Ash sticks" and used by "nine-tenths" of the players in the World Series. As pitcher and then as first baseman, he was not only an early proponent of gloves (once seen as "unmanly") but deliberately wore a black one for greater prominence. Having boosted the popularity of baseball gloves on the mound and at first base, he then happily supplied them by the thousand to an eager public.

Like that other great huckster of his age, P. T. Barnum, Spalding was a master of marketing hyperbole. The firm warned against unscrupulous counterfeiters of "official" Spalding goods. "First be sure it's a Spalding—then go buy" was their slogan. Their baseballs were sold in red sealed boxes with instructions to check that the seal wasn't broken before opening. An article in Spalding's *Guide* even alerted players to a rash of counterfeit catchers' masks that were "liable to disfigure a player for life."

By October 1888, having firmly established the Spalding brand and developed a multimillion-dollar business from scratch, he set his sights on the next big thing: bringing "America's game" to the world. For Spalding and others in the age of Manifest Destiny, baseball represented everything unique and noble in the American character. As he later ticked off in his autobiography—alphabetically, no less—baseball was "the exponent of American Courage, Confidence, Combativeness, American Dash, Discipline, Determination, American Energy, Eagerness, Enthusiasm, American Pluck, Persistency, American Spirit, Sagacity, Success, American Vim, Vigor, Virility." (What, no Zeal?)

Spalding decided to take all that American goodness— and, by the way, Spalding sporting goods—on a world tour. For six months an entourage of 20 major-league players barnstormed the globe, from the deserts of Egypt and Ceylon to the green fields of Australia and New Zealand and the cricket pitches of England. As with his earlier 1874 ramble, the trip had great PR value, with 42 games played before some 200,000 people. But the cricket-loving masses of the Anglo-colonial world were, again, largely unmoved. One British reporter stated that Spalding's beloved game was "as much out of place in England as a nursery frolic in the House of Commons."

Spalding and his band of travelers returned to the United States, nevertheless, as heroes. Three hundred guests, including Teddy Roosevelt and Mark Twain, packed into Delmonico's in New York to toast Spalding's "feat of pluck." Countering the pinched views of the English press, Twain famously mused about the idea of attempting to bring baseball, "the very symbol, the outward and visible expression of the drive and push and rush and struggle of the raging, tearing, booming nineteenth century . . . to places of profound repose and soft indolence."

Spalding's tour had confirmed for him that baseball symbolized everything that was great about America. In the years that followed, the notion that baseball might have English roots became unconscionable to Spalding—even though as a younger man he had, along with most of his contemporaries, accepted England's influence on the game. At the same time, baseball luminary Henry Chadwick, editor of Spalding's *Guide*, began authoring pieces there about baseball's English roots. This got Spalding's attention and set him off on his final quest: to brand baseball "Made in America" once and for all.

After taking apart Chadwick's arguments in the pages of the *Guide*, in 1905 Spalding announced the formation of a national commission to collect evidence and settle the question of baseball's origins. He handpicked like-minded friends and colleagues, including two members of Congress and A. G. Mills, the former president of the National League. Old-timers sent in random, rambling stories of playing old-cat or tip-cat or some other such game as kids, but none of it added up to a clear historical picture. Not until the editors of the *Beacon Journal* in Akron, Ohio, received a letter from a mining engineer named Abner Graves written in response to an article written by Spalding. "The American game of Base Ball," Graves declared succinctly, "was invented by Abner Doubleday of Cooperstown, New York."

Prompted by Spalding for more details, Graves sent a second letter to the commission in which the plot thickened. He described a scene from his childhood in the rural upstate New York town. He recalled playing marbles with a group of other boys when Doubleday approached them about a new game called "base ball" and drew a diagram in the dirt with a stick to explain its rules. Graves added that unfortunately "there is not one chance in ten thousand that a boy's drawing . . . would have been preserved."

Luckily for him and for Doubleday's legacy, Spalding's commission didn't require such evidence. Doubleday was a Civil War hero who had fired the first cannon at Fort Sumter and whose brigade had played a pivotal role in the Battle of Gettysburg. Spalding noted that "it certainly appeals to an American's pride to have had the great national game of Base-ball created and named by a Major-General in the United States Army." And there was another, more bizarre, connection between Spalding and Doubleday that might have helped convince Spalding to embrace him as the father of the game. As David Block has uncovered, the two men were both, at different points in time, members of the Theosophical Society—a California-based occult society concerned with apparitions and other supernatural manifestations.

The commission issued its conclusions at the end of 1907. Baseball, they declared, was of American origin and "the first scheme for playing it, according to the best evidence obtainable to date, was devised by Abner Doubleday at Cooperstown, N.Y., in 1839."

The decision was made and the story of Doubleday was folded neatly into the official lore and history of the game. Chadwick continued to protest, but no one was interested in his messy English version of events. Americans hailed the decision and textbook writers and historians happily turned it into another fact for schoolchildren to memorize. The Baseball Hall of Fame was built in Cooperstown in 1939 on the centennial of the game's mythological founding, and a U.S. Postal Service commemorative stamp followed soon after.

Aside from all the evidence presented earlier for baseball's steady evolution from English children's games, there are just a few other problems with the Doubleday tale. In 1839, when Doubleday was supposed to be scratching double plays into the dirt at Cooperstown, he was actually a cadet attending West Point 100 miles away. Doubleday left 67 diaries and wrote numerous magazine and newspaper articles in his later years, but only once, in passing, did he even mention the game of baseball.

So what about that other Abner—Mr. Graves? Who was this guy who claimed to be there at the moment of the game's immaculate conception? Well, according to his own colorful accounts over the years, he led an exciting life. At the age of 14 he sailed around Cape Horn. In 1852 he was one of the first riders on the pony express—inconveniently before the service actually started. And what he didn't share was just as interesting. He'd been hospitalized in insane asylums twice in his earlier years. In his coup de grâce, at the ripe old age of 90, Abner—described by Spalding's commission as a "reputable gentleman"—shot and killed his wife Minnie in an argument over the sale of their house. He was committed to a Colorado state asylum, where he died two years later.

Today, no historian or scholar of any repute subscribes to the Doubleday version of baseball's origins. And yet the myth persists. As recently as 2010, Major League Baseball commissioner Bud Selig confessed in an Internet posting, "From all of the historians which I have spoken with, I really believe that Abner Doubleday is the 'Father of Baseball.'" (One might wonder which historians the commissioner has been speaking with: is he conferring in the off-season with Byzantine scholars . . . or historians of the Norman invasion?)

Selig's a smart guy, so I'm guessing he knows the history of his sport better than he lets on. So why does he make statements like this, and why would he lay a wreath on Doubleday's grave in Arlington Cemetery as he did ten years ago? Why, for that matter, do millions of people still go on pilgrimage to remote, rural New York State to perpetuate a fraud that was exposed more than 60 years ago?

The exhibit panels on Abner Doubleday in the Hall of Fame answer these lingering questions as well as anything I've read: "In the hearts of those who love baseball, he is remembered as the lad in the pasture where the game was invented. Only cynics would need to know more." As the baseball-loving evolutionary biologist Stephen Jay Gould once pointed out, most people, given the choice, will choose creation myths over history every time. "For creation

myths . . . identify heroes and sacred places, while evolutionary stories provide no palpable, particular thing as a symbol
for reverence, worship, or patriotism."

One of the many wonders of baseball is that after being tested and tried in every possible way—the scandals,
the drug tests, the player strikes, the multimillion-dollar
contracts—we still believe deeply in the myths and the rites
of the game. We still sing "Take Me Out to the Ballgame" in
the seventh-inning stretch with sincerity. We still believe the
curse of the Bambino was real (it had to be something!). We
still never, ever talk about a "no-hitter" or a "perfect game"
in progress. We still recite the ERAs and RBIs and OBPs
of players long dead like numerological incantations. And,
despite our more rational selves, we still keep a special place
in our hearts for Abner Doubleday, a man who was far more
expert with a rifle than a bat.

On the playing field in Newbury, I was finally hitting my
stride and warming to 1860s rules. I scored a single and drove
in a run with a line drive to right center field, my legs sup-
pressing muscle memory itself so as not to overrun first base.
I cleverly bunted the ball backward behind the catcher, exploiting that quirky loophole in the rules while it still lasted.
Playing outfield in the hot afternoon sun, I resisted the urge
to chase a pop ball, walking up leisurely instead to scoop it
off the bounce for the out.

When the game ended, no one was certain of the score
and no one really cared—we were gentlemen at play, after
all. A truck pulled up from a local microbrewery that fielded

their own vintage club (yep, "The Brewers"), just in time to reinvigorate our feeling of social fraternity. The takeout pizza arrived next in a beat-up sedan bouncing over the lumpy pasture. It wasn't quite a Knickerbockers feast, but it would serve just as well.

Just then, my cell phone rang.

"It's your wife calling from the distant future," warned one of my teammates. "Don't answer it!"

For vintage ballplayers, as for Yogi Berra, "the future ain't what it used to be," and its nagging call is usually best ignored, especially on a hot Saturday in summer. That's certainly how Scott Westgate feels. Scott, whom I spoke with by phone (being a weekday, he answered), is a Michigan mortgage broker and the current president of the Vintage Base Ball Association (VBBA), the organizing body for creatively anachronistic ballplayers. Much as he loves modern baseball, having played all through high school, he feels the game lost its soul somewhere in its journey to the present.

"Baseball was once a celebration of life. Two towns would have a summer get-together and it would culminate with a game in an open field—not for competition but for exercise, for friendship, to have an entertaining event. That's all changed."

The VBBA, Scott said, came together several years ago as a brotherhood of guys who wanted to promote, perpetuate, and re-create the game of baseball "as it was meant to be played." But all is not well in Scott's version of the past.

"More and more we're facing pitchers who are supposed to be playing by 1860 rules, but they're putting spin on the ball, or have a special hurl to deceive the hitter, which is not how it was supposed to be played. Now we're trying to hold on to the bound rule as it makes for a more gentlemanly game. But you've got guys out there diving for fly balls and barehanding it like they're Dwight Evans or something."

Picking up on the desire for a more competitive vintage game, Jim Bouton, former major-league pitcher and tell-all author of *Ball Four*, a few years ago started a rival league— the Vintage Base Ball *Federation*—that plays by 1880s rather than 1860s rules. That means overhand pitching, padded gloves, and called balls and strikes.

Scott's not a fan and seems genuinely alarmed at the prospect of newfangled 1880s competitiveness creeping into and corrupting his beloved old game. "We need to keep ingraining in our members that this is not meant to be a competition. It's just supposed to be a game."

Chapter Seven

PLAYED IN AMERICA

Football combines the two worst elements
of American life. Violence and committee
meetings.

GEORGE WILL

Baseball," said former tight end Jamie Williams, "is
what America aspires to be. Football is what this
country is." If baseball is by nature nostalgic, pas-
toral, playful, and free, American football is progressive,
industrial, aggressive, and regimented. In baseball, players
round a circuit of bases, oblivious to time, with the goal of
getting everyone safely home, right where they started. In
football, players advance their forces along the gridiron, battling through opponents and against the clock to gain yards
and touch the ball down in enemy terrain.

These two great American sporting traditions couldn't be
more different. In a sense, they've come to reflect competing
visions of American life—one drawn to the past and to the
idea of simpler times, the other hurling brashly toward the

future. By every reasonable measure football, and the future, are winning out.

Half of the U.S. population watched the Green Bay Packers defeat the Pittsburgh Steelers in Super Bowl XLV, setting a new record for American television viewership. Throw in the millions who watched from bar stools or paid $200 to stand in the parking lot of Cowboy Stadium, and we're talking more than 163 million people.

When these numbers were announced, the annual debate arose once again in the media and in online discussion boards: which of our two national sports deserves the much-coveted title of "America's game"?

The issue's been settled for years, if not decades. The 2010 Major League Baseball World Series averaged just 14 million viewers a game, the second lowest turnout ever for a broadcasted series. According to the 2010 Harris Poll, just shy of one-third of Americans identified professional football as their favorite sport, compared to just 17 percent for baseball. The last time baseball and pro football were tied in the poll was 1985. Football, the NFL boasted in a 2009 PR campaign, backed up by a 29-page white paper analyzing the league's business and media dominance across every conceivable measure, is "America's Choice."

If football is today our "biggest civic tent," as historian Michael MacCambridge describes it, the one thing all Americans can still agree upon, in 1869 there was no such consensus on football or any other sport. The year was a pivotal one that saw the official formation of professional baseball, which began barnstorming the hearts and minds of a growing nation. The Cincinnati Red Stockings, the sport's first fully salaried club, went 57–0 to complete the only perfect season in baseball history. Every social club and fraternity of any worth had its baseball club, including the leading East Coast colleges and universities, where formal athletic programs were still in their infancy. Young veterans returning from Civil War battlefields brought back to campuses a newfound passion for athletic competition, which the faculty still regarded as a frivolous distraction from academic studies. While intramural "rushes" and other contests were common on campuses, organized intercollegiate contests were largely unheard of.

In 1866 Rutgers University had hosted its first intercollegiate athletic event—a game of baseball against Princeton University, known then as the College of New Jersey, and situated a mere 20 miles away. Although they'd never faced each other over a ball before, the two neighboring colleges already had an intense and bitter rivalry. For years, the two student bodies had struggled over possession of an old Revolutionary War cannon, staging midnight raids to capture and recapture the prize until Princeton finally sealed the deal, and the cannon itself, in several hundred pounds of cement.

Having lost the cannon battle, Rutgers students turned next to baseball, the most popular sport on campus. The result was the same: an embarrassing 40–2 routing on their home turf. And so, in the fall of 1869, in a last-ditch effort to avenge defeat and restore the pride of their alma mater, a group of Rutgers students issued a challenge to Princeton to play a three-game series of football. The challenge was formally accepted by William Gummere, captain of Princeton's baseball team who a year later would enter the annals of that sport as the first base runner to steal second base with a hook slide, throwing himself feetfirst under the tag of his opponent.

The two colleges didn't have football teams to speak of, but like other leading East Coast colleges at the time they had their own intramural traditions that stretched back to the early 1800s. Yale played a game as part of the mass freshman-sophomore rush, celebrated in poetry for its "breaches of peaces, and pieces of britches." Harvard had a similar rite, in which plenty of crimson was spilled, known as Bloody Monday. And Princeton students played an annual game called "balldown" that pitted students with names A–L against those with names M–Z.

Given their proximity, Princeton and Rutgers had developed similar though not identical traditions, allowing the captains to settle quickly on the series rules. The field was to be 360 feet long and 225 feet wide. There would be 25 men to a side and the round rubber ball, supplied by the host team, would be advanced by kicking only. Any throwing or running with the ball was forbidden, as were tripping and holding. Goals would be scored, as in modern soccer, by kicking the ball between two posts (with no crossbar) set eight feet apart. The game hosted at Princeton would follow Princeton's code, which allowed a player who caught the ball on the fly or first bounce a free kick from a clear space of 10 feet (a rule perhaps influenced by baseball's bound rule?). The games at Rutgers, however, would follow their code, which did not allow for free kicks.

As Parke Davis described the scene on game day, "the jerky little 'dummy' engine that steamed out of Princeton that memorable morning of November 6, 1869, was crowded to the aisles and platforms with a freight of eager students." The Rutgers students met their rivals at the New Brunswick station, gave them a tour of town, and shot a few games of billiards before heading to College Field. There were no uniforms to put on, though the Rutgers men wound their scarlet scarves around their heads to form "turbans." The players, none of whom weighed much more than 150 pounds, simply stripped off their coats and hats and took to the field in their street clothes. A thin but boisterous crowd of 100 spectators showed up to watch.

The teams' strategies were crude at best. Two men from each side, called "captains of the enemy's goal," took position directly in front of the opponents' goal where they awaited an opportunity to knock a goal in. The remaining 23 were split between "fielders" who took up fixed defensive positions in the back field and "bulldogs" who pursued the ball. Princeton won the coin toss and "bucked" or kicked off the ball from a "tee of earth." The inexperienced kicker missed his mark, sending the ball off to the sidelines, where the Rutgers men "pounced on it like hounds" and forced it down and through the posts to score the first goal. "Big Mike," a Civil War veteran from the Princeton squad, responded, scattering the Rutgers defense "like a burst bundle of sticks" to put the visiting team on the board. Further into the game, Big Mike and Rutgers' George Large (no nickname required) chased the ball into a fence serving as makeshift seating for fans, taking fence and fans down into a crashing heap and eliciting cheers of approval from those in safer seats. The teams traded goals back and forth to tie the game at 4–4. By the rules agreed upon, the first team to score 6 would win.

At that point, the Rutgers captain shifted tactics. Observing that Princeton was using its height advantage to block high kicks, he ordered his men to keep the ball close to the ground. With short low dribbles and passes that wouldn't be out of place on a modern soccer pitch, Rutgers scored the final two goals to win the historic contest 6–4. Contrary to a recollection by one of Princeton's players of being run out of town, the day "closed with a supper," according to Davis, "in which both teams participated together, interspersing songs and speeches with the deliciously roasted game birds from the Jersey marshes and meadows."

Though the spectators, especially Rutgers fans, were delighted with the rough-and-tumble affair, the local media was less than impressed. An editor of the *Bergen County Gazette* described it as a "jackass performance" by young men for whom it should be more essential to "construe correctly a page of Homer or of Virgil than to be able to kick a football powerfully."

A week later, Princeton returned the favor in game 2 of the series, shutting out Rutgers 8–0 in a decisive win that's been unfairly forgotten by all but a handful of Princeton boosters. The deciding game 3, scheduled for just after Thanksgiving, was never played. Just two weeks into the first season of college football, faculty at both schools had had enough of the new game and its jackass performances. They swooped in and shut down the series, alarmed at the "great and distracting interest aroused" by this new football fever.

They had no idea.

When I saw the headline of a recent *New Yorker* article on football's concussion crisis—"Does Football Have a Future?"—I had to chuckle. Seriously? If you include earlier forms of the game, people have been asking the same question for going on, let's see, 700 years or so.

"Yes," I muttered to myself while turning the page, "next question."

From literally the first appearance of the word "football" in the English language, critics of the game in its multitude of forms have been eager to predict, if not usher in, its demise. Writing back in the 1950s about English football in particular, Morris Marples captured perfectly the game's history of moral siege:

> At one time it was banned as a threat to military training; at another condemned by some as a violent and unseemly pastime, dangerous alike to person and property; praised by others as a manly exercise, of potential educational value. To the Puritans it was a sin, especially if played on the Sabbath; to the cultivated gentleman of the nineteenth century a vulgar amusement, fit only for the common herd; to the schoolboy of whatever century, we may suspect, the best of games.

Here's to the schoolboys! If NFL football is "America's Choice" today, it is thanks, in part, to the elite offspring of 19th-century English society who preserved an embattled and dying tradition behind the ivy-covered walls of their public schools. The late 18th and early 19th century had seen an all-out attack on traditional mob football across the British Isles. The mayors of Derby, a town with an ancient street-ball tradition much like the Kirkwall Ba', attempted to purge the game several times, declaring in 1796 after a player was accidentally drowned during the annual mêlée that football was "disgraceful to humanity and to civilization, subversive of good order and Government and destructive of the Morals, Properties and very Lives of our Inhabitants."

The game hung on in Derby until 1847, when another mayor led troops in on horseback. He was stoned by the crowds but beat them back and read them the original Riot Act, which empowered authorities to clamp down on any unlawful gathering of more than a dozen people. The Derby game was never played again. Only in the peripheries and backwaters, places like the remote skerries and isles of Orkney, did football stubbornly persist. There, and in the elite public schools, where natural selection was the only law consistently observed.

Britain's public schools were the "ludic zoos of the age," as David Goldblatt characterized them, preserving endangered games and diversions long after they'd been snuffed out elsewhere. Left to their devices, the boys in these rarified academies demonstrated an endemic predisposition to violence and brutality. At Harrow, an exclusive London school that counts eight former prime ministers among its alums, students indulged in a common pastime known as "toozling," which involved the torture and killing of small songbirds. Long before quarterback Michael Vick was prosecuted in federal court for animal cruelty, it was a well-known fact that "no dog could live on Harrow Hill." The heat of the scrum was the perfect Darwinian testing ground for separating boys from men and establishing the social pecking order.

Each school had its own rules for playing football, determined largely by the grounds available for play. Harrow's muddy pitches inspired a slow game with a flat-bottomed ball that could skid through the puddles. Students at Westminster and Charterhouse in London played in brick-covered cloisters, where pushing, shoving, dribbling, and some handling of the ball were acceptable but not tackling, throwing, or high kicks. Eton developed a unique "wall game" on a field 120 yards long but just 6 yards wide, bounded on one side by an 8-foot-high brick wall and on the other by a ditch. One goal was a garden door and the other an old elm tree. When school officials temporarily banned the wall game owing to excessive injuries, the students took to a nearby field and modified play to emphasize a more open game of running, dribbling, and kicking.

Meanwhile, in the sweeping expanse of green known as Old Bigside, the boys of Rugby School were playing an entirely different kind of football that allowed for carrying of the ball, lateral passes, and tackling. The school and its rough, chaotic game gained notoriety in the 1857 novel *Tom Brown's Schooldays*:

The two sides close, and you can see nothing for
minutes but a swaying crowd of boys, at one point
violently agitated. That is where the ball is, and there
are the keen players to be met, and the glory and
the hard knocks to be got: you hear the dull thud of
the ball and shouts of "Off your side." "Down with
him," "Put him over," "Bravo." This is what we call a
scrummage, gentlemen, and the first scrummage in a
School-house match was no joke.

As students arrived from these schools for university at
Oxford or Cambridge, debate naturally erupted over which
rules of football to play by. Negotiations to find a compro-
mise between Rugby's catch-and-run game and the dribble-
and-kick game played at Eton and other London schools
broke down repeatedly. Committees even debated such questions as whether "hacking" an opponent's shins should be
allowed. One defender of that brutal but effective tactic for
tackling argued that to get rid of hacking would "do away
with the courage and pluck of the game, and I will be bound
to bring over a lot of Frenchmen who would beat you with a
week's practice."

The impasse was settled, more or less, in 1863 with the
formation of the Football Association and the adoption of
the Eton rules for the official "Association" game. "Association" was later abbreviated as "soccer" to distinguish it from
rugby football, which was codified eight years later with the
establishment of the Rugby Football Union.

While football was fracturing in two back in its birthplace, on the other side of the Atlantic an intercollegiate consensus was emerging around the soccer variety of the game.

Riding a wave of popularity out of the 1869 Rutgers-Princeton series, football quickly spread through the college circuit. Columbia played Rutgers the next fall and Yale joined the pack in 1872 with its first game against Columbia. The following year, the Eton team visited Yale, only to be humbled at their own game, 2–1. Despite its explosion of popularity, the new game had its early detractors within the Ivy League. Cornell's president, Andrew D. White, declined permission for his students to leave campus for a game, famously declaring, "I will not permit thirty men to travel 400 miles to agitate a bag of wind."

In an effort to hammer out a common set of rules to govern college football in the United States, Princeton called a conference in New York City in 1873. Princeton, Rutgers, Yale, and Columbia all participated and together formed the Intercollegiate Football Association. The rules firmly decided against any throwing or carrying of the ball, establishing "association football," or soccer, as the official American intercollegiate game. Football in the United States was moving down the same track as football in England until one renegade institution derailed and diverted it forever.

For years Harvard had favored the "Boston Game," a homespun variety of football made popular years earlier by members of the Oneida Club, a ragtag group of schoolboys who met after school on the pitch in Boston Common. Before the other colleges got around to codifying their rules of play, Harvard had established its own rules around the Boston Game, including rule 8, which permitted "any player to catch or pick up the ball but not to run with it unless pursued by an opponent and then only so long as pursued."

In 1874, some players at McGill University in Montreal caught wind that Harvard was playing a game resembling the rugby game they'd adopted, so they issued a challenge for a two-game series to be played at Harvard. The first, won by Harvard 3–0, was played following Harvard's rules. The second, which followed the rugby code rules and allowed for tackling, ended scoreless. But everyone who played and watched that second game walked away convinced of its superiority to anything they'd seen before. "Football will be a popular game here in the future," read a comment in the next day's Harvard *Advocate*. "The Rugby game is in much better favor than the somewhat sleepy game now played by our men."

Flush with excitement over their newly hybridized game, Harvard next challenged Yale. But the archrivals, who played two very different kinds of football, first had to agree to a set of "concessionary rules." Harvard managed to win most of the concessions, and the two met in New Haven in November of 1875 for the first occurrence of "The Game," an annual Ivy League rite that has been repeated 127 times. Following Harvard's lead, the teams played according to modified rugby rules, which allowed for running with the ball and tackling. In concession to Yale and their soccer style of play, only kicked goals, not touchdowns, would count toward the score. And, following an innovation Yale had picked up from the visiting Eton team, the sides were reduced from 15 to 11 men.

The Crimson won, 4–0, the only victory they'd savor over the next 15 years of the rivalry. When the team met for their next appointed contest a year later, a 17-year-old freshman halfback named Walter Camp took to the field for the Bulldogs. Over the next 20 years or so, Camp, as player and then head coach for Yale, would almost singlehandedly close the distance between 19th-century rugby and the modern game of the gridiron. Rule by rule, committee decision by committee decision, Camp transformed the game.

Much has been made of American exceptionalism in the sports we uniquely play, and uniquely reject. When seen as a positive (mostly by Americans, of course), exceptionalism means we are a nation born of revolution, "founded on a creed," as G. K. Chesterton wrote, and driven by a deep-seated belief in our unique destiny to champion individual rights and freedoms. More often, however, the term is used to decry America's perceived unilateralism, the go-it-alone swagger of our economic policies and military interventions, and the fact that we prefer the gladiatorial combat of American football to the "beautiful game" of soccer that unites the rest of the world in ludic harmony.

American football, more than any sport, has emerged as the symbol of this exceptionalism—the game that Americans love and the rest of the world loves to hate. The fact that we play and watch our homegrown game religiously while ignoring the lingua franca of world soccer is perceived by many as a nose-thumbing rejection of the global community and the spirit of internationalism. ESPN correspondent Sal

Paolantonio happily fueled this perception and thumbed his nose at the world in his jingoistic tract *How Football Explains America*, an in-your-face takedown of Franklin Foer's global exploration, *How Soccer Explains the World*:

> Kicking it. That's what the rest of the world does. And that's what I mostly thought about soccer: a game played by a bunch of guys who wish they could pick up the ball and throw it and would like to do whatever it takes to prevent the other guy from doing so. . . . No throwing, no blocking, no tackling— and most important, very, very little scoring. Not American.

Not surprisingly, the international press savaged the author. Under the memorable title "Worst Sports Book Ever?" a review in the English newspaper *The Guardian* suggested "football no more explains America than spotted dick or the Eton wall game or crown green bowling or the 'donkey choker' meat pie sandwich explains the English. It's just that nobody else likes the stuff."

The heated rhetoric around football's exceptionalism and capacity for "explaining" America belies a more complex history. American football emerged not as a rejection of the world or the "global game" that soccer has only since become, but as an assertion of local tradition over the latest foreign export. Before 1863, when the English Football Association was formed, there was no single set of rules for playing football, just hundreds of local variations and traditions that had developed in all their quirky glory over centuries. Most of these—like the Ba', *la soule*, rugby, and the Boston Game—allowed some form of ball-handling, if not running and tackling as well. It wasn't until 1866 that it was ruled illegal in soccer for players other than goalkeepers to catch the ball, and despite rulings to the contrary, tackling players and "grassing" goalies was common practice well into the 1880s. To arrive at the elegant, fast-passing game that it is today, soccer had to break with its high-contact, ball-handling roots, just as American football had to replace the scrum with the scrimmage.

As David Goldblatt recounts, in the late 19th century, as England looked to spread its newly sanctioned game of soccer to its colonies and former colonies, it was the nations once closest to the crown that rejected the game. Kiwis, having sampled the game's many manifestations over the years, chose rugby. Australia had imported football early in the 1850s, before its rules were settled upon, and, as Goldblatt puts it, "like the continent's unique flora and fauna it evolved in isolation." Aussie Rules football merged soccer, rugby, old folk football, and possibly some Aboriginal influences to form a distinctly antipodean pastime. In Ireland, soccer didn't stand a "tinker's chance," as my father used to say, arriving at the very moment the island was rising up against British rule. It was viewed as a Protestant game and a symbol of cultural imperialism infiltrating through sport. So the Irish clung all the harder to their Gaelic football (and to the ball they were allowed to handle), a folk game they'd played for the past 500 years. Canada already had a national game, lacrosse, and when it came to football, followed the lead of the elite Ivy League colleges to the south (and vice versa, given McGill's influence on Harvard). By 1891, Canadians had formed the Canadian Football Union, essentially taking up American football with a few different rules.

Far from being a lone holdout, the arrogant exception, the United States was in good company. We'd been incubating our own versions of football on town greens, sandlots, and college campuses since the Pilgrims landed. By the time professional soccer arrived on U.S. shores in 1894 with the formation of the short-lived American League of Professional Football Clubs, it was too late. For soccer to have then found its way into the hearts of Americans, it would have had to fight its way past sports that were already deeply enshrined in our national culture. Baseball was our summer game and national religion. Basketball was the new winter game, serving the sporting needs of our struggling masses. And we already had a game we called football, thank you very much, played with hands and feet and an oblong ball.

John Heisman, who along with Walter Camp inhabits American football's pantheon, pioneered many cherished features of the game, including the dramatic pregame locker-room oration. With kickoff minutes away and the fight songs echoing down the stadium tunnel, Heisman was known to pace in front of his men, waving a football in their faces.

"What is this?" he'd ask, quickly answering his question before anyone dared to propose the obvious.

"It's a prolate spheroid. An elongated sphere in which

the outer leather casing is drawn tightly up over a somewhat smaller rubber tubing."

He'd pause for effect as the definition sunk in, the players wondering perhaps whether they'd be expected to recite it back.

"Better to have died as a small boy than to fumble this football."

That Heisman should have thrown around a term like "prolate spheroid" in the tense moments before a game is less unlikely than it might appear. He had, after all, relentlessly pressured Camp as the head of football's rules committee to legalize the forward pass in 1906. And it was the forward pass, and the need for an aerodynamic ball that could spiral effortlessly through the air toward its distant target, that drove the evolution of the ball toward its signature bullet-shaped form. It was the prolate spheroid that made the genius of the modern game possible, and Heisman wanted his players to appreciate the weight of that genius every time they handled the ball.

For much of sports history, people simply played with whatever they had available. The Egyptians made balls of papyrus, the same material they used to make boats and sandals and to wrap the occasional mummy. The Aztecs and Maya were lucky enough to have natural rubber—and human heads—in considerable supply. The French relied on beard hair and wine corks, both also in considerable supply, for their tennis balls. And the English had their livestock. The first footballs were pig bladders inflated by mouth and tied at the end like balloons. These "pigskin" balls were irregular in shape, somewhere between oval and round, and easily punctured. Local shoemakers made leather covers that laced up to protect the pigskin bladders.

One such shoemaker was Richard Lindon of Rugby, England, who, along with shoeing the town and students of Rugby, served as the local ball maker. Lindon's wife was stuck with the unenviable job of inflating the fresh "green" bladders, a hazardous task given the prevalence of diseased swine. She eventually contracted lung disease from too many bad bladders and died.

Charles Goodyear saved football, and presumably many lives, in 1844 with his patent for vulcanized rubber. The significance of his new invention for the world of sports was immediately apparent. Goodyear soon after introduced the first balls with rubber bladders. It's been suggested that the new, more responsive rubber balls helped transform soccer from a power-kick game to one focused on dribbling and controlling the ball. From his small shop in Rugby, Lindon ran with the new invention, perfecting the design for an eight-panel "India Rubber" ball and inventing a brass pump to spare future wives. The boys of Rugby soon came to him asking for a ball that better suited their unique carrying game, so Lindon created an egg-shaped, four-panel "Big-Side Match Ball," direct ancestor to Heisman's prolate spheroid. Thus began a productive dialectic as the ball adapted to match the game and as players exploited the physical properties of the ball in ways that opened up new possibilities for play.

. . .

The distance from Lindon's quaint shoe shop to the Wilson football factory in Ada, Ohio, is vast in nearly every sense—temporal, cultural, geographical. If Rugby, England, is on one end of football's history, Ada is on the other. With a population just under 6,000 and a tidy 10-block Main Street that gives way to endless fields of corn and soy, Ada's about as close as you can get to the warm, beating heartland of football. Though American football was born in the Ivy League colleges of the Northeast, it came of age in the towns and small cities of the Midwest—and in Ohio in particular. In the early years of the 20th century, the Ohio League became one of the first professional football leagues, giving rise to such legends as Jim Thorpe. In 1920, the direct predecessor of the National Football League was conceived on the floor of an auto dealership in Canton, just 150 miles due east of Ada. Fourteen managers from 10 professional teams in Ohio and surrounding states sat on the running boards of cars and drank beer out of buckets as they cooked up the most lucrative business venture in sports history.

As deep as Ohio's football roots run, the most intimate connection between the game and the Buckeye state is to be found right here in Ada. I arrived in town on a cool September day to trace the path of the football, from the feedlot to the gridiron, and to meet the modern-day heirs to Lindon's legacy. There was a buzz of cheerful anticipation in the air. Students at Ohio Northern University, Ada's other anchor institution, were arriving for the fall semester—"the onslaught," as the waitress at Little Mexico Café cheerfully described it. Football season was about to kick off and the

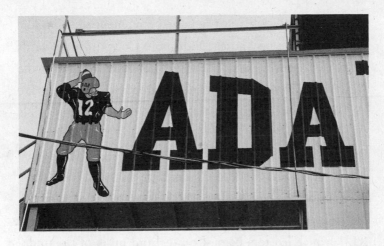

Ada High School Bulldogs were coming off a 12–1 season as Northwest Ohio Conference Champions.

It didn't take long to locate the factory. The town water tower, which loomed a few blocks east of Main Street, reads ADA on one side and WILSON NFL on the other. I found the unimposing one-story brick factory at the tower's base and entered the fake wood–paneled plant office. Dan Riegle, the 57-year-old plant manager who's an honest to god Mike Ditka look-alike, got up from behind a large metal desk to greet me. Dan's been punching the clock here for 28 years, which it turns out makes him a relative newcomer.

He handed me a pair of protective glasses and we stepped onto the factory floor.

"We've produced every football used in the NFL right here since 1955," Dan shouted over the rhythmic din of machinery. "Every Super Bowl touchdown, every interception, every great moment in football history for over fifty years has been with a ball made where you're standing."

I paused to let his nearly casual statement sink in. The ball Johnny Unitas and the Baltimore Colts drove 80 yards in 13 plays to win the 1958 NFL championship against the New York Giants in the "Greatest Game Ever Played": made in Ada. The ball Dwight Clark caught on a high impossible leap off a Joe Montana pass to win the 1982 NFC championship for the San Francisco 49ers: made in Ada. The cursed (for this Pats fan) ball that Giants wide receiver David Tyree inexplicably pinned against his helmet off a 32-yard Eli Manning pass with less than two minutes left in Super Bowl XLII, which led to a come-from-behind upset of the undefeated New England Patriots: made, tragically, in Ada.

Dan broke my reverie and held up a large cowhide that he'd pulled from a stack of 20 or so. "There's the head. There's the butt. There's the legs," he pointed out, perhaps assuming a city boy like me wouldn't otherwise be able to make heads or tails of it.

"Every NFL football starts its life on a feedlot in Nebraska, Iowa, or Kansas," said Dan.

"So, are these from grain-fed or grass-fed cows?" I asked, jokingly.

"Pure grain-fed American beef cows," replied Dan.

"Wilson might want to consider producing organic, grass-fed footballs," I mused. "Could be the next big thing."

Dan looked at me stone-faced. "I suppose."

Unlike Spalding Inc., started by A. G. Spalding both to promote and capitalize on the popularity of baseball, Wilson was founded, rather ingloriously, to make a few extra dollars off cow parts. Incorporated in 1913 by the Chicago meat-packing firm Sulzberger and Schwarzchild, the company was first established to make creative use of slaughterhouse by-products. It started with cow gut tennis strings, violin strings, and animal suture and expanded from there into footballs and basketballs.

From the feedlots, the cowhides are treated at a plant in Chicago where the hair is removed, the skins are stamped to create the signature stipple pattern found on every ball, and a tack is applied using a proprietary formula that gives quarterbacks a better grip. From there they make their way to Ada, where 150 workers perform the alchemy of transforming cowskin into pigskin.

One of those workers is Sharon Mullins, who's worked here for 40 years. I watched her use a metal form and a large press to punch oval panels out of a skin, avoiding holes or other imperfections. Typically, 10 footballs can be made from a single cow. In every NFL game the teams go through around 40 regular balls and 12 kicking balls. That's five or so cows to service a single NFL game!

Down the line is Peg Price, a spry 43-year veteran who's worked every part of a football you can work. Today, she's a "splitter," which means her job is to split the thick skin panels on a machine to make them lighter. Like everyone else in the Wilson plant, Peg is paid by the piece, so she cranks along at a lightning pace, not missing a beat while she talks.

"I make sure to work on all the Super Bowl balls," she told me, "'cause I want to be sure they're done right!"

"The specs for NFL footballs haven't really changed in

my twenty-eight years here," said Dan. "We could probably engineer a ball you could easily kick eighty yards, but you have to protect the integrity of the game."

I find it comforting to know that despite all the cheating scandals involving videotaping and signal stealing, the piece workers of Ada are keeping the game honest by making balls with technology that, for the most part, wouldn't be out of place in Lindon's cobbler shop.

The NFL takes patriotic pride in the fact that every one of their balls is "Made in the U.S.A." by skilled workers who've been at it for decades. (By contrast, it's only fair to note, 70 percent of the world's stitched soccer balls are made in the Pakistan city of Sialkot, where workers make around $5 a day and where child labor was still rampant as late as the 1990s.)

Further along the football assembly line we met Glen Hanson, a bookish-looking gentleman in his early 60s, hunched over an industrial sewing machine with protective glasses and ear muffs. He was busy stitching the four panels of a football together, just as he's been doing for 36 years.

I asked Dan if he's concerned that most of his experienced workers are close to retirement age.

"You bet!" he responded, pointing to Glen, who was guiding a ball by hand as the machine hammers out stitches. "How am I going to find a young person willing to spend six months training and then sit every day and stitch footballs? No one's interested in working that hard anymore."

Once the ball's stitched up it's time to turn it right-side out again. As we approached the ball turner, Dan pulled me

Footballs ready to be "turned" at the Wilson Football Factory in Ada, Ohio.

aside. "I wouldn't ask him too many questions. He's kind of grumpy."

After watching his routine for a few minutes I could see why—it was hard, mind-numbing work turning footballs right-side out all day long. The turner took one ball at a time, placed it in a little steamer box for a few minutes to soften the leather. He then used a metal rod to turn it right-side out, making sure to stretch it out properly. He stuck a polyurethane bladder inside and sent it along to be laced by hand, put into a metal mold, and inflated to 13 psi, the mold ensuring that the final product is the same consistently sized prolate spheroid as every other ball.

Once the balls are turned and inflated, they get inspected by Barbara, the strong safety of the production line. She is the last line of defense before the ball leaves the plant and makes its debut on the gridiron. Barbara weighs each ball on a scale to make sure it's between 14 and 15 ounces, and she uses a tailor's measuring tape to check that it's 21 inches around the middle, 28 around the ends.

According to Dan, in all his years on the job he's never had an NFL ball sent back. "Of course," he added, "some quarterbacks are harder to please than others. . . ."

"Like who?" I pounce eagerly, looking for some dirt.

"Not naming names, but let me put it this way: if the quarterback throws for three hundred yards and four touchdown passes, it's all him. He's amazing. If he gets intercepted a few times in the same game, it's all the ball. Too slippery, not inflated right, or some other excuse."

Barbara spun a finished ball in her hands, eyeing it down its length to see if it was ready for prime time. "After a while you just get a feel for whether a ball's ready for game time or not," she said, scrutinizing a finished ball. "You can throw me a ball and I can tell by catching it whether it's off by an ounce."

The radical innovation of the Ada production line—with stampers, splitters, stitchers, turners, inspectors, and managers each playing their role to improve quality and output—is the science of specialization. That, along with some relatively basic machinery, enables the 150 workers of the Wilson Football Factory to produce more than 700,000 identical, top-quality footballs a year. As Michael Mandelbaum has pointed out, the same principles of production and division of labor are at the very core of the way football is organized and played.

As the game was assuming its modern form in the late 19th century, the science of organizational management and specialization was first being championed by industrialists like Frederick Winslow Taylor, who codified what he called the four principles of scientific management:

1. Replace rule-of-thumb approaches with work methods based on a scientific study of the tasks.
2. Scientifically select and train each worker rather than leaving them to train themselves.
3. Cooperate with the workers to ensure that the scientifically developed methods are being followed.
4. Divide work nearly equally between managers and workers, so that the managers apply scientific management principles to planning the work and the workers actually perform the tasks.

Walter Camp, every bit a product of his industrial age, understood exactly how Taylor's principles might apply to the game of football. Even as a young man, he approached the game, as Michael Oriard has put it, from a uniquely "managerial and technocratic perspective." Growing up in Yale's backyard in New Haven, Connecticut, Camp had a natural knack for sports, competing not only in football but in baseball, rowing, swimming, and track and field.

When Camp first started playing for Yale in 1876, football was still emerging from the preindustrial chaos of the scrum, a disorderly "shoving match," as he characterized it. As the hard-working captain of the team during his junior and senior years, Camp imposed a "method, not men" strategy. When he struggled to hold on to the large, watermelon-shaped ball in a game, he took to carrying it around to classes all day. When his teammates twice bucked his strategy and broke curfew, he resigned the team, rejoining only after they pledged their loyalty to him and his program for winning games.

By the age of 19, Camp was already a thorn in the side of the Intercollegiate Football Association (IFA), the governing body of college football, submitting proposals for major changes in the game's rules. For two years he lobbied to reduce the number of players from 15 to 11, a move Yale had been pushing for ever since Eton's visit years earlier. This change, he argued, would open up the field and allow for a faster-moving, more strategic game with greater scoring potential. It would also have the benefit of making the game consistent with soccer and rugby, each of which fielded 11 on a side. The committee rejected his proposal twice. When they met again in October 1880, Camp finally broke down their resistance. And he was just getting started.

At that same meeting, Camp proposed and pushed through a second concept that would revolutionize American football, severing its ties to other forms of football once and for all. It was called the scrimmage. Although the term—in common use from at least the early 1800s—was just an etymological tweak on the more familiar "scrummage" of rugby, the change itself was momentous. It effectively ended the tyranny of the scrum by introducing the radical notion of possession into the game. Here's how the original amendment was inscribed in the IFA's rulebook:

> A scrimmage takes place when the holder of the ball, being in the field of play, puts it down on the ground in front of him and puts it in play while onside, first, by kicking the ball; second, by snapping it back with his foot. The man who first receives the ball from the snap-back shall be called the quarterback, and shall not then rush forward with the ball under penalty of foul.

Prior to the amendments, when a man was tackled, possession was literally up for grabs. The ball was placed on the ground in the tangled mass of the scrum where the players would push and shove and try to heel it out to a teammate on the periphery. With the introduction of the scrimmage, the ball was now snapped back with the heel (and later the hand) to the quarterback who—not yet allowed to rush or pass it forward—could hand it off to a teammate to run with. In other words, possession could be retained by one team long enough to execute an offensive strategy. Camp saw this invention as the decisive turning point for his sport, describing the scrimmage as "the backbone to which the entire body of American football is attached." He went on to elaborate on the significance of the break with football's rugby past:

> What is, therefore, in the English game a matter of considerable chance is "cut-and-dried" in the Ameri-

can game; and the element of chance being eliminated, opportunity is given for the display in the latter game of far more skill in the development of brilliant plays and carefully planned manoeuvres.

Camp was a pragmatist and knew all too well that the new rule would be meaningless if it wasn't enforced—if there wasn't a stiff penalty for breaking it. The line of scrimmage secured a firm hold the following year when the rules committee assigned an "offside" penalty for crossing it too early. The first or second time a team was offside, the snap would be replayed. If it occurred a third time, possession would turn over to the other team.

Of course, the danger of Camp and the IFA making the rules up as they went along is that each rule change brought with it unforeseen, and often unwelcome, consequences. While the scrimmage provided for possession of the ball, it failed to address the question of its surrender. Major problems with the new rule became clear when Princeton and Yale met in 1880 for a much anticipated matchup in two inches of wet snow at New York's Polo Grounds. As described by Parke Davis, the second half began with the Yale offense aggressively pressuring Princeton's goal. That's when Princeton's too-clever captain, seizing upon a loophole in the new rules, ordered his players to just hold the ball—no kicking, no passing. Princeton held possession for nearly the entire second half and the game ended with no score and 4,000 freezing cold and sorely disappointed spectators.

The "block game," as this strategy was called, resulted in

the most excruciating games in football history. One newspaper described the strategy as an "unmitigated evil." Fans responded to the scoreless, plodding performances by throwing garbage on the field. Camp was as unhappy as anyone with the situation. One of his main complaints about early football had been what he deemed the "cowardly" team play that privileged defensive tactics over a strong offensive attack. The new abuses, he later wrote, "so disgusted spectators that it was absolutely necessary to make a change."

The change came—not a moment too soon—in the 1882 rules committee. Camp persuaded his colleagues to adopt a system of "downs" that required the team in possession to advance the ball in a limited number of attempts—or relinquish possession. "If on three consecutive fairs and downs a team shall not have advanced the ball five yards or lost ten," read the latest amendment, "they must give up the ball to the other side at the spot where the fourth down was made." With the system of downs came the need for referees to measure the gain or loss of yardage. Camp then ignited fierce debate with his suggestion that the field be chalked with lines every five yards.

"But the field will look like a gridiron!" exclaimed the Princeton committee representative, E. C. Peace.

"Precisely," responded Camp, and fields across the country got their familiar battle stripes.

After college, Camp took a job as a clerk at the New Haven Clock Company, a family business, where he worked for years while serving as the unpaid coach of the Yale football team. When his day job made him late for practice, which frequently happened, he'd send his wife Alice ahead to take notes that he'd review at home. Rising in the company to the position of president, Camp applied the familiar order and regimen of the production line to his coaching method and to the game he set about shaping.

As Mark Bernstein has pointed out, it's no coincidence that American football was the first major sport to be played against a clock. When Princeton met Rutgers in that first intercollegiate game, the team that scored six points first won the match. By the 1880s, when the United States first standardized time zones, game periods were being timed and referees were armed with stopwatches. Ever since then, the outcome of game after game has been decided by minutes and seconds. It's impossible now to imagine a football game where time is not the most unforgiving opponent on the field.

Having deftly crafted the chessboard and the rules of engagement, Camp next set about developing the unique capabilities of each piece arranged on it. "Division of labor," he wrote, "has been so thoroughly and effectively carried out on the football field that a player nowadays must train for a particular position." The "quarter-back," he wrote in his groundbreaking manual, *American Football*, is a "position in which a small man can be used to great advantage." Halfbacks and backs require "dash and fire," while for the center, or snap-back as it was called, "brain and brawn are here at their highest premium." In those early days of organized athletics, training was still a novel concept. Players showed up on campus in the fall, fat, tan, and happy, and started playing ball. But soon scientific regimens were introduced and preseason training became standard protocol.

In his manual, Camp dedicated several appendices to evaluating the merits of various training systems and diets. Following the "J. B. O'Reilly" system, for example, an athlete should rise at 7:00 AM, "get a good dry-rubbing, and then sponge his body with cold water." His breakfast "need not always consist of a broiled mutton-chop or cutlet," which, to my taste at least, leaves the door open to a wide array of possibilities. Dinner served at 1:00 PM was ideal, and "any kind of butcher's meat" with vegetables was fine as long as there was no pastry served. Water was the only drink to be allowed the American athlete, though English athletes were forgiven in this area due to the fact that "the climate and the custom in England favor the drinking of beer or claret." A light supper at 6:00 PM was great so long as it didn't "consist of slops or gruel." The athlete's day should end with lights out at 10:00 PM in a room with an open window, with a "draught . . . if possible, though not across the bed."

He even had opinions as to the level of table service required for an athlete in training. When asked by another coach to diagnose a team situation in which several star players were "manifestly out of sorts," Camp sat down to dinner with them and quickly pinpointed the problem. "The beef—and an excellent roast it was, too—was literally served in junks, such as one might throw to a dog." Some boys were accustomed to a certain level of dining, he asserted, and their appetite and physical condition could suffer from poor table service.

In Camp's vision of football, nothing could be left to the vagaries of chance. And all the fresh air, mutton chops, and fancy flatware paid off. In his eight-year career as head coach, first at Yale and then at Stanford, Camp lost only five games. In 1888, his first year as Yale head coach, the Bulldogs outscored their opponents a staggering 698–0.

With relentless attention to detail, in the smoke-filled huddle of IFA committee meetings, Camp and his fellow rule makers regulated football into existence, converting it in less than a decade from a raucous free-for-all into an obsessively methodical sport. Rules were enacted and put to the test on the field, then brought back to the scrutiny of the committee to be fine-tuned or thrown out. The snap of the scrimmage replaced the scramble of the scrum. Random pasture gave way to the calculated geometry of the gridiron. Time became the most ruthless player on the field, forcing decisiveness and action. Specialization turned the passions of the mob into the precision of the machine, with each man selected and trained to play his part. Plays were called, signals devised, and the quarterback assumed his starring role as "director of the game," opening a door for the Tom Bradys and Peyton Mannings of the future to step through.

Rule by rule, committee by committee, Camp's grand vision of order unfolded on the gridiron. But as the game became more open, methodical, and scientific, it also, ironically, became more violent. The 1880s saw running games unlike any that have been seen since. In 1884, Wyllys Terry of Yale ran 115 yards for a touchdown against Wesleyan, setting a record that will stand forever thanks to the field being shortened soon after. And in an effort to discourage blocking and prevent neck injuries in what was becoming an increasingly physical game, Camp pushed through a proposal in 1888 to allow tackling below the waist for the first time.

It was Harvard football adviser and avid chess expert Lorin Deland who in 1892 conceived one of the most brutal plays to ever appear on the field. Deland, who had never played football and only witnessed his first game two years earlier, turned to the history books—and to Napoleon's military tactics in particular—to devise his take-no-prisoners play known as the "flying wedge." "One of the chief points brought out by the great French general," Deland noted, "was that if he could mass a large proportion of his troops and throw them against a weak point of the enemy, he could easily defeat that portion, and gaining their rear, create havoc with the rest."

In the second half of the annual Harvard-Yale game, Deland lined up his squad in a unique V formation stretching 25 yards behind the ball. At the time, there was no requirement at kickoff to kick the ball a certain distance, so the kicker lightly tapped the ball, then scooped it up and ran with it. Nine other players formed a protective wedge around the runner and bore down on one of Yale's weakest defensemen, trampling him to the ground in what was known as a "mass momentum" play. Deland's strategically violent play, described at the time as "half a ton of bone and muscle coming into collision with a man weighing 160 or 170 pounds," kicked open a hornet's nest of controversy around football that wouldn't subside for another 20 years—and has never really gone away. Amos Alonzo Stagg, on his way to becoming a coaching legend at the

University of Chicago, called the play "the most spectacular single formation ever." "It was a play," wrote a reporter for the *Boston Herald*, "that sent the football men who were spectators into raptures."

The standard-issue equipment of the time offered victims little protection from the crushing impact of the flying wedge. To protect their heads, players wore only a knit cap, a strap-on nose guard, and, for a brief spell, fashionably long hair. Rubber cleats were tacked onto street shoes, and the earlier canvas "smock" was replaced by tougher moleskin trousers with sewn-in padding. Coaches and players experimented with new forms of protection as the game became more physical. The first padded leather "head harness" appeared in 1896, and patents were filed soon after for variations on the theme, including a pneumatic helmet that borrowed from ball design by encasing the head in a rubber sack inflated with a hand pump. Among Deland's many innovations was a one-piece leather suit that made it harder to grip and tackle his players. One particularly industrious halfback of the era showed up on the field for a championship game greased from shoulder to knee, prompting the creation of a rule that lasted in the books for years that "No sticky or greasy substance shall be used on the persons or clothing of the players."

As the bloodied bodies of 20-year-old men were dragged off the field, public opinion quickly turned against the game. Rugby had always been a rough, even occasionally brutal sport, and controversy had dogged it from day one. But in the Progressive era of the late 19th century, when muckraking journalists and social activists were busy reforming social ills and political corruption wherever they could find them, football was a ripe target for reform. The game was exploding in popularity on college campuses across the country and becoming as integral to the celebration of Thanksgiving as church and turkey. By the 1890s, an estimated 5,000 games involving 110,000 participants were being played on Thanksgiving in every corner of the United States. The holiday, lamented one writer, "is no longer a solemn festival to God for mercies given. It is a holiday granted by the State and the nation to see a football game." Weekend games and tailgate parties were already entrenched fixtures of the college experience. And yet, in its "evolved" form, football presented society with an uncomfortable paradox: a game that was more violent in its modern form than it had been before: a game that had been scientifically, if unwittingly, engineered to be more deadly. New training methods made for stronger, bulkier, and more specialized players. New helmets padded their confidence more than their heads as they hit harder, more precisely, and with greater coordination than before. The best coaches devised mass plays like the flying wedge to achieve maximum impact and damage. So much for progress.

A widely read *New York Times* editorial from December 1893 titled "Change the Football Rules: The Rugby Game as Played Now Is a Dangerous Pastime" called for reform, documenting story after story of players who'd been killed on the gridiron. Another *Times* editorial went so far as to compare football to lynching. *The Nation*, amid all the frantic editorial voices, was the game's staunchest critic, calling

"Out of the Game," from *Harper's Weekly*, 1891.

over and over again for nothing less than its complete abolition. In just one Saturday in November 1893, the magazine reported a host of injuries and deaths, referring to football as a "murderous game":

> Captain Frank Ranken of the Montauk football team had his leg broken in two places . . . Robert Christy of the Wooster University died from a kick in the stomach. . . . At the game at Springfield . . . Mackie punched his head into Stillman's stomach . . . Beard stepped "unconsciously" on Wrightman's head, and Acton hit Beard a smart blow on the chin.

Harvard-Yale games were particularly prone to carnage. When he played for the Bulldogs, Frederic Remington, the flamboyant western artist and sculptor, was known to dip his uniform in blood from a local slaughterhouse before games to make it "more businesslike."

Charles Eliot, Harvard's president, emerged as the leading spokesman of the reform movement. Along with other prominent college presidents at the time, Eliot was at the forefront of building what Mark Bernstein describes as a "new empire of the mind" governed by science and reason. Football had no place in Eliot's vision of the university. Though claiming to appreciate the value of athletics in moderation, Eliot saw football as, at best, an unwanted distraction from academics. At worst, he argued, the game brought out violent tendencies in both players and spectators that had no place in civilized society. "To become brutal and brutalizing," he wrote, "is the natural tendency of all sports which involve violent personal collision between the players."

In a foreshadowing of recent medical inquiries into collision-induced brain trauma, the *Journal of the American Medical Association* in 1902 supported Eliot and the reformers with a report suggesting that football was becoming a public health concern. Reviewing that season's "very respectable record of casualties, enough to supply a respectable Spanish-American War," the editors reported 12 deaths, several fatal injuries, 80-plus serious injuries. "To be a cripple or lunatic for life is paying high for athletic emulation."

Although he regretted the reports of injury and death, Camp thought them exaggerated and quickly turned his focus on mounting a defense of his beloved sport. Even as other coaches pushed for the abolition of mass momentum plays, like the flying wedge, Camp defended the strategy as a "piece of clever headwork." Contrary to Eliot, Camp believed that football built character and "manliness" in young men, preparing them to live lives as leaders. Like many contemporaries, he believed in the "survival of the fittest" and viewed the gridiron as a proving ground. His views on the subject were unquestionably influenced by his close friend and brother-in-law, William Graham Sumner, the leading proponent of Social Darwinism.

To build his case for football, Camp sent out a questionnaire to hundreds of former players, coaches, doctors, and administrators to gather objective evidence on both the dangers and benefits of the game. He captured and published the testimonials in *Football Facts and Figures: A Symposium of Expert Opinions on the Game's Place in American Athletics*, a 230-page manifesto for football as a safe, valuable, and morally upright pastime. It has been suggested since that Camp discarded 20 percent of the responses in order to arrive at the right conclusion.

In Camp's report, a professor from Yale presented his findings that football was an "intellectual game," presenting evidence that Ivy League football players had higher academic achievement than those who played baseball or rowed. One former player declared that "besides the 'humanities' which were dinged into me in the classroom, I value what some would be pleased to call the 'inhumanities' dinged into me on the football field." Along with the physical benefits, carefully delineated in a chart comparing lung capacity and leg and neck girth of players and nonplayers, the "moral effects" of the game were touted, including courage, self-control, respect for authority, and manliness. Football, one expert argued, produced "God-fearing men, upright in action and clean of speech." Harvard's surgeon, Dr. Conant, downplayed the injuries caused by the game, concluding that most consisted of ankle and knee sprains. The coach at Pennsylvania even suggested that many players who got hurt were "playing baby on the field."

Camp sent copies of his study to a number of influential leaders, including Theodore Roosevelt, serving at the time on the U.S. Civil Service Commission. Roosevelt was a fan of rough sports and regarded football as the best way for a young man to build character. After reading the study, he wrote Camp a letter of support, concluding that football's risks were no worse than those of boxing or polo. "I would rather see my boys play it, than see them play any other [sport]." The opponents of the game were, in his view, "timid." And though he was open to reasonable reform of the game, he quoted another Yalee and future president, William Howard Taft, who said that he preferred reformers "who ate roast beef and were able to make their blows felt in the world."

Eliot and other vocal critics regarded football as a primitive throwback, out of place in a progressive age dominated by science and reason. But the new gilded class harbored concerns that their college-graduate sons, doted upon and spoiled with money and idle time, were coming up soft and losing their edge and pluck in the process. In a chest-thumping call to arms for Harvard's graduating class of 1895, Oliver Wendell Holmes exhorted the elite of the effete to embrace blood sport as part of the "soldier's faith":

> Out of heroism grows faith in the worth of hero-
> ism. . . . Therefore I rejoice at every dangerous sport
> which I see pursued. . . . If once in a while in our
> rough riding a neck is broken, I regard it, not as a
> waste, but as a price well paid for the breeding of a
> race fit for headship and command.

Holmes's call to the wild was well received and continues to be heard. As Michael Oriard has documented in *King Football*, every attempt over the decades to make the game less violent has run into concerns over "sissifying" the game. Football was always a man's game, a sport that defined and celebrated the masculine ideal. In the postwar boom of the 1920s, for example, college football's rugged violence was regarded by many as a healthy counterbalance to an increasingly feminized culture where men sported raccoon coats, listened to jazz, and attended tea parties. "Modern life," as Oriard puts it, "was *soft* . . . football was *hard*."

The flying wedge only lasted a couple of years before being abolished, but in its wake came a host of other momentum plays and backfield strategies designed to take out vulnerable defensemen. The era of "trench warfare" reached a new low point in 1905, a season in which 18 young men died and 159 were seriously injured. Roosevelt, now president and father of two sons about to play college ball, felt the need to intervene, as much to save football as to save lives. He called Camp and other representatives from the Big Three—Harvard, Princeton, and Yale—to the White House with the intent of making the game "not soft but honest." The attendees pledged to follow the spirit and law of the rules. But the brutality continued. Harvard tackle Karl Brill made news when he quit the team, declaring, "I believe that the human body was not made to withstand the enormous strain that football demands. It is a mere gladiatorial contest." That season, Columbia University, Northwestern, Union College, and the Massachusetts Institute of Technology dropped their football programs. Stanford and the University of California went back to rugby, a more acceptable alternative to what American football had become.

Along with its brutality, another strike against football for its critics was the rising professionalism in the college game. More than 30 years after baseball's first professional association was formed, football supporters, including Camp, still held fast to the amateur ideal and decried the "tramp athletes" and "ringers" some college teams were recruiting on the sly. As early as 1894, seven of Michigan's 11 starters weren't even enrolled in the school but were farmhands or steelworkers brought in to work the gridiron on weekends. Critics saw brutality and professionalism going hand in hand, as gate receipts drove a "win at any cost" mentality into the sport—a mentality reformers have fought in vain ever since.

Attempts at real reform began in earnest in 1906 when 38 schools came together to form the Intercollegiate Athletic Association (ICAA), later renamed the NCAA. The purpose of the rules that emerged that year were, as a *New York Times* report stated, to " 'open up the game'—that is, to provide for the natural elimination of the so-called mass plays and bring about a game in which speed and real skill shall supersede

"Football of the Future," from *Harper's Weekly*, November 1889.

so far as possible mere brute strength and force of weight." An extra referee was added to enforce existing rules against kneeing, kicking, punching, and other excessive roughness. The requirement for a first down was bumped up to 10 yards. But the greatest innovation that emerged to nudge football toward modernity was the legalization of the forward pass.

The forward pass was nothing new. Players had experimented with it for years, but the limitations and penalties imposed on throwing the ball made it more of a desperation play than a core strategy. Passes could only be thrown from five yards behind the line of scrimmage and had to be thrown to either side of center. Incomplete passes resulted in a 15-yard penalty on first and second downs and a turnover on the third. If a pass went out of bounds, possession went to whichever team retrieved it first. The forward pass became an instant game-changer in the 1906 season, even though the best quarterbacks could only throw the watermelon-shaped ball 20 yards or so. Amos Alonzo Stagg claimed that by that first season he was already running 64 different forward-pass patterns.

To encourage the more open and safer passing game, the NCAA in 1912 reduced the size of the football to dimensions that Barbara, the Wilson football inspector in Ada, could almost sign off on: "It shall be tightly inflated. . . . Circumference, long axis, from 28 inches to 28½ inches; short axis 22½ to 23 inches. Weight, from 14 to 15 ounces." That same year the committee shortened the field to add end zones and permitted touchdown passes over the goal line for the first time, giving quarterbacks a new target and the prolate spheroid a reason to exist.

Not everyone was a fan of the passing game, though. Walter Camp fought it tooth and nail, and as late as the 1930s Jock Sutherland, University of Pittsburgh's coach, stated that "throwing laterals is an attempt to sissify a man's game and there is no fun in getting over the ground that way." Pitt, unlike their softer competitors, was, he declared with testosterone-laced bravado, "a sock-it-to-'em school."

With mass plays a thing of the past, and the forward pass opening up the game to hundreds of new play patterns, football evolved into the game of "contact ballet" it is today. But as Camp learned early on as he tweaked and tested new rules, changes designed to make the game safer can also have the opposite effect. Helmets, introduced as protection and required in the NFL starting in 1943, are today used as weapons. Tackles that used to take place over short distances and involved mostly arms and shoulders are now high-speed helmet attacks. And the same forward pass that rescued football from the brink in 1906 created more room for players to gather deadly speed and momentum. Troy Polamalu, the All-Pro Steelers safety who has been dragged to the ground more times than he can count (including once by his wild mane of Samoan hair), has pointed to the passing game as it's evolved as a reason for the rise in head injuries, including the seven concussions he's had:

> In the past, it was a style of ball that was three yards and a cloud of dust, so you didn't see too many of these big hits, because there wasn't so much space between players. I mean, with the passing game now, you get four-wide-receiver sets, sometimes five-wide-receiver sets. You get guys coming across the middle, you get zone coverages. You know, there's more space between these big hits.

According to Timothy Gay, author of *The Physics of Football*, an average defensive back's mass combined with his speed—40 yards in 4.56 seconds—can produce up to 1,600 pounds of force on collision. And that assumes the other guy is standing still.

Less than two weeks after Super Bowl XLV, Dave Duerson, the Pro-Bowl safety who helped lead the Chicago Bears to a Super Bowl victory in 1985 and did the same for the New York Giants in 1990, committed suicide by shooting himself in the chest. In a final text message to his family, he wrote: "Please see that my brain is given to the NFL's brain bank." Duerson had deliberately spared his brain so it could be studied for signs of chronic traumatic encephalopathy, or CTE, a degenerative brain disease linked to repeated concussions and head trauma in football.

To date, some two dozen retired NFL players, including Duerson, have been found to have suffered from CTE, which can only be identified by autopsy. Most of them battled depression, many had run-ins with the law, and several ended their lives by suicide. "Iron Mike" Webster of the Pittsburgh Steelers took to living in train stations and tazing himself to relieve chronic pain. Fellow Steelers lineman Terry Long killed himself by drinking antifreeze, and his teammate Justin Strzelczyk died in a high-speed police chase by driving head-on at 90 mph into a tanker truck. After years of repeated collisions on the gridiron, the brain tissue of these large, muscle-bound men was found to resemble that of an 80-year-old suffering from Alzheimer's disease.

The "concussion crisis," as football's latest come-to-Jesus moment has been called, has exposed the iceberg beneath the game's long-stormy surface. We always knew the game was rough, even too rough at times. We saw the hits and the blood and the stretchers on the field, and we heard the sports commentators report on the medical implications of each collision, how long a player would be off the roster while he recovered, how therapy was progressing. But the research coming out of

Boston University's Center for the Study of Traumatic Encephalopathy reveals through a battery of brain scans a more sinister, hidden toll. Young lives are being irreversibly altered by years of "dings" to the head, each ding cheered on by millions of loyal fans and rewarded with higher-paying contracts. Long after the Super Bowl rings are handed out, brains and families are being ravaged by depression, domestic violence, and suicide caused by a disease with a single preventative measure: avoid padding up and stepping foot on the gridiron.

And it isn't just seasoned NFL or college players who are affected. Between 1982 and 2009, the National Center for Catastrophic Injury Research reports 295 fatalities directly or indirectly attributable to playing high school football. In early 2009, at a turning point in the safety debate, Boston University researchers held a press conference to report their findings of the early signs of CTE in the brain of an 18-year-old high school player who had suffered multiple concussions. With several million preteens playing Pop Warner football every fall, what had been regarded by some as the price paid by a few overpaid professional athletes in a rough sport was now looking more like a public health concern.

The crisis reached a fever pitch during a weekend in October 2010 when a Rutgers player was paralyzed from the neck down and three brutal helmet-to-helmet hits resulted in concussions, blood, and stretchers on the field. NFL officials vowed, once again, to enforce rules against tackling above the neck or leading with the helmet. Taking century-old positions for or against the game as it is now played, newspaper editorials and radio talk shows probed whether football had indeed become too violent.

"Should You Watch?" asked the headline of one editorial questioning the moral culpability of couch dwellers.

The Green Bay Packers were applauded later that season for putting the long-term health of star quarterback Aaron Rodgers ahead of winning after he took a hard hit to the head in an important late-season game against the Detroit Lions. But in the days leading up to their Super Bowl appearance against the Packers, Steelers linebacker James Harrison chided his opponents and the league's crackdown on head-to-head tackles, suggesting that they "lay a pillow down where I'm going to tackle them, so they don't hit the ground too hard." And for all the fans who applauded the new level of vigilance, there were just as many who derided efforts to tame the game, like this online poster responding to a Roger Abrams article on "5 Ways to Make Football Safer":

> I think it's safe to say that Roger Abrams doesn't play (or enjoy) football. Unnecessary violence? Really? What about boxing? UFC and MMA fighting? How many men have died in NASCAR? They don't race because it's the safe thing to do. We love the contests of men pitted against men. If you don't have the stomach for it, Doc, change the channel. Tiger Woods needs the fans. As for me, I'll continue to watch and play my gladiatorial pastimes. Men will be men . . . all the rest can watch, play golf or just knit.

Why, with its inherent brutality and violence, is football "America's Choice"? And how much does its enormous popularity and ascendancy have to do with the violence itself? These are questions that have been keeping us up at night since the game's inception. They emerge whenever the casualties once again start to mount and we're forced to contemplate what Michael Oriard calls our "competing desires for danger and safety, violence and beauty—savagery and civilization in their many guises." They subside when the long arm of regulation tilts the balance back toward the socially acceptable.

Those competing desires are present in many sports, and have been for centuries, if not millennia. Just as dolphins and other mammals in the wild have been known to risk death just to play, we humans have always engaged in sports that test our physical and psychological limits. We've learned that it's on those outer limits where we feel most fully alive, and where, as Peter Marin writes, we are "stripped morally to the bone." The anthropologist Clifford Geertz described such experiences as "deep play," where the stakes of participating are so high as to be considered irrational. It's a concept that the ancient Maya and Aztecs clearly understood and took to its ultimate, ritualistic, spectacular end.

Football's violence—disciplined, controlled, and, with unfortunate exceptions, surgically deployed to stop the ball—is undeniably part of its widespread appeal, perhaps even its "special glory," as George Stade described it. Every Sunday we wince and yet can't look away as potentially life-altering collisions explode on our televisions. Every Monday we share and replay them on YouTube as often as we can stand to watch. Fantasy merges with reality as our favorite players become avatars on the screen, acting out in cathartic bursts of violence the urges and desires we may all secretly harbor but thankfully restrain. Until 2011, when the game was modified to help educate young people about the dangers of concussions, *Madden NFL*, one of the best-selling video games of all time, would allow players who got concussed to stay in the game. Ambulances could be seen running over players on their way to attend the wounded.

And yet as spectators, we're riveted not so much by the blood and gore but by the heroic aversion of it and the narrow escapes that define the magic of the game. We delight at football's artful and precarious interplay of refined strategy and raw athleticism, crisp movement and crumpled mass, delicate grace and brute force. Ben McGrath of *The New Yorker* captured this poetic balance beautifully in his description of a successful punt return by DeSean Jackson of the Philadelphia Eagles with 14 seconds left in a tied game against the New York Giants:

> It's all there in the replay: the exuberant Jackson hurling the ball twenty rows deep into the stands; the angry Giants coach, Tom Coughlin, throwing his headset in disgust and tearing into his dumbfounded rookie punter; the blocked tacklers lying on the field like soldiers. Setting aside regional partisanship, you don't root for the man carrying the ball to be tackled at moments like this. You stop breathing and root for the near-miss. Averted danger is the essence of football.

Averted danger, deep play, the tense coexistence of primitive impulses and modern restraint—all delivered to the comfort of your living room in HD. What more could any sports fan ask for?

But what's been most troubling about football's recent concussion crisis is the realization that the dramatic narrative that unfolds on the gridiron may not be the whole story. What's unsettling is our lingering sense that the drama and the danger may continue on, unresolved, long after the clock has run out and the season has ended and players we cheered on have long retired. When instant replay is not enough and postmortem brain scans are required to complete the picture and conclude the drama, is it still play?

Chapter Eight

NOTHING NEW UNDER THE SUN

When it's played the way it's spozed to be
played, basketball happens in the air, the pure
air; flying, floating, elevated above the floor,
levitating the way oppressed peoples of this
earth imagine themselves in their dreams.

JOHN EDGAR WIDEMAN

James Naismith had a deadline. Fourteen days to create a new sport that would sweep America within a decade, defy the limits of race and gender, provide a fast track out of poverty, generate $4 billion in annual U.S. revenue, and within a century be played by 200 million people worldwide.

Invent basketball. Two weeks. Go.

The expectations, of course, weren't quite so ambitious when Luther Gulick, director of the YMCA Training School in Springfield, Massachusetts, tapped the

30-year-old Naismith to help with a challenging gym class he was leading. Soon after arriving at the school as a student in 1891, Naismith, a Canadian-born theologian turned phys-ed instructor, was recruited to deal with a class of 18 future YMCA administrators—"the incorrigibles," as they'd been dubbed. The school had been established just a year earlier to train young men in the fundamentals of starting and operating YMCA centers across the United States and internationally.

Their course of study required just one hour of gym class every day. In the fall, that meant a mixture of indoor calisthenics and some outdoor football. In the spring there was baseball to keep things interesting. But through the long, gray months of the New England winter, the men, most of whom were pushing 30, were trapped in a dark gym, 65 by 45 feet, doing military marches and Swedish calisthenics and playing endless games of sailors' tag.

Naismith felt their pain. "The trouble is not with the men but with the system we are using," he told his professor. These men were used to playing team ball games and competitive sports and needed "something that would appeal to their play instincts." What was needed was a game that would be "interesting, easy to learn, and easy to play in the winter and by artificial light."

Go for it, Gulick replied, in so many words. You've got until Christmas break.

Under the gun, Naismith, an accomplished athlete, spent the first 12 days experimenting with the sports he knew to meet Gulick's vision for success:

... a competitive game, like football or lacrosse, but it must be a game that can be played indoors. It must be a game requiring skill and sportsmanship, providing exercise for the whole body and yet it must be one which can be played without extreme roughness or damage to players or equipment.

First, he tried a form of touch football, but these were men who lived for the scrum and loved to tackle. "To ask these men to handle their opponents gently was to make their favorite sport a laughing stock." Next up was soccer, but windows were threatened, clubs and dumbbells were soon flying off the wall, and the game quickly degraded into a "practical lesson in first aid." Indoor lacrosse proved even more dangerous, given the cramped quarters and lack of stick-handling skills. "Faces were scarred and hands were hacked," and another game got tossed aside.

Naismith was dejected. With just two days left, he was preparing to admit defeat when he recalled a psychology seminar where Gulick had waxed on about his theory of invention, borrowing from a biblical passage from Ecclesiastes: "There is nothing new under the sun. All so-called new things are simply recombinations of the factors of things that are now in existence."

So he began, methodically and obsessively, to break down the elements of popular games, examine them in isolation, and look for ways to recombine them.

His first brilliant decision? The game had to involve a ball. All competitive team games used a ball, so his must as well. But what kind of ball—small or large? Games with small balls, like baseball, cricket, and lacrosse, he noted, also required sticks, which made them harder to learn and more expensive to take up—characteristics that didn't meet the needs of the YMCA. So he settled on a large ball, like the ones used in rugby or soccer.

Next, he considered why football, the most popular large-ball sport of the time, couldn't be played indoors. Naturally, it was because you couldn't have players' faces repeatedly mashed into the gym floor. And tackling, he reasoned, was necessary in football because players were allowed to run with the ball and had to be stopped . . .

"I've got it!" he recalled later of the eureka moment when he stumbled upon the essential, unique premise of the game. The player in possession of the ball would not be allowed to run, but would have to pass or bat it to a teammate. Great, so far, but if that was the whole point of the game, he reasoned, it would be little more than a game of "keep away," which he knew wouldn't hold the interest of the incorrigibles. These men needed to be able to score goals, compete, and win.

Having neither time nor the patience of his subjects to waste on testing his ideas, Naismith played out experiments in his mind. "I mentally placed a goal like the one used in lacrosse at each end of the floor." He quickly dismissed the idea, fearing that such goals would make the game too rough.

That's when he remembered a quirky childhood game he played behind the blacksmith shop at Bennie's Corners, Ontario, called Duck on the Rock. It involved putting a small rock, or "duck," on top of a large boulder as the target, with each player standing 20 feet back behind a line launching their rock to dislodge the duck. The best way to do this and still retrieve your rock without getting tagged was to toss it in an arc.

"With this game in mind, I thought that if the goal were horizontal instead of vertical, the players would be compelled to throw the ball in an arc." And if the goals were put up high enough, the defense couldn't simply swarm around the goal but would have to secure possession earlier by stealing a pass.

It's tempting to think that, as some have alluded, Naismith might have drawn some remote inspiration from *ulama*, where, following one set of rules, the Aztecs and Maya knocked the ball through an elevated stone ring to score. He could, plausibly, have read John Lloyd Stephens's popular account 50 years earlier of discovering the ruined ball court in the ancient city of Chichén Itzá or seen artist Frederick Catherwood's drawings of the crumbling stadium and its ornately carved rings. But there's no evidence he ever did. And a good thing too, perhaps, or we might be sacrificing losing teams at half-court today!

Day 13 ended and Naismith went to bed dreaming of the game he was about to transfer from his head to the hardwood. "I believe that I am the first person who ever played basketball; and although I used the bed for a court, I certainly played a hard game that night."

The next morning he went early to his office, grabbed a soccer ball, and began looking about for something to use as a goal. He sent the building superintendent, Mr. Stebbins, off to the basement to find some boxes, but Stebbins returned instead with the now-famous peach baskets, sparing us the fate of "boxball" and setting us down the path to the *swish*, one of sport's most sublime sounds. He tacked the baskets to the balconies on either end of the gym—which just happened to be at that magical, dunkable height of 10 feet—posted a sheet with 13 rules to the bulletin board, and prepared to make history.

History was, at first, none too pretty. The 18 men scrambled and grabbed for the ball, fouls were committed, faces were scratched. "It was simply a case of no one knowing just what to do," said Naismith. This was not yet, and wouldn't be for decades, the aerial ballet of pivot plays, jump shots, and the crashing of boards. In fact, for the first four years or so there weren't any boards to attack, not until the goaltending of fans sitting in the balcony became enough of a problem that backboards became standard equipment. When a basket was scored, a rare and heroic act at the time, the referee had to climb a ladder to retrieve the ball or would release it with the pull of a chain.

There was no limit to the number of players, with some teams fielding as many as 50 men spread out the length of the court. "The fewer players down to three," wrote Naismith in his first description of the game in 1892, "the more scientific it may be made, but the more players the more fun, and the more exercise for quick judgment." And there was no strategy or plays to set up other than passing continuously until a player was freed up close to the basket. When plays did begin to emerge, they were as often a creative workaround to poor gym conditions as the product of any strategic genius. The

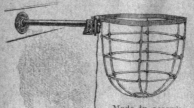

SPALDING'S
BASKET BALL GOAL.

FOR IN OR OUTDOOR USE.

Made in accordance with the lates rules governing the game and the most substantial goal in use. Made entirely of wrought iron and heavy wire The ball is released from basket by pulling cord inside and returns automatically to place. Price Complete . . . . **$20.00.**

SPALDING'S
REGULATION BASKET BALL.

Fine Leather Cover and best Red Para Rubber Bladder.

No. **5 A.** Basket Ball. . . **$4.00.**
No. **5 B.** Best all Rubber Ball. **1.25.**

Our Complete Illustrated Catalogue Mailed Free to any Address.

A. G. SPALDING & BROS.,

NEW YORK. PHILADELPHIA. CHICAGO.

1894 Spalding advertisement for the company's first regulation ball and innovative quick-release basket.

first players to "post up," for example, did so around two steel posts fortuitously placed on the floor of an old YMCA gym in Trenton, New Jersey.

Though it's hard to imagine basketball without the dribble, Naismith never envisioned that players would actually bounce the ball—nor would he have had any reason to. The balls of his time weren't designed to bounce well or predictably. For the first two years, basketball had no specialized ball but was played with a soccer ball. Contrary to the Spalding Inc. website, which claims that "Naismith asked A. G. Spalding to develop the very first basketball," the first game balls were actually produced down the road from Springfield in 1894 by the Overman Wheel Company, a bicycle manufacturer known for its popular Victor/Victoria "safety" bicycle. Their ball was slightly larger, heavier, and lumpier than a modern regulation ball, made from leather panels encasing a rubber bladder. Several times a game it would have to be unlaced in order to pump up the bladder. In 1919, Joe Schwarzer, a Syracuse All-American and early professional player, recalled the quirks and challenges of playing with those early balls:

> The ball was four pieces of leather sewn together, with a slit in the center where they put the bladder in and laces over that. When you shot the ball, you could see it going up by leaps and bounds depending on how the air would hit the laces. And of course because it didn't bounce as well as today's ball, it was harder to dribble.

It was a lot harder to shoot. When you were shooting fouls, for example, you could almost tell when the ball went up what was going to happen by watching the laces. If it hits the rim on the laces, God knows what would happen. So when you shot, you wanted the ball to rotate just once, and you didn't want the laces to hit the rim.

Neither Overman nor Naismith ever attempted to patent the basketball. Naismith never even patented the game he invented, writing later in life that "my pay has not been in dollars but in the satisfaction of giving something to the world that is a benefit to masses of people." It's remarkable, really, that it took 25 years for Spalding to step in to capitalize on Naismith's magnanimity and Overman's oversight. In 1929, George L. Pierce of Brooklyn, acting as "Assignor to A. G. Spalding & Bros," was issued patent no. 1,718,305 for the "Basket Ball." Five years earlier Pierce and Spalding had also patented an improved football.

Lumps and laces aside, players found creative ways to advance the first basketballs, rolling, bouncing, or even batting the ball over their heads to get it out of a corner. "It was not uncommon," wrote Naismith of basketball's lawless early days, "to see a player running down the floor, juggling the ball a few inches above his head." Gulick, who was responsible for codifying the early YMCA rules, attempted to ban the dribble in 1898, arguing that "a man cannot dribble the ball down the floor even with one hand and then throw for goal. He must pass it. One man cannot make star plays in

Early basketball action, ca. 1910.

this style." For the first three decades or so, dribbling (mostly double-dribbling, actually) was an inelegant defensive move that large players used to muscle their way toward the basket. I think that despite all the changes time has brought to the sport, most coaches today would still agree with Gulick's essential philosophy: "the game must remain for what it was originally intended to be—a passing game."

That first game ended 1–0 on a 25-foot set shot by future YMCA executive secretary William R. Chase. Naismith's invention was a hit with the incorrigibles, and, as he later wrote, "word soon got around that they were having fun in Naismith's gym class." Within weeks 200 spectators were lining the gallery for lunchtime games. At Christmas break, students took the popular game back to small towns across the country. Under the understated title "A New Game,"

Naismith's 13 rules were published in the January 1892 issue of *The Triangle*, a YMCA publication that went out to every U.S. branch. Within months, games were taking place at YMCAs from Brooklyn to Crawfordsville, Indiana, and in just a few years college ball was underway. From Springfield, the game spread with viral speed through the YMCA's international network to Europe, South America, Japan, China, and the rest of the world.

I once spent three gloriously fruitless weeks on a boat in the Bahamas searching for the spot where Columbus first set foot in the New World. I had old maps, fragmentary accounts of the Genoese navigator's first voyage, diligently dull reports from archaeological digs, and a healthy supply of sunscreen. Though it's been the focus of countless expeditions, there's not much knowledge to be gained from finding the spot. It doesn't much matter which scrubby cay he and his crew first planted a cross upon, declaring it and all that lay beyond its shores property of the Spanish crown. What matters is everything that followed.

And yet there was, and always is, the romantic allure of finding *the spot*, that holy grail of discovery for any archaeologist or historian, whether they'll admit to it or not. The spot on the African savannah where humans first walked upright. The spot in the Fertile Crescent where agriculture got its start. The spot between the Tigris and Euphrates rivers where blunt reed was first applied to clay tablet to carve the written word. The spot where the first baseball bat struck a ball and where the circuit of bases was first run.

For most historical events or evolutionary turning points, including that first line drive, there's either no spot to uncover or way too many to count. But that's never stopped us from searching, as baseball historians continue to do in their quest for the earliest, first appearance of baseball on American soil. Sometimes our pilgrim urge to stand on sacred ground is so compelling that we invent spots, like Plymouth Rock and Cooperstown, and persuade ourselves to believe.

That's why I experienced a rare thrill, an archaeologist's tingle of discovery, when I found myself standing on the cracked pavement at the corner of State and Sherman Streets in Springfield, Massachusetts, beneath the flickering golden arches of McDonald's, inhaling the output of frialator vents that rattled in the cold December wind. I was standing on *the spot*. Never mind that the spot was on, as I'd been warned, "the wrong side of town," a drug-ridden neighborhood where the liquor stores offer check-cashing services and where a recent drive-by shooting in broad daylight had left a 21-year-old man dead and a 13-year-old boy with a bullet in his leg. Even such tragedy couldn't keep me away. This was, after all, the undisputed spot where Dr. James Naismith—the original Dr. J—tacked up his peach baskets to the balcony of a cramped YMCA gym long since torn down, divided 18 men into two teams, and gave the world "basket ball."

Like most wannabe discoverers, I was of course merely retreading well-worn ground. Though largely forgotten and neglected like so much in Springfield, the site of basketball's invention has long been known. In its heyday, this western Massachusetts city was one of the most important industrial centers in the nation. Straddling the banks of the Connecticut River at the nexus of major roads leading to New York, Boston, Montreal, and other major ports, Springfield was chosen by George Washington in 1777 as the site of the fledgling nation's first armory. Here, Thomas Blanchard developed a lathe that could turn out interchangeable parts for the mass production of rifle stocks, an innovation that sparked the development of assembly line production. The armory turned out the first musket as well as the famous Springfield rifle, cranking out 200,000 a year to supply Union forces during the Civil War. "From floor to ceiling, like a huge organ, rise the burnished arms," wrote Henry Wadsworth Longfellow of the polished guns packed in racks. At its production peak during World War II, the armory employed 14,000 men and women to turn out M1 Garand rifles.

Aside from firearms and free throws, the "City of Firsts," as it has been called, gave us the first American-English dictionary (Merriam-Webster), the first gasoline-powered car (Duryea Motor Wagon Co.), the first successful motorcycle (Indian), and *The Cat in the Hat*, by way of native son Theodore "Dr. Seuss" Geisel.

The city's downward spiral began in 1968 with the Pentagon's controversial decision to close the armory. As with so many other manufacturing centers, "white flight" to the suburbs drained the inner city of population and tax revenue as close to 50 percent of the industrial employment dried up. Urban blight spread and gang violence and crime peaked in the late 1990s and early part of the millennium. Beset with mismanagement and corruption, the city faced financial collapse and was taken over by a state-controlled finance board for five years to get it back on track. In 2008, even as it was showing signs of recovery, Springfield showed up on a Forbes list of America's "Fastest Dying Cities" alongside depressed Rust Belt centers like Flint, Michigan, and Youngstown, Ohio.

In 2002, as part of a major redevelopment plan, the Basketball Hall of Fame opened a gleaming new $103 million, 80,000-square-foot facility on a strip of land wedged between I-91 and the Connecticut River. The Hall of Fame, which had its humble beginnings decades earlier on the campus of Springfield College, deserves credit for sticking with the city at its low point. Today hundreds of thousands of visitors a year from all over the world circle the Hall of Fame's steel dome to pay homage to giants of the game and gawk at Michael Jordan's oversized shoe collection. But most never see Springfield. They get whisked safely from offramp to onramp without ever needing to set foot, or drop a dollar, in the city of the game's birth—and without ever seeing the spot where it all began.

Aaron Williams wanted to change that.

A lifelong resident and civic leader who lives near State and Sherman, Williams always knew the game was invented nearby, but like most people had never thought about where. When he learned that the first tip-off took place right down the street from his house in Mason Square, he formed a coalition of neighborhood groups and business leaders, enlisted the help of the Hall of Fame, and began raising money for a monument.

"People see [the Square] as one of the poorest communities in the state. I see it differently," he told the local newspaper.

For Williams, the area's storied past could help restore pride where pride was in short supply. He also thought a monument might attract visitors and spur some economic development. Williams knows all too well his neighborhood's reputation for crime might keep some visitors away, but he exudes an unshakeable "build it and they will come" idealism that carried the project to completion.

"How do you calm fear?" he asked a reporter at the unveiling. "You show them history."

That December day as I stood under the board announcing a special on "Sausaqe and Eqq McMuffin" (a thinly veiled plea for *g*s, no doubt), I thought how fitting it was for McDonald's—which has over the years employed the likes of Michael Jordan, Larry Bird, LeBron James, and Dwight Howard to hawk the counterintuitive levitational powers of the Big Mac—to have planted their corporate flag in this hallowed spot and claimed it as their own. Naismith, who by the 1930s was already decrying the commercialization of his game, would be pivoting in his grave. The board outside the franchise should actually read, I thought to myself, "Basketball: Billions and Billions Served."

But no flag had been planted. There were no photos, no plaque, not even a commemorative Happy Meal toy—nothing to acknowledge the spot and its importance. I asked a young man wiping down tables if he knew of any markers. He stared at me blankly and then called over his manager, who seemed annoyed at being pulled off the McNugget line.

"Nothing here," he said. "But they just put up a statue of some people across the street."

I dodged four lanes of traffic and trudged through a hard crust of blackened snow to find a modest bronze sculpture of a white man and a young black boy playing ball together—the manifestation of Williams's vision. The man wears a turn-of-the-century uniform with the number 18 on his back. He's bounce-passing (somewhat anachronistically, since they didn't do that back then) the ball to the boy, who wears 91 on his back and Jordans on his feet. The game being played is not across space but across generations, cultures, and race—an assist from past to future. On the surrounding Plexiglas panels, a black-and-white photo of the first team, a cluster of tank tops and walrus mustaches, is exposed by passing headlights, then fades back into the dark.

When I spoke to Williams later about his role in making the monument a reality, he humbly played down his role. "Hey, I just didn't want another kid to walk by that spot every day dribbling a ball and not know what happened here."

When Naismith first set foot on that same spot in the fall of 1891, he was fresh from studying for the ministry at McGill University in Montreal. A devout Christian and talented athlete, he found himself as a young man torn between his desire to serve God and play ball. At McGill, he was a star football player, and while in Montreal he had picked up the Indian game of lacrosse, playing for the Montreal Shamrocks, one of the first professional teams. His friend and coach at Springfield College and the University of Chicago, Amos Alonzo Stagg, later told Naismith that he chose to play him at center because "you can do the meanest things in the most gentlemanly manner." At the time, with controversy brewing over violence in football, playing that and other rough sports was viewed by some as inconsistent with a Christian way of life. Naismith's teachers at the seminary disapproved of his double life on the gridiron and were none too pleased when he took to the pulpit one Sunday after a rough game against Ottawa with two black eyes.

But Naismith saw things differently. To him, the lessons learned in the heat of the scrum—lessons about self-control, sportsmanship, decency—were as important as anything he could deliver from a pulpit. He was, in this regard alone perhaps, of a mind with French existentialist Albert Camus, who wrote that he owed to the soccer of his youth "all that I know most surely about morality and obligation." It became clear to the 30-year-old Naismith "that there were other ways of influencing young people than preaching." He figured that "if the devil was making use of [athletics] to lead young men, it must have some natural attraction, and that it might be used to lead to a good end as well as to a bad one." Forced to choose between the ministry and athletics, he found a way to merge the two at the YMCA.

The Young Men's Christian Association got its start in London in 1844 with the first U.S. branches opening in Montreal and Boston in 1851 dedicated to "the improvement of the spiritual, mental, and social conditions of young men." The Y movement emerged to deal with the seismic social and demographic changes that were sweeping western Europe and North America with industrialization. As men left farm and country, and often families, behind to take new factory jobs in the cities, the traditional social fabric began to unravel for many. At the same time, millions of immigrants poured into East Coast cities in search of new opportunities and new lives.

"These young guys were staying in rooming houses together, or homeless on the streets, with no families to look after them," said Harry Rock, director of YMCA relations at Springfield College, whose campus office is in an 1894 redbrick Victorian gymnasium building. "They were getting into alcohol, prostitution, gambling, crime. So the Y formed to serve these wandering souls and keep them on the straight and narrow."

With rented space, they opened reading rooms and meeting houses where men could come off the street to read hometown newspapers, join Bible classes, attend lectures, and get counseling.

"They quickly learned that Bible classes were a tough sell to these young guys," said Rock. "Think about it. You don't say 'Come to the Y to build your Christian character.' You say, 'Come in and work out or play ball.'"

And so in 1869 the first YMCA gyms opened in New York, San Francisco, and Washington, D.C., with programs that dusted off Civil War military calisthenics. The whole idea of exercising indoors was still a new concept for most Americans, though the elite universities had begun building their own indoor facilities to train athletes in the winter months. Borrowing from exercise systems well established in Germany and Scandinavia, the new gyms were outfitted with dumbbells, pulleys, Indian clubs, parallel bars, running tracks, and other elaborate apparatus. Once incandescent lighting became broadly available in the 1880s the popularity of indoor recreation and sports began to find some traction.

After just a few years, there were nearly 400 YMCA gyms throughout North America. But with the expansion came serious management issues. Pay was poor and turnover high for the secretaries who ran the facilities as well as the physical education directors in charge of programs. Charged with "watching for the souls of men," many secretaries failed to watch their budgets as well, leading to financial collapse for many branches. Clearly some training was needed. So Robert McBurney, the general secretary, turned to a colleague and Springfield minister, David Allen Reed, to set up a YMCA Training School. Reed, who was already training Christian lay workers, managed to lure the school to town with a building site ready for construction—at the corner of State and Sherman.

"To win men for the Master through the gym . . . to win the sympathy and love of men; to be an example to others."

That was Naismith's earnest response on his application to the YMCA Training School to the question, "What is the work of a YMCA physical director?" A holy roller with a theology degree who played college football and led phys-ed classes to help pay for college, Naismith was the ideal candidate for the new program. He took immediately to Professor

Gulick, four years his junior but a man on a mission. Gulick was head of the physical education program and a leading advocate of "muscular Christianity," a popular movement of the age embraced by Teddy Roosevelt and satirized by H. L. Mencken.

For centuries, the body, with its unholy needs and urges, was regarded as the source of all evil. Gulick and his muscular Christians, however, argued it was only the *flabby* body that was the source of all evil. Only the strong man who took care of all aspects of himself was fit to do God's will. Writing of the merits of "vibratory exercise," Gulick, a kind of evangelical Jack LaLanne, lamented the debilitating effects of the modern age on the manly form:

> Many business men at forty are fat and flabby; their arms are weak, their hands are soft and pulpy, their abdomens are prominent and jelly-like. When they run a block for a train, they puff and blow like disordered gasoline autos. Men get into this condition because they sit still too much; because they eat more than they need, and because they drink.

He envisioned the complete man as one who balanced mind, body, and spirit. And he captured that vision in his creation of the iconic YMCA triangle—where spirit rests on top, mind on the left, and body on the right. "A wonderful combination of the dust of the earth and the breath of God" is how he described the logo that has survived six marketing redesigns over the past century or so.

The new game of basketball not only embodied perfectly YMCA principles, it was exactly the draw the young organization needed. From YMCA gyms, basketball quickly spread to church halls, Masonic temples, armories, public schools, city playgrounds, and other urban institutions. It began as and has remained an urban game, born of the spirit of social reform and designed to keep kids off the streets and out of trouble.

That's been the mission of the Dunbar Community Center for the past century. The Dunbar is a legendary neighborhood gym that's spitting distance from the spot on the outskirts of Mason Square. It began its life as a residential learning center for young black women going into domestic service in nearby mansions, and today serves as a safe haven for kids who might not have one otherwise.

"For two or three hours they're not getting robbed, not getting shot. They're playing ball, having fun," yelled Mike Rucks, the gym's 56-year-old athletic coordinator, over the afterschool din of squeals and sneakers.

It's never been just fun and games at the Dunbar, though, Mike admitted. The gym has a hard-earned reputation as proving ground, or burial ground, for up-and-coming players in the region.

"They used to say around here that you hadn't played till you'd played, and survived, Death Valley."

Death Valley is the name for the Dunbar's original gym, now closed and replaced by a shiny new facility that can accommodate the center's ever-expanding youth programs. Mike led me down the hall, where he fumbled for keys and unlocked a dented door. He flipped the lights on in the gym, which had reverted to a storage area, revealing colorful murals and an old-school court hemmed in by tiled walls and a stage located just a few perilous steps behind the boards. The gym earned its name as much from the talented house players who repeatedly schooled visiting teams as it did from the court's hard edges that drew plenty of contact in heated games.

"Man, we had some great throw-downs in here. Place would be packed, people lining the walls, talking trash: 'You can't play. Your mother can't play.'" One of the visitors who ventured into the Valley and climbed out intact was a young man named Julius Erving, who came up in the late 1960s while he was a student at the University of Massachusetts in Amherst.

Lots of great, lesser-known players got their start here too, said Mike. Players with nicknames like "Gimp" and "Treetop." Some who made it, like Travis Best, a talented guard from Central High who once scored 81 points, a state record, in a single game. He went on to play for Georgia Tech, the 1999–2000 Indiana Pacers team that lost in the NBA Championship to the LA Lakers, and various Euro teams. And then there were the ones whose hoop dreams were cut short. Mark Hall, three-time state champion who went on to play for Minnesota and was drafted to the Atlanta Hawks in 1982 but struggled with addiction and died from a cocaine overdose six years later. And Amos Hill, whom Mike and others describe as one of the most talented players to ever come through the Dunbar. "He never had some of the breaks growing up that kids have today, though," Mike said, shaking his head.

"I blame some of the coaches as much as anyone. They'll use a kid, tell 'em what they want to hear. I see it around here. Once the kids turn fourteen, that's when the vultures start swooping in." He's become so disgusted by the coaches who prey on young talent that he'll only coach up to age 13.

The stories of youth basketball's dark underbelly and coaches and recruiters behaving badly are far too commonplace. In his devastating book *Play Their Hearts Out*, *Sports Illustrated* writer George Dohrmann went undercover to report up close on the corruption that's rampant in a sport where players start being ranked at the age of 10. He tells the story of Demetrius Walker, now playing for New Mexico, who was described by *Sports Illustrated* in 2005 as "14 going on LeBron." Walker's Amateur Athletic Union (AAU) coach, Joe Keller, professed selfless concern for his charge's well-being, arranging for him to be homeschooled by a tutor, caring for his well-being. "I'm not going to get a thing out of this," Keller told *Sports Illustrated* in 2004. But as Dohrmann later exposes, Keller had arranged for homeschooling so Walker could repeat eighth grade and remain eligible for his AAU team. There was no tutor, and for an entire year the boy received no instruction at all. And it turns out Keller's real aspiration was to get a cut of Walker's contracts once he made it to the big leagues. "Within six years," he later boasted to Dohrmann, "I am going to be a millionaire."

Mike has seen as bad and worse in the 30 years he's been hanging around the Dunbar. And he knows enough not to underestimate the make-or-break effect coaches and mentors like him can have on the lives of the kids who pass through his gym. He shares a philosophy, and coincidentally most of a name, with Holcombe Rucker, the renowned New York City Parks Department employee who in 1946 took responsibility for the playground cage at Harlem's St. Nicholas Projects and turned it into his own private laboratory.

"Ruck," as he was known by everyone, believed that basketball could be a one-way ticket out of the ghetto for talented black youth. And for the ones who never made it, it could be a way to learn life lessons that would help them succeed elsewhere. In the absence of city funding, he begged and borrowed balls, recruited volunteer refs, and set up a teen-targeted summer league and a legendary tournament. The Rucker, as the park was dubbed, wasn't the place to refine your passing game. It was all about in-your-face streetball theatrics and flash. As Nelson George paints the picture in his book *Elevating the Game*, players picked quarters off the rim after a layup and performed 360-degree dunks years before any Nike ad showed them how.

Surprise visits by the likes of Dr. J, Wilt Chamberlain, and Nate "Tiny" Archibald would set up one-on-one challenges where a local underdog could show his stuff and maybe, just maybe, get recruited to the pros. "This was on-the-job training when no jobs were available," wrote Kareem Abdul-Jabbar of playing at the Rucker. "These were philosophers out there, every one-on-one a debate, each move a break through concept, every weekend a treatise. I took the seminar every chance I could."

And for Ruck it was all about education. "Each one teach

one" was his motto, and every chance he had he'd do just that, bending kids' ears about staying in school and the value of education. Between games, he'd teach impromptu English lessons, look over kids' homework, and choose players based on report card scores. It's been said that through his efforts 700 kids received scholarships to help pay for college.

The coaches across Springfield at the small New Leadership Charter School have had outsized success with the same kind of education-first philosophy. The middle and high school with 500 students opened its doors in 1998 in the heart of one of Springfield's most challenged neighborhoods. But unlike other public schools in the city, there are no metal detectors to pass through and no police presence—just vigilant teachers, parent volunteers, and kids who, for the most part, steer clear of the worst trouble.

At the Dunbar I'd been told, "Go over to New Leadership. They've got a story you need to hear." Even though the school was only a mile and a half away and I had the right address, it took me forever to find it. After looping the block a couple of times, passing empty lots and the occasional boarded-up, derelict house, I spotted a young man standing on the steps of an old brick Catholic school waving to me. New Leadership, I learned, leases the building from the archdiocese and doesn't have a sign of its own.

Joseph Wise, the studious-looking 29-year-old dean of students and girls basketball coach, greeted me on the stone steps, wearing a crisp white shirt and bright striped tie. He hurried me into the school's tiled lobby.

"This is not an area you want to be lost in," he cautioned.

Having grown up in New York City in the 1970s, I have pretty high standards for what I consider to be urban blight. I shrugged his comment off, thinking he was taking me for just another white kid from the suburbs. "It honestly doesn't seem that bad."

"Oh, don't be fooled," he laughed. "It's plenty bad!"

The school, Joe told me as we walked down the hallway past trophy cases, is focused on "character development and college prep—in that order." And they're guided by a simple mantra that appears everywhere: "Success is the only choice." So far, at least, it seems to be working. All 28 students in their first graduating class went on to college—a remarkable statistic in a city where only half of the students who start high school ever graduate.

Joe walked me down the hall to Coach Gee's office, a storage closet behind the gym. Dusty trophies shared precious shelf space with toilet paper and cleaning supplies. Capus Gee, a broad-shouldered 52-year-old with a resounding laugh, doubles as boys basketball coach and head of maintenance. As we talked, balls repeatedly pounded the plywood board separating the office from the gym on the other side. Coach Gee recalled with visible pride the early days starting up New Leadership's basketball program.

"Back then classes were happening in modulars and the only 'gym' we had was a cornered-off area of the cafeteria. Every practice I'd be calling around to churches all over the city, looking for a place to play. Half the time we'd be locked out, so we'd put the balls down and run laps outside instead.

No surprise our kids could outrun the other teams every time."

Things haven't changed much since then. The school's lease requires them to be out by 2:30, so they have to find other homes for afterschool activities. The girls team practices in a tiny grade school gym, with lunch tables pushed against the walls, and the boys JV team has use of a half-court at another gym.

About the time the program was getting off the ground, Springfield cut its budget for school sports by a third, leaving a gaping hole in a program that only charges players $10 to register and has to make up the difference.

"We didn't ask for more help from the city. We just wrapped our arms around each other and did it ourselves," said Coach Gee.

"Most of these kids are being raised by a single parent, or often a single grandparent. Some families can't even come up with a $10 registration fee—or it's either that or pay for the heat to be on. But everyone chipped in and cooked dinners to sell. Heck, I even cooked!"

The team raised $3,500 to close the budget gap that year and it showed the community what they could do when they all came together around a cause.

"Ever since, our end-of-the-year banquet has become famous. Other schools with big budgets are eating crackers and cheese. We have fried chicken, ribs, every kid gets a trophy and a nice hoodie. They leave feeling good about themselves."

Coaches Gee and Wise live for basketball, trading stories of local heroes and high school stats. But for them it's just part of a bigger, more important picture. Playing ball is just a way to build a kid's character and confidence, teach them about discipline, teamwork, and other life lessons. And they know that for some kids, it's the magic carrot that keeps them in school, off the streets, and out of trouble. As a policy, the coaches see progress reports for their players every two weeks and hold them accountable.

While every coach would pay lip service to the same philosophy, Coach Gee knows too many coaches who are more likely to put winning first. He shared the story of one of his most promising players—"kid was fast, great jump shot, you name it"—who was struggling in school and had to be held back. Another high school's coach lured him with the promise that if he joined the school's program he wouldn't need to repeat his year. The student left New Leadership but ended up getting held back anyway, so he transferred to another school and got held back again. Now he's 20 years old, taking freshman classes, and trying to figure out where the road leads from here.

I asked him if he knew of Amos Hill and what happened to him.

"Everyone who knows Springfield basketball knew Amos Hill. Most gifted athlete that ever came out of Springfield. But the same thing happened to him, only worse. Do you know he got all the way through high school and couldn't read or write? No wonder the poor guy drank himself to death."

"Our kids know school and home come first," added Joe.

"If you want to play for the team, you need to keep your grades up and do the right thing at home."

In 2004, the first year of New Leadership's boys basketball program, with no seniors to play and no gym to call their own, the varsity team won the western Massachusetts conference for their division and went on to be the first charter school to play in a state title game.

"That win was big for the boys team," said Coach Gee. "But that was just the beginning. Then Qisi joined the girls team and put New Leadership girls basketball on the national map."

"Qisi" is Bilqis Abdul-Qaadir, an honors graduate from New Leadership, now playing as a second-year point guard for the Division I Memphis Tigers. And if there's anyone walking the streets of Springfield today who embodies the full legacy of James Naismith, Bilqis has got my vote.

In 2009, she finished her senior year at New Leadership with a staggering 3,070 career points, shattering the state record set 18 years earlier by University of Connecticut and WNBA star and TV commentator Rebecca Lobo. It was beyond unlikely that Bilqis could come out of a tiny unknown Division III charter school like New Leadership to surpass Lobo's long-standing record by 300 points. It was astounding that she stood only five feet, three inches, 13 inches shorter than Lobo, when she set the record. But the most powerful part of her story, and the part she's most proud of, is that she did it all while staying true to her beliefs as a devout Muslim woman. For four years, Bilqis drained jump shots, sunk buzzer beaters, and took the lane through a wall of much

taller players with her arms and legs fully covered and a traditional *hijab* scarf wrapping her head.

I visited Bilqis at her Springfield home on an early summer
day. Aidan came along, lured by the promise of a visit to the
Hall of Fame. Bilqis was home from Memphis for a few weeks
of family time before returning for training. She met us in the
front yard of her yellow-sided house wearing a Gap sweatshirt
and a black head scarf and greeted us with a shy smile and
polite handshake. She's soft-spoken and humble but exudes
a kind of don't-mess-with-me determination and confidence,
all characteristics that seem to run in the family. Her father, a
limo driver, was in the driveway washing his car. Her mother,
who has run a day-care center out of the house for 30 years,
was busy minding her grandchildren, who were chasing each
other in circles. Both are converted Muslims who have raised
their eight children within their adopted faith.

From as early as Bilqis can remember, she had a basketball in her hands and an uncanny ability to find the hole in
any defense.

"We had a little-tike Nerf hoop in the living room," she
said, showing Aidan the spot where it was set up. "My brothers would play against me on their knees."

"Really? How many brothers?" Aidan asked.

"At least two. I was *always* being double-teamed, but
that's how you learn, right?"

From there it was driveway ball, AAU programs, and
countless miles of road trips—but academics always came
first. Her mother chose to homeschool her youngest rather

Bilqis Abdul-Qaadir playing for New Leadership, 2009.

than subject her to the Springfield public school system, where her older brothers had gotten "mixed up in stuff." When eighth grade came around, her AAU coaches encouraged her to attend one of the large public schools with established basketball programs. But her mother was having none of it. So off she went to New Leadership, a school with no girls basketball program to speak of and no gym to call its own.

It helped that her brother Yusuf had found both academic and athletic success there, having helped lead his varsity team to the 2004 state championship. As Bilqis was entering her new school, her brother was heading to Division II Bentley College on a full scholarship.

"That girl *defined* scrappy," recalled Joe of the four-foot, ten-inch, 80-pound girl who showed up that year to play on his new team. "Her jersey was hanging off her. But then she goes out in her first game and scores forty-three points, sixteen steals, ten assists. We were all like—whoa!"

In her freshman year, following Islamic law, she had to begin covering up. There was never a question of whether she would. She was devoted to her faith and to the sacrifice and discipline it required of her. That included playing on an empty stomach while fasting during Ramadan, pulling over on the side of the road or ducking into the nurse's office to pray five times a day. But covering up was still a huge hurdle for a self-conscious teen to overcome, let alone a rising athlete like Bilqis.

She remembered the first day her mother dropped her off at practice in her new attire. "I was crying, I was so scared. I didn't know what my friends were going to say."

She also didn't know about Under Armour.

"My mom and I were still figuring out what I should wear. I had these heavy cotton sweatpants, long cotton shirts, cotton head scarf. I was so hot and uncomfortable."

Her coaches stood behind her commitment. They began researching light, breathable fabrics, looking for the perfect balance between high-tech comfort and *hijab* modesty. But there was still the social discomfort of being a symbol of Muslim identity in post-9/11 America. Enough referees questioned her attire that the team had to carry a letter of permission from the Massachusetts Athletic Association. Although she wasn't the first Muslim woman to play at that level, the precedent wasn't encouraging. The previous year, University of South Florida co-captain Andrea Armstrong was forced to quit the team when her conversion to Islam and adoption of the dress code led to a reprimand from her coach and hate mail from fans.

I asked Bilqis if she'd experienced similar incidents with spectators or rivals.

She shrugged the question off. "Most players and fans were totally respectful, but there were definitely some who said things."

Her mother, who'd been sitting in the kitchen within earshot, chimed in.

"It was hard to watch sometimes. I remember once, she was taking the ball in from the sideline and behind her some idiot yelled 'Terrorist!' I hate to say it, but that kind of thing happens off the court too."

Her father, who wears his gray beard long following

Muslim custom, relayed a recent experience of his own from the day when the news broke of Osama bin Laden's killing.

"I go into the store to get the paper and the owner holds up the headline and asks me if I'm going to cut my beard now. Then he says, 'Only kidding.' Can you believe that? Why would he think that's funny?"

Bilqis never let the insults and trash talk get to her, though, and in four years never got a technical foul. Her standard line, coming back to the bench after an incident was, "It's okay." Then she'd go back in and unleash buckets of fury in response. By the end of her freshman year she had topped 1,000 points and by senior year she was averaging 40 points a game. The recruitment letters started arriving in the mail.

"They were double-teaming her when she *didn't* have the ball, literally stuck to her like glue," Joe said. "When she got the ball she'd have to drive through triple teams or more but she'd always find a way to the basket. I'd never seen anything like it. It was the Qisi show."

Bilqis started her senior year with 2,300 points—just 400 points shy of Lobo's record—and word began to spread.

"Scouts started calling, ESPN started calling, there was a fever building around her quest for the record," said Joe.

But beyond the media swirl, the greatest effect was within the community. Bilqis became a household name and a symbol of pride, not just for Muslims, and not just for the black community, but for a city in need of a hero—a basketball hero, no less. By mid-January she was within 38 points of the record and playing at the Hoop Hall Classic tournament at Springfield College. Rebecca Lobo arrived with her family, wishing luck to her heir apparent as TV cameras rolled.

"I wasn't really focused on the record," said Bilqis. "I just wanted to win the game."

New Leadership was down by 18 with 31 seconds left. She had 36 points when she fired an open three-pointer from 24 feet and it bounced out. She'd have to wait another game for her big moment.

The next game was supposed to be at the small elementary school gym that New Leadership borrowed for home games, but it needed to be moved to Commerce High to accommodate the crowd of more than 1,000. Bilqis was nervous that night, knowing recruiters, WNBA coaches, reporters, and the mayor of Springfield were all going to be in the stands. It took a long time for her to catch her rhythm and get on the board. Finally she got fouled and put up her 2,711th point, anticlimactically, on a free throw.

As she pursued the record and became a media sensation, Bilqis had to get comfortable with the idea of being more than just another talented ballplayer. She came to embrace her role as a symbol of hope and inspiration for people. She knew that every time she stepped out on the court she was opening minds and challenging stereotypes of Muslim women. And she played her part knowing that she was just building on a long legacy, that she owed a debt to a long list of pioneers who "cleared the lane" for her and made her achievement possible.

Senda Berenson, the "founding mother" of women's basket-ball, arrived at Smith College in Northampton, Massachu-setts, in 1892 at the age of 24 to be "director of physical culture." A Lithuanian immigrant who had come to Boston with her family when she was seven, Berenson found her-self cordially accepted but socially isolated as the only Jewish staff member on a Christian campus of 800. One former stu-dent's description of her gives a hint of the kinds of bias she confronted. "She was smart and attractive, and not particu-larly Jewish . . . I mean some Jewish people are very different-looking from others and she was very attractive looking and perfectly dressed."

Berenson was intelligent and focused, a woman with a mission: "Many of our young women are well enough in a way, yet never know the joy of mere living, are lazy, listless and lack vitality," she wrote of the challenge she had come to take on. Like Naismith, she inherited her own group of in-corrigibles and was challenged to find physical activities that were both fun and appropriate for a young Victorian woman to engage in. She came upon Naismith's article in the *Tri-angle* newsletter about the new game that he'd invented in Springfield, just 20 miles south, and decided to give it a try with her class.

According to Naismith's accounts, women were already playing at the YMCA Training School before Berenson staged the first organized game. A few teachers who had been com-ing by at lunchtime to watch the men play asked Naismith whether he saw any reason why women couldn't play as well.

"I told them that I saw no reason why they should not," he replied. "I shall never forget the sight that they presented in their long trailing dresses with leg-of-mutton sleeves, and in several cases with the hint of a bustle. In spite of these handicaps, the girls took the ball and began to shoot at the basket."

Naismith's openness to having women play his game was progressive for the time. Women had, of course, been playing ball and chipping away at the glass ceiling of sports for centuries. As early as 1427, a young Flemish woman named Margot, dubbed the "Joan of Arc of Tennis," became the sensation of Paris for humbling the city's best male *jeu de paume* players while playing both backhand and forehand—without a racket. A century or so later Mary, Queen of Scots, an avid golfer, ran afoul of the church for hitting the links just a few days after her second husband's passing. Women were joining the scrum in folk football games for as long as there are records of the games, though they were barred from formal Association play until the late 1890s. And Jane Austen in 1798 was among the first to write of the joys of baseball, with organized women's teams following around 70 years later.

Despite this proud if erratic history, the idea that girls and women could withstand and even benefit from the rigors of athletic competition was still regarded as controversial. Members of the "fairer sex" were seen as physically and emotionally frail, their bodies designed by nature for childbearing and little more. Women were not allowed to vote or own property. And the prevailing attitudes of the day toward sexuality dictated that they be bound in tight corsets and wrapped in yards of fabric, making basic movement a chore. "Until recent years," wrote Berenson, "the so-called ideal woman was a small waisted, small footed, small brained damsel, who prided herself on her delicate health, who thought fainting interesting, and hysterics fascinating."

When Berenson started at Smith, however, attitudes were slowly beginning to shift. Women had begun to expand beyond their traditional roles as wives and mothers to fill new jobs in teaching, social work, and factories. Writing in 1903, Berenson captured the sea change that was under way and how it placed new demands on women:

> Now that the woman's sphere of influence is constantly widening, now that she is proving that her work in certain fields of labor is equal to men's work and hence should have equal reward, now that all fields of labor and all professions are opening their doors to her, she needs more than ever the physical strength to meet these ever increasing demands. And not only does she need a strong physique, but physical and moral courage as well.

This new game of basketball, she determined, was exactly what her young Smith women needed to get them in shape for a new century. Designed to reward skill and agility rather than brute force, the game was deemed fitting for women in a way that football or even baseball was not. So on a gray March day in 1892, she posted a note on the outer door of the gym that read "Gentlemen are not allowed in the gymnasium during basket ball games." An unexpected crowd filed into the gym with school colors and banners to watch the freshman and sophomore classes play the new game. Berenson hung wastepaper baskets on either side of the gym and divided the teams. Then, in tossing the ball in the air for the first tip-off, she struck the arm of the freshman captain and dislocated the girl's shoulder. "We took the girl into the office and pulled the joint into place, another center took her place, and the game went on," wrote Berenson.

Clearly, this was not going to be easy.

But basketball seemed to instantly tap a deep vein of excitement and liberation in every woman who played, pro-

Senda Berenson tossing up the ball, Smith College, 1903.

ducing the same "feeling of freedom and self-reliance" that suffragist Susan B. Anthony credited to bicycling, another popular women's activity of the time. Early teams captured this feeling in their names: The Atlantas, a San Francisco high school team named for the fleet-footed Greek goddess. The Amazons and Olympians at Elizabeth College in North Carolina. The Suffragists and Feminists, African American schoolteacher teams in Richmond, Virginia. Although Berenson's version of the game—with rules modified to minimize physical contact—accommodated prurient notions of feminine decorum, it wasn't long before women broke out beyond the genteel elite college scene.

The 1920s and 1930s marked an early high point for women's suffrage and sport. Women won the right to vote, Amelia Earhart crossed the Atlantic by plane, and Mildred "Babe" Didrikson barnstormed her way into the American mainstream. Didrikson, who grew up in the gritty oil town of Beaumont, Texas, and went on to be a basketball star, pro golfer, and Olympic gold medalist, symbolized a new breed of woman athlete unfazed by middle-class stereotypes of femininity. When asked by a reporter if there was anything she didn't play, she quipped, "Yeah, dolls." Working-class women like Didrikson, used to the physical demands of laboring in factories or on farms, enjoyed the exercise, fun, and camaraderie that basketball offered and didn't much care what the men thought of that.

Requiring just a ball and a makeshift hoop, the game spread rapidly through small rural towns, Indian reservations, and city projects. Social mores of every kind were repeatedly challenged and battle lines drawn. In Iowa, when the high school athletic association voted in 1925 to end women's competition, one coach famously declared, "Gentlemen, if you attempt to do away with girls' basketball in Iowa, you'll be standing in the middle of the track when the train runs over!" That train made a lot of stops before it finally arrived in 1972 in the form of Title IX and, despite attempts to derail it, it's stayed on track ever since.

Seven decades before Bilqis had to grit her teeth through anti-Muslim taunts, a team called the Philadelphia SPHAs endured similar slurs and threats on the court, but played on. The SPHAs, which stood for South Philadelphia Hebrew Association, got their start in the tough "cager" days when courts were ringed by wire or rope cages to prevent players from diving into spectators' laps after loose balls. Until 1913, out-of-bound rules matched those of Walter Camp, awarding the ball to whichever team chased it down first. This was not by a long shot the no-contact sport Naismith had envisioned. Joe Schwarzer recalled returning home after his first cage game with rope burns across his back. Strategically positioned ladies were known to stab opposing players through the mesh with hatpins, and in coal regions of Pennsylvania fans would heat nails with miner's lamps and throw them over the net at players.

And that was just the standard treatment. As a Jewish team that proudly stitched the Star of David and the Hebrew letters samekh, pe, he, aleph to their jerseys, the SPHAs had to deal with far worse. "Coffins and hangmen's nooses would sometimes be painted on hometown floor to mark their spots, and in one hall the team was greeted with signs around the balconies saying, 'Kill the Christ-Killers,'" recalled one player. The SPHAs began as a team of Jewish grade school kids that took on, and defeated, all comers in Philadelphia's settlement houses. Like the kids from New Leadership, distant karmic heirs to their hardwood chutzpah, the SPHAs lacked a home court and were known as the Wandering Jews. They nevertheless wandered their way into seven American Basketball League titles between 1933 and 1945, at the same time their brethren in Europe were being shipped to concentration camps.

Before Bill Russell, Elgin Baylor, Wilt Chamberlain, and the era of black ascendancy, the cage was dominated by Jewish stars like Nat Holman, Eddie Gottlieb, and Harry Litwack who made up nearly half the players in the league.

Why were the Jews so good? Well, if you followed the logic of Paul Gallico, a top sportswriter of the time at the *New York Daily News*, it was because "the game places a premium on an alert, scheming mind, flashy trickiness, artful dodging and general smart-aleckness." Others, in the days before height was seen as a critical advantage, even suggested that the shorter Jews had "God-given better balance and speed." When Jews faded from the game, handing the ball off to blacks in the 1950s, the same kind of pseudo-genetic theories were dusted off to explain the "natural" athletic ability of African American superstars.

To say that basketball was a Jewish game before it was an African American one would be to miss the point entirely. It was, and remains at heart, a city game. Whoever ruled the asphalt ruled the game. As Red Auerbach, the cigar-smoking son of Russian Jews who coached the Boston Celtics to nine NBA championships from 1956 to 1967, described growing up in the tenements of Williamsburg, Brooklyn, in the 1920s: "Everywhere you looked, all you saw was concrete, so there was no football, no baseball, and hardly any track there. Basketball was our game."

In March 1939 it was the New York Renaissance Big Five who ruled the asphalt and led the game as world champions. The Rens, called by John Wooden "the greatest team I ever saw," were the first all-black professional basketball team. They got their name from the Renaissance Casino and Ballroom at 138th Street and Seventh Avenue, where a second-floor ballroom served as their home court. The team was formed in 1923 by Smilin' Bob Douglas, a West Indian entrepreneur who grew up playing cricket and soccer but fell in love with basketball the first time he saw it played and decided to form his own team. Through the 1920s and 1930s the Rens were the toast of Harlem, playing for well-off tuxedo and ballgown-wearing blacks who came out to enjoy an evening game followed by dancing.

The Rens invited team after team to Harlem and one by one sent them home in defeat. Wrote the editor of a black newspaper, "It is a race between white teams to see which one can defeat the colored players on their home court, but so far, none of them have been successful." That race was ended in 1925 by the Original Celtics, setting off one of the greatest early rivalries in basketball. Contrary to their name, the Celtics (no relation to the Boston Celtics) were an ethnic hodgepodge of Irish, Jewish, and German players who'd grown up together in the projects of Hell's Kitchen. Over the next several years, the two teams traded wins in front of as many as 10,000 fans, and in the process found friendship and mutual respect.

When the American Basketball League was formed in 1926, it invited the SPHAs and other teams made up of urban ethnic minorities to join up. But the Rens and other black teams were rejected, and would be for another 20-plus years. In solidarity for their rivals and friends (and, Kareem Abdul-Jabbar argues, because there was more money to be made elsewhere), the Original Celtics refused to join the league. Through the 1930s, whenever the Celtics faced the Rens, Celtics center Joe Lapchick would hug Tarzan Cooper of the Rens in front of the crowd as a gesture against racism, eliciting boos and even death threats. "When we played against most white teams, we were colored," said Bob Douglas years later. "Against the Celtics, we were men."

Barred from organized league play, the team took their show on the road, barnstorming through small towns in the Midwest and South. During those Jim Crow days when blacks were forced to drink from separate water fountains and attend separate schools, signs outside many gyms might as well have read, "Black men can't jump—here." In some states, like Georgia and Alabama, interracial play was banned by state ordinance. In others, games featuring the Rens against all-white local teams got the most return at the gate. To pay the bills in those Depression years, they maintained a grueling schedule, traveling continuously between January and April and playing games every day, with two games on weekends. Douglas later estimated the team covered 38,000 miles a year at their traveling peak.

In small rural towns, the Rens often found themselves shut out of hotels and restaurants after traveling hundreds of miles. Gas station owners with rifles would refuse to fill their bus. Eyre "Bruiser" Saitch, a star of the team and pioneering black tennis champion, recalled how they "slept in jails because they wouldn't put us up in hotels. . . . We sometimes had over a thousand damn dollars in our pockets and we couldn't get a good goddamn meal." Inside the small-town Masonic halls and school gyms where they played, things weren't any easier. Referees routinely called more fouls against them than their white competitors. In one game against the Chicago Bruins, the Rens got called for 18 fouls while the Bruins had zero. When their manager protested an unfair call, a riot squad had to be called in to save the team from being killed.

Despite the odds, in 1932–1933 the embattled Rens posted a 120–8 record, with six of those losses to the Celtics. In one grueling 86-day stretch that year, they played and won a near-impossible 88 games. By 1939, they were a national phenomenon, so it was no surprise when they were tapped to be one of a dozen teams to compete in Chicago in the first World Professional Basketball Tournament. The organizers wanted to field the best teams in the country, black and white, league-affiliated and not. The winning team would get $1,000 and the world champion title. The Celtics lost in the first round, and the SPHAs were forced to withdraw due to injuries. In round one the Rens trounced a team called the New York Yankees and went on to face their neighborhood counterparts, the Harlem Globetrotters.

The two all-black barnstorming teams had followed very different paths to the championships. The Rens played the game hard and straight up, determined to win on their terms and show that blacks had the same abilities as whites. The Globetrotters, a team with equally talented players, were formed by promoter Abe Saperstein to entertain whites. Their version of basketball, full of clowning and trickery, was a form of black pantomime that played to white stereotypes and paid off handsomely at the box office. The Rens resented being overshadowed by the Trotters and their traveling minstrel show. Said Bob Douglas in 1979, "I would never have burlesqued basketball. I loved it too much for that."

There was no burlesque or pantomime that day, however. Just two teams battling to become world champions and prove they had it in them. The Rens came out on top and in front of a mostly white crowd of 3,000 went on to defeat the white Oshkosh All-Stars to seize the title. Blacks everywhere celebrated the symbolic victory. After the game, Douglas held a banquet for his team and handed out championship jackets that read COLORED WORLD CHAMPIONS. John Isaacs, the team's six-foot guard, asked to borrow a razor and carefully cut out the word "colored." Douglas protested that he was ruining the jacket, but Isaacs just replied, "No, just making it better."

In a sense, "making it better" has been basketball's aspiration all along, part of the game's founding DNA. Of all the major sports played in the world today, it's the only one that was invented wholesale, and the only one designed to serve a social purpose. The father of basketball was no seer and no genius of the hardwood. He didn't foresee the need for the dribble or the jump shot. He admitted only to having played the game twice and to have preferred wrestling for exercise and other sports for watching. He naively argued that basketball was a game to be played, not coached, and true to his belief remains to this day the only coach in University of Kansas history with a losing career record.

From his early experiences on the gridiron, however, he knew that whenever people face each other over a ball there's always more at play than the game itself. The field or court is a stage where morality plays are regularly acted out, risks are taken, courage and character are put to the test. Naismith was an idealist and optimist who saw mostly the positive potential of his game to lift young people up, shape them—mind, body, and spirit—for the better. He fought for the right of women to play his game and at University of Kansas stood by his protégé and legendary black coach John McLendon against the school's entrenched racist policies. "Sportsmanship," he once told his daughter-in-law Rachel Naismith, "is shown as much in fighting for rights as in conceding rights."

Looking back years later, McLendon reflected on Naismith as a mentor, providing what may be the best definition on record of what it means to be a good coach:

> Naismith believed you can do as much toward help-
> ing people become better people, teaching them

the lessons of life through athletics, than you can through preaching. So he had that in the back of his mind that a coach is supposed to make a difference between what a person is and what he ought to be. Use interest in athletics as sort of a captive audience type thing, you've got him, now you have to do something with him.

Bilqis has learned firsthand the give and take of the game, and how the hard-won victories and bitter losses always go hand in hand. Though it's not been easy playing in *hijab* and dealing with name calling and ignorant questions, her spiritual journey has also given her a decisive advantage over other players in the stretch.

"Praying five times a day, fasting through Ramadan—it's given me the structure and discipline to do whatever needs to be done," she said.

It didn't take long for Aidan to pick up on that inner toughness, and to admire her for it. Standing under the dome in the Hall of Fame after visiting Bilqis, taking in all the legends who have graced the game, Aidan asked, "Do you think Qisi will ever make it here?"

"Who knows," I answered.

"I hope she does," he added.

After setting the Massachusetts record, Bilqis was inundated with recruitment letters and offers by NCAA finalists like Boston College and the University of Louisville. They rolled out the red carpet on campus visits and offered all the usual perks. But she chose instead to go to the University of Memphis, a lower-ranked upstart. I asked her why she'd made such an unlikely choice.

"They were interested in me and my religion. They showed me the campus mosque. Some of the big-time schools don't care about academics or your personal life, just basketball. That isn't for me."

Bilqis arrived at Memphis to great fanfare only to sit out her freshman year with a torn ligament in her knee. That gave her plenty of free time to answer the Facebook messages that streamed in from Muslim girls as far away as Indonesia who have been inspired by her story. In her second season, with a senior guard ahead of her she didn't get much floor time and found herself losing some confidence in her shot. When I spoke with her, she wasn't so sure whether she had a bright basketball future ahead or not.

"I'd still like to play in Europe, but my WNBA dreams have kind of fizzled out. That's okay 'cause I was never dependent on basketball. I've got a lot of other stuff I want to do with my life."

"Be a special guest of the president at the White House" was never on that life list, but in July 2010 she added it and checked it off all at once.

"My dad told me there was a letter for me with gold lettering and the presidential seal," she recalled of the day when the invitation arrived. "I seriously thought he was just messing with me."

It was an invitation from the White House to celebrate *iftar*, the feast breaking the Muslim Ramadan fast, with President Obama and 70 other honored guests. When Bilqis arrived wearing a purple head scarf, she was given a tour of various rooms and was then told to find her seat.

"I saw my name card and looked at the setting next to me, which said 'President Obama.' Next thing I know I'm sitting knee to knee with the president of the United States talking about maybe playing one-on-one someday. I was like pinching myself!"

In his recorded remarks, President Obama singled out Bilqis, calling her "an inspiration not simply to Muslim girls; she's an inspiration to all of us." He then teased her about her height.

"She's not even five feet, five inches. Where is she?" he asked, looking across the room.

Bilqis didn't miss a beat. "Right here," she answered, standing tall.

BACK TO BASICS

Around the time I was finishing this book, I spent several days of vacation with my family at a lodge deep in the Ecuadorian rain forest. We were escaping a particularly cold and dreary April up north, the kind that mocks every hope of spring's return. We were also escaping the worst start to a season the Red Sox had committed since the end of World War II—a season that would end abruptly and tragically. It couldn't have been a better time to seek refuge and solace amid sun-kissed orchids and frolicking toucans. While I wasn't consciously fleeing my subject matter, it nevertheless felt good to take a break and get as far away from the 24/7 world of sports news as I possibly could.

I'd been traveling and writing on and off for nearly four years, feeling pangs of guilt at the supreme irony of missing more than a few of my kids' ball games so I could research and write about the importance of ball games. Over those intervening years, Aidan had grown up fast. The seven-year-old who was happy playing endless games of catch in the backyard with his dad transformed seemingly overnight into a hard-core, highly competitive preteen who's working on his six-pack and can kill an hour in the driveway practicing his lefty jump shot.

The innocent, all-consuming delight he took in playing ball is thankfully still there. I see it when he's trying to beat his own record for spinning a basketball on his finger or messing around playing Nerf ball with his friends. But now, that delight competes for attention with drills, zone formations, travel leagues, and intensive summer clinics. With little pressure to perform from either of his parents, he's more innately competitive than I ever was, taking every loss personally, pushing himself to excel, dreaming as kids do of making it to the big leagues.

As for his odyssey-inspiring query, he hasn't exactly been waiting around for an answer. In fact, he can't believe he ever asked "such a dumb question" in the first place.

"Why do we play ball?" he teased me one day when I'd been hunched over my desk way too long. "I've got one word for you: F-U-N."

I never lectured him on my findings and I knew better than to try. There are few things more annoying for a kid Aidan's age than having his father sit him down to explain the world to him. Instead, I just leaked tales of my adventures whenever I had the chance, hoping they might somehow add up to an answer. Back from Gulf World in Florida, I showed him pictures and told him about playing catch with dolphins, how playing makes them smarter and more able to survive in the wild—and how our distant ancestors might have expanded their own cognitive rosters by throwing fastballs with rocks.

"So you're saying I should just go play and not bother with school?" he challenged me, flexing his neurons.

Watching the World Cup together, we talked about the Uppies and the Doonies, about the good old days when Tusker's head was as good as a ball and the beautiful game wasn't quite so pretty, but anyone who was daring enough could join the scrum and win the trophy of a lifetime. When the Celtics faced the Lakers for the 12th time in the 2010 NBA championships we discussed rivalries, how they define us versus the other guys, and give us a deep tribal sense of belonging. Why it's okay to hate the other team with every fiber of your being, but you should always be kind and take pity on their fans. They had, after all, simply drawn the short straw by stepping foot on the wrong side of town or being born in the wrong city or country. Poor buggers.

After playing tennis together one day, I showed Aidan Renaissance engravings of men in powdered wigs and pantaloons swinging rackets at homemade balls on a palace court.

"Back then," I joked, "not everyone got to play tennis. A low-class kid like you would have been lucky to be the king's ball boy."

"Not if I had to wear a wig like that I wouldn't!" he shot back in disgust.

Like this, during the commercial breaks of games or on long car rides to tournaments we talked about how games divide and bring us together, how they ground us in timeless traditions and connect us across generations, how they bring out the best and the worst in us: love and loyalty, violence and deception.

From our father-son trip to basketball's birthplace, Michael Jordan's size 13 shoes and Bilqis Abdul-Qaadir's head scarf will forever be merged seamlessly in his memory. Each impressive in its own right. Each a part of what's made the game great.

Having stood in that ancient stone stadium at the ruins of Cobá in the Mexican Yucatán, Aidan learned firsthand that it was the ancient Olmec and Maya, not the Greeks, Romans, or Egyptians, who were the first to develop a true, widely played sport with a ball. And having heard me recount the story of the *Popol Vuh* while he stared at that skull in center court, he knows that those early games once served as potent magic, capable of keeping the sun and the stars and the seasons in motion—ensuring all was right with the world.

And (rolling heads aside), have things really changed so much? Would spring still arrive across America if baseball's opening day didn't somehow conjure it? Could we be truly thankful on Thanksgiving without football or know it was New Year's in Orkney without the Ba'? Is there not, despite the doping and cheating and all the other scandals, some lingering magic in the Olympics and in the World Cup, that grand global rite that calls on the world every four years to stop conflicts, set aside political differences, and gather together around a ball?

• • •

Our jungle lodge, with its thatched bamboo huts lit by candlelight and tiki torches, could easily have served as a set for *Survivor*. The few dim electric bulbs on site were hydro-powered by the Class V river surging just outside our cabin. That meant no computers, no TV, no ESPN. Just the soothing hum and drone of cicadas.

Aidan had been eaten alive by mosquitoes the night before, so I was dispatched by my wife to find some Benadryl to ease his suffering in the nearest village a couple of miles away. I passed up a ride in the lodge owner's truck and pulled myself across the river on the ingenious wooden gondola that served as the only connection between the forest and the outside world. I walked the dirt path, scanning the canopy on either side for signs of the rare birds the local naturalist had trained me to look for. The pocket of rain forest we were in was world-renowned for its diversity of bird life. A steady stream of quiet, ExOfficio-wearing, binocular-wielding birders arrived regularly in this remote outpost determined to bolster their life lists. I, on the other hand, had never quite gotten beyond the pigeon-sparrow dichotomy that summed up bird life in New York City.

As I walked along, however, I began to hear a cacophony of distant calls and squawks. I approached stealthily, fantasizing ungenerously about spotting some absurdly rare specimen that the birders back at the lodge had traveled thousands of miles to tick off their list.

"Oh yeah," I'd mention casually halfway through lunch, "I think I spotted one of those long-wattled umbrellabirds today. Actually a few of them."

But as I got closer to the source of the calls, I realized they were coming not from the trees but from inside a small house on the edge of town. In a spare living room open to the road, at least 15 people were gathered around and screaming at a tiny television set. They were watching a soccer match.

"*¿Quién juega?*" I inquired in Spanish, thinking it must be LDU or Emelec, Ecuador's two archrival clubs.

"*Los Diablos Rojos y Newcastle!*" called out an agitated teenager, using one of a multitude of nicknames for Manchester United.

"Go Reds!" I yelled, pumping my fist inside the door. The teenager and his friends echoed my call back in broken English. The game being scoreless, I continued my way down the road.

Once in town, it became apparent that everyone in this small Ecuadorian village was watching the same regular season Premier League game between teams hailing from industrial towns in the north of England. Even at the drugstore I had to tear the owner away from his radio to get service.

Jarring as it was to have my jungle reverie shattered by refrains of "Take Me Home United Road," it was a more likely scene to come upon than a pair of mating umbrellabirds. Football is, after all, a national obsession in Ecuador, as it is throughout South America. This tiny country has had oversized success in the game, having qualified for two of the past three World Cups, despite their entire national league bringing in revenues lower than what the top European players take home in their paychecks. LDU, the Liga Deportíva

Universitária, has managed to beat more prominent Brazilian and Argentinian teams. And its rival, Emelec, is cresting on a recent infusion of Venezuelan oil money, thanks to Hugo Chávez becoming best buddies with the Ecuadorian president.

As much as Ecuadorians love their national teams, however, they may love their "Diablos Rojos" even more. United is, after all, the most lucrative and popular sports franchise on the planet, worth an estimated $1.8 billion in 2010 according to *Forbes* magazine. Their international fan base numbers in the tens of millions, and they can count as corporate sponsors a Chilean winemaker, a Turkish airline, a Thai brewery, and the capital city of South Korea.

But Ecuadorians have a more personal reason to love United, and that is Reds' star winger and native son Antonio Valencia, or "Toño Maravilla," as he's known here. Valencia's roots are in the rain forest, having grown up in an Amazonian town founded by Texaco in the 1960s. As a child, he played barefoot on recently logged fields, the same fields that Chevron, now owner of Texaco, last year paid a record $9 billion in fines for contaminating.

I may have thought I was wandering innocently through the Garden of Eden, but this Eden was, it turns out, squarely within United international territory.

When I arrived back at the lodge for lunch, my fellow tourists were gathered on one end of the table having a heated discussion about marmot distribution in the tropics. My family was on the other end cooking up a scheme to go ziplining for the afternoon. Once there was a break in the conversation, I mentioned stumbling unexpectedly upon the football match.

"Who was winning?!" asked an Aussie birder in his 60s who'd been fighting through brush with his wife since 5:00 AM and looked like it.

"No score yet," I said.

Hoping to stimulate discussion of something other than birds, I mentioned how funny it was to find such rabid fans of a UK franchise here on the other side of the globe.

"Actually, I know exactly how they feel," confessed the Aussie. He was born and raised near Birmingham, England, and so, despite having moved to Australia two decades ago, remained an unrepentant, uncurable, diehard supporter of West Bromwich–Albion.

"It's ridiculous, really, when you think of it. I follow every game and when they lose it sets me off on a depression that can last days."

His wife nodded and rolled her eyes next to him.

"When I'm back in England I go to every game I can and it's like my father's next to me just like when I was a kid. I can hear him yelling and goading the other team. Brings me to tears at times I'm embarrassed to admit."

"Isn't it wonderful to have that kind of connection," suggested a German woman down the table who hadn't said a word since we arrived.

"Is it?" asked the Aussie, visibly embarrassed by how emotional the topic made him. "I suppose it is, but it's just as much a burden now, isn't it?"

His wife nodded again.

"How about you?" I asked a Scottish ecologist from Edinburgh who was honeymooning with his wife.

"Hearts or Hibernian?" asked the Aussie, citing the two big Edinburgh clubs.

"To be honest, I'm more of a migratory bird guy," admitted the Scotsman.

I suggested that having the patience to wait for birds to return from multiyear migrations made him highly qualified to be a Scotland supporter come World Cup time.

From there the conversation went down the familiar paths it goes down whenever Americans and Europeans get to talking about sports. None of them could *possibly* understand how we Americans could be so enamored of the helmet-to-helmet combat that we call football, even though we don't use our feet . . . blah, blah and so on.

"You're just jealous because we've figured out how to keep the blood on the field," I shot back, noting that at their worst the Maya and Aztecs had nothing on the Chelsea Headhunters, the vicious hooligan firm linked to the West London football club.

Then there was the usual ribbing about baseball being just a duller knockoff of cricket.

"Cricket? Oh, you mean Flemish hockey?" I teased back, drawing mostly quizzical looks.

As the banter continued, I noticed that a young man had pulled up a stool nearby and was following the conversation intently. He stood out from both tourists and other Ecuadorians with his jet black hair, small stature, and seriously ripped upper body. He was a young Huaorani Indian named

Dogaka Berua who had traveled for days by dugout canoe and bus from his home deep in the Amazon to visit Tom, the lodge owner, an old friend of his family.

The Huaorani traditionally live as hunter-gatherers in the rain forest, many wearing no clothes to speak of and hunting wild peccaries with blowguns and poisonous arrows, fishing with spears and nets, and gathering tubers. Their first encounter with the outside world, in 1956, didn't go well for anyone. Five evangelical missionaries landed on a river beach near one of their villages to initiate contact and were speared to death. Since then, most of their groups have had regular contact with the outside world and now live in permanent settlements, where oil companies and illegal loggers continue to encroach on their lands.

Earlier that day, I'd missed out on seeing Dogaka scale the smooth trunk of a 40-foot tree using just his arms and feet to shimmy up, something he'd normally do to get a good blowgun shot at a monkey.

Seeing he was absorbed in our sports conversation, I seized the chance to ask him what games the Huaorani played. I knew several Amazonian tribes had once played games with rubber balls. The Otomac, for instance, played a game where the men used their shoulders and the women used wooden bats to knock a rubber ball back and forth in a court. According to an 18th-century missionary, the women struck the ball so hard at the men that their poor spouses' backs were being repeatedly injured, "which these hens celebrate with laughter." The Chiquito of eastern Bolivia played a Ba'-like game with one half of the village pitted against the other as they knocked a small rubber ball back and forth using only their heads. Each point was awarded a corn cob and the winning side earned the right to get drunk on *chicha*, an alcoholic beverage, while the other side watched.

Dogaka said that as far as he knew the Huaorani had no such games, though they did sometimes make rough balls from tapped rubber and kick them around. Other favorite games, he said, were arrow-shooting contests and rolling a termite mound down a hill while racing it to the bottom.

"But none of them compares to football!" he declared, smiling through missing teeth.

Soccer had been introduced to Huaorani communities years ago and had become instantly popular. In 2001, controversy was stirred up when one recently contacted group of Huaorani granted an Italian oil company rights to build an oil well and pipeline through their lands in exchange for a trifle of goods, including 50 kg of rice, 50 kg of sugar, two blocks of fat, a sack of salt, 15 plates and cups, $200 worth of medicine—and two soccer balls. A local environmental group decried the raw deal as "an insult to the collective rights of this indigenous nationality," which it surely was, not to mention exploitative and sleazy.

But without belittling the deal's impact on both people and environment, it was also profoundly telling that two soccer balls, of all things, were the only nonessential commodities the Indians requested. And who could blame them? If I'd been making do with termite mounds and was suddenly turned on to the wonders of the modern ball, I'd dig deep to get my hands on a couple.

Probing further, I asked Dogaka what it was about football that he and other Huaorani loved so much. He paused, self-conscious of suddenly being the focus of attention. Then he earnestly explained, dodging and moving his feet in a dribble motion, how it feels to kick the ball as hard as you can across an open field, and to run fast and stay balanced while nestling the ball safely between your feet. How it's just as fun to juggle the ball, bounce it off your head or kick it back and forth with a friend. We all listened, riveted, as though hearing of this thing called soccer for the very first time. And in a way, that's how it felt.

"It's kind of like a monkey hunt," he concluded with a flourish, eliciting laughter from the group.

"Come on, Dogaka, a soccer ball is *way* more forgiving on the chase than a monkey," I argued.

He ceded the point.

Aidan sat at the other end of the table, taking it all in, wondering no doubt if we'd all lost our minds listening to an Amazonian tribesman wax on about the finer points of a game he played every weekend back home.

Then he broke the silence, "We should have brought a ball with us."

I was about to suggest we go throw some rocks when Dogaka stepped in to rescue the moment.

"Want to learn how to climb a tree?" he asked.

Aidan leapt up and ran off with him, the rest of us in close pursuit, all heading into the forest to find a good climbing tree. There wasn't any point to it, no monkeys to hunt or fruit to pick up top. A waste of good energy really, and kind of dangerous too. It would do just fine. It would be fun.

Acknowledgments

I f book writing were a sport, it would be most like baseball: a team effort that nevertheless comes down to you alone at the plate facing either humiliation or victory. In thanking my own team, I must first turn to my agent, Robert Guinsler, who saw something in me and my idea when it landed on his desk at Sterling Lord and took the first leap. In the long journey from raw idea to crafted form, I was fortunate to have the enthusiasm and insight of a tag team of editors at Harper Perennial. George Quraishi opened the door to HP and helped launch the effort before leaving and delivering me into the expert hands of Barry Harbaugh. Barry immediately saw what I was trying to accomplish, and his calm guidance helped bring out the best in the book and in me as a writer.

The research for this book was far too much fun to call research. It was exploration of the rambling, pre-GPS kind where a few tips, a hunch, or a reckless whim can lead to great discoveries and stories. I drew inspiration and learned so much from the athletes and aficionados I met along the way, individuals whose love of their games is infectious, especially Graeme King, Bobby Leslie, Matty Ronaldson, Chuy

Páez, Freeman Bucktooth, Alfie Jacques, Jeremy Thompson, Jeff Turner, Brian Sheehy, and Bilqis Abdul-Qaadir. They welcomed me into their lives and onto their playing fields and shared their time and knowledge so generously. This book would have been plodding history were it not for the life they breathed into it.

Wrapping their stories in historical and scientific context meant standing on the shoulders of many great historians, anthropologists, and scientists. Most I encountered only through scholarly works liberated from the remarkably complete stacks of Harvard University's libraries. Others I had the good fortune to lean upon directly for their wisdom and expertise, including Stan Kuczaj, Allan Guttmann, Wolfgang Decker, John Robertson, James Brady, Sergio Garza, Manuel Aguilar, Lawrence McCray, Mark Bekoff, Tom Quesenberry, Jeff Monseau, Harry Rock, and Yves Carlier.

Every writer needs sanctuaries where he can retreat from the demands of daily life. Writing this book while working full-time and attempting to be a halfway decent husband and father made it not only helpful but essential to get away. I am deeply indebted to Preston Browning and his late wife, Ann, of Wellspring House for opening their home to me and to other writers and artists. Many ideas were unlocked and blocks unblocked there in Ashfield. When I was at the deadly midpoint of my project, my glass half empty and the end nowhere in sight, the MacDowell Colony rescued me with a fellowship that reenergized my work and made me feel that what I was doing might actually matter. In subsequent moments of doubt, I needed only to conjure the lunch basket deposited daily on my studio porch to feel restored. I am so grateful for that experience and for the extraordinary people I met there.

At every step I received moral support and sound advice from many good friends, family members, and fellow writers, including James Bernard, Nick Buettner, Dan Buettner, Dan Finamore, Val Fox, Lawrence Kessenich, Jen Krier, Bill Landay, Toby Lester, all the Logans, David McLain, Stephanie Pearson, Bernadette Rivero, Bill Shutkin, Emily Sohn, Amy and Scott Sutherland, and Jerome Thelia. I also owe thanks to my fellow "athenistas"—especially Pierre Valette and Rob Cosinuke—who have shown understanding and support for my double life.

To my mother, Mary Fox, I attribute the hard-working Irish scrappiness that got me through the toughest points. She not only taught me how to play tennis but how to play to win. I owe thanks and many drinks to my brother and fellow writer, Joe Fox, for being there as a friend and sounding board whenever I needed it and for making our wintry Scottish sojourn so memorable.

My kids are my greatest source of joy, and that joy infuses every page of this book. Aidan unwittingly launched my journey with his insatiable curiosity and love of all things sport-related. Amelia cheered me on throughout and kept me company on my dolphin visit. We had such fun, as we always do on our adventures together. My hope is that they'll read this book and be inspired to find wonder in simple things and unexpected places.

Finally, I offer my deepest gratitude and love to my wife,

Steph, who told me I could do this when I was almost sure I couldn't, who said it was going to be amazing when I was thinking it might just be okay, and who unselfishly shouldered so many extra duties so I could achieve this goal. You made this—like so many good things—possible.

Notes

Prologue: Warm-Up

8   **According to a 2004 study:** Juster et al., "Major Changes Have Taken Place in How Children and Teens Spend Their Time."

1: Play Ball

13   **"It is already known to me":** James, *The Principles of Psychology*, p. 675.

14   **"of limited immediate function":** "Taking Play Seriously," *New York Times*, Feb. 17, 2008.

14   **"purposeless activity, for its own sake":** Cited in Allen Guttmann, *From Ritual to Record*, p. 3.

14   **"not serious":** Huizinga, *Homo Ludens*, p. 13.

14   **"an occasion of pure waste":** Roger Caillois, *Man, Play and Games*, p. 5.

14   **In his schema:** Stuart Brown, *Play*, pp. 17–18.

15   **"have not waited for man":** Huizinga, *Homo Ludens*, p. 1.

15   **According to Marc Bekoff:** Marc Bekoff, "Social Play and Social Morality," p. 838.

16   **Studies of young mammals:** "Taking Play Seriously," *New York Times*, Feb. 17, 2008.

16   **One of the most dramatic:** Ibid.

17   **"a central paradox":** "The Play's the Thing," From book review in *The Atlantic*, May 2010.

21   **In one study:** Cited in "The Serious Need for Play," *Scientific American Mind*, Feb.-March 2009.

21   **In another study:** Brown, *Play*, p. 33.

21   **A recent study conducted:** "How Sports May Focus the Brain," *New York Times*, March 23, 2011.

22   **Neuroscientist Sergio Pellis:** "Taking Play Seriously."

23   **EQ is defined:** Lori Marino, "Convergence of Complex Cognitive Abilities in Cetaceans and Primates," p. 59.

27   **Vanessa Woods, a researcher:** From phone interview conducted Jan. 20, 2009.

28   **"In a dangerous world":** Diane Ackerman, *Deep Play*, p. 4.

30   **In the 1960s:** Richard Lee, "What Do Hunters Do for a Living, or, How to Make Out on Scant Resources."

30   **"keep bankers' hours":** Marshall Sahlins, *Stone Age Economics*, p. 34.

31   **"A ball, similar to the one":** W. E. Harney, "Sport and Play Amidst the Aborigines of the Northern Territory." *Mankind* 4 (9): 377–379. Cited in Blanchard.

31   **the Copper Inuit:** Blanchard, *The Anthropology of Sport*, p. 150.

32   **Buzkashi achieved brief fame:** Azoy, *Buzkashi: Game and Power in Afghanistan*.

36   **"[His] comrades are roused up":** Cooper, "Buddies in Babylonia," p. 78.

37   **The ancient Greeks played it:** Neils et al., *Coming of Age in Ancient Greece*.

37   **"Give the word":** Percy Gardner, *Catalogue of the Greek Vases in the Ashmolean Museum*.

38   **The actual balls used:** Wolfgang Decker, *Sports and Games of Ancient Egypt*, pp. 111–116.

41   **Every city had its stadiums:** Guttmann, *Sports: The First Five Millennia*, p. 19.

41   **"Nausicaa hurled the ball":** Harris, *Sport in Greece and Rome*, p. 81.

42   **"He caught the ball and laughed":** Stephen J. Miller, *Arete*, p. 116.

2: From Skirmish to Scrum

50   **"a soft and musical inflection":** Muir quote cited on Orkneyjar.com: The Heritage of the Orkney Islands.

50   **"Hundreds of years ago the people of Kirkwall":** John D. Robertson, *The Kirkwall Ba'*, p. 215.

55   **The origin of the Uppie and Doonie division:** Ibid., p. 6.

59   **"A round ball and a square wall":** Guttmann, *Sports: The First Five Millennia*, p. 40.

60   **As one British scholar has humbly pointed out:** Morris Marples, *A History of Football*, p. 4.

60   **One of the earliest mentions of a football-like game:** Francis Peabody Magoun, *History of Football*, p. 1.

61   **"drove balls far over the fields":** Ibid, p. 4.

61   **"After dinner all the youth of the city":** Marples, *A History of Football*, p. 18.

63   **"seven balls of the largest size":** Robertson, *The Kirkwall Ba'*, p. 286.

64   **"We'll surely hae guid tatties":** Ibid., p. 160.

67   **the only time women played a ba':** Ibid., pp. 115–122.

73   **"died by misadventure":** Magoun, *History of Football*, p. 4.

74   **"Neyther maye there be anye looker":** Teresa McLean, *The English at Play in the Middle Ages*, p. 8.

74   **"Whereas our Lord the King"**: Magoun, *History of Football*, p. 5.

75   **"dangerous and pernicious [game]"**: Cited in William J. Baker, *Sports in the Western World*, p. 54.

76   **"In the face of moral preachments"**: Ibid., p. 55.

3: Advantage, King

80   **"And those standing at the one end"**: Heiner Gillmeister, *Tennis: A Cultural History*, p. 1.

81   **"On Easter Day, after dinner"**: Robert Henderson, *Ball, Bat and Bishop*, p. 50.

83   **"the French are born with rackets"**: Baker, *Sports in the Western World*, p. 67.

83   **In 1596, there were 250 *jeu de paume* courts**: Guttmann, *Sports: The First Five Millennia*, p. 63.

85   **Your typical lawn tennis ball**: Feldman, *When Do Fish Sleep?*, p. 36.

86   **They used dog hair instead**: Gillmeister, *Tennis: A Cultural History*, p. 77.

86   **"and not containing sand, ground chalk"**: Baker, *Sports in the Western World*, p. 66.

88   **Looking at the near-finished product**: Yves Carlier, *Jeu des Rois, Roi des jeux*, p. 37.

91   **In fact, he loved tennis so much**: Julian Marshall, *The Annals of Tennis*, p. 18.

93   **"Let us leave the nets to fishermen"**: Baker, *Sports in the Western World*, p. 86.

98   **"played all day with them at ball"**: Malcolm Whitman, *Tennis Origins and Mysteries*, p. 26.

99   **"13th June 1494"**: Gillmeister, *Tennis: A Cultural History*, p. 21–22.

103   **"Some members of the clergy"**: Ibid., p. 32.

103 **"priests and all others in sacred orders"**: Henderson, *Ball, Bat and Bishop*, p. 54.

104 ***The Book of the Courtier***: Baker, *Sports in the Western World*, p. 60.

104 **"Water which stands without any movement"**: Roman Krznaric, *The First Beautiful Game*, p. 38.

105 **Henry II built his courts at the Louvre:** Baker, *Sports in the Western World*, p. 65.

107 **Molière's troupe of comedians:** Carlier, *Jeu des Rois, Rois des Jeux*.

4: Sudden Death in the New World

112 **"He was decapitated":** Elizabeth Newsome, *Trees of Life and Death*, p. 84.

113 ***pallone*, a handball game:** Anthony Fischer, *The Game of Pallone*.

114 **"I don't understand how when the balls hit the ground":** Mártir d'Anglería, *Décadas del Nuevo Mundo*.

114 **"Jumping and bouncing are its qualities":** Duran, *Book of the Gods and Rites and the Ancient Calendar*, p. 316.

114 **For 3,500 years or so:** Laura F. Nadal, "Rubber and Rubber Balls in Mesoamerica," p. 24.

116 **"Rubber is the gum of a tree":** Toribio de Benavente, cited in Tarkanian and Hosler.

116 **"The balls are made from the juice":** Mártir d'Anglería, cited in Tarkanian and Hosler.

117 **In the 1940s Paul Stanley:** Tarkanian and Hosler, "An Ancient Tradition Continued."

118 **At El Manatí:** Nadal, "Rubber and Rubber Balls in Mesoamerica," p. 27.

126   **One match on record from 1930:** Ted Leyenaar, "The Modern Ballgames of Sinaloa."

126   **"I do not know how to describe it":** Bernal Díaz del Castillo, *The Discovery and Conquest of Mexico*, p. 269.

127   **"The playing of the ball game began":** Bernardino de Sahagún, *Primeros Memoriales*, p. 200.

127   **"The man who sent the ball":** Duran, *Book of the Gods and Rites and the Ancient Calendar*, p. 315.

129   **"On a lucky day, at midnight":** Antonio de Herrera Tordesillas, *Historia General de los Hechos*.

131   **Though it was first recorded:** Dennis Tedlock, *The Popol Vuh*.

132   **"Life is both taken and renewed":** Mary Ellen Miller, "The Maya Ballgame."

134   **According to a 17th-century account:** Ralph L. Beals, *The Acaxee.*

138   **In what almost seemed a sadistic homage:** "Mexico Cartel Stitches Rival's Face on Soccer Ball," Associated Press, January 9, 2010.

5: The Creator's Game

144   **As early as 1374:** Baker, *Sports in the Western World*, p. 46.

144   **"There is a poor sick man":** Cited in Stewart Culin, *Games of the North American Indians*, p. 589.

145   **"They have a third play with a ball":** Ibid.

146   **In this way, the Iroquois confederacy:** Donald Fisher, *Lacrosse*, p. 14.

147   **In 1763, a group of Ojibwe:** Ibid.

155   **In 1878, a group of Mohawk and Onondagan Indians:** Ibid., p. 58.

156   **"the fact that they may beat the pale-face":** George W. Beers, *Lacrosse: The National Game of Canada*, p. 55.

159   **"a fighting band of Redskins":** Fisher, *Lacrosse: A History of the Game*, p. 172.

161   **"In his dream, the boy saw":** Thomas Vennum, *American Indian Lacrosse*, p. 30.

162   **Traditionally, the outcomes of games:** Ibid., p. 36.

163   **"Sometimes, also, one of these Jugglers":** Cited in Culin, p. 589.

168   **"On one side of the green the Senecas":** Vennum, *American Indian Lacrosse*, p. 104.

169   **"didn't seem to be so much a point of the game":** Ibid., p. 110.

171   **In 2010, lacrosse in the United States:** Sporting Goods Manufacturers Association, *U.S. Trends in Team Sports*, 2010 edition.

6: Home, with Joy

175   **"every prospect of becoming [America's] national game":** George B. Kirsch, *The Creation of American Team Sports*, pp. 21–23.

175   **"he sometimes throws and catches a ball":** David Block, *Baseball Before We Knew It*, p. 237.

177   **"This is not a museum, it's a church":** Bernard Henri-Lévy, "In the Footsteps of Tocqueville," *The Atlantic Magazine*, May 2005.

178   **Baseball Reliquary:** Dorothy Seymour Mills, *Chasing Baseball*, pp. 48–50.

178   **"Well—it's our game":** Walt Whitman, from Horace Traubel, *Walt Whitman in Camden*.

179   **A letter sent to the Hall of Fame:** Block, *Baseball Before We Knew It*, p. 101; and SABR Protoball Chronology, Up to 1850.

179   **Romanian Oina Federation:** SABR Protoball Chronology, Up to 1850.

180 **Danish researcher Per Maigard:** Donald Dewey, "The Danish Professor and Baseball."

182 **"To shote, to bowle":** Block, *Baseball Before We Knew It*, p. 230.

184 **"In the winter, in a large room":** Ibid., p. 140.

185 **working trap-ball into the saucy mix:** Richard Thomas Dutton, *Women Beware Women and Other Plays*, cited in SABR Protoball Chronology, Up to 1850.

185 **What about cricket, then:** Block, *Baseball Before We Knew It*, p. 144.

186 **"to avail themselves of passing the Fourth":** Warren Goldstein, *Playing for Keeps*, pp. 132–33.

189 **"When the batsman takes his position":** Peter Morris, *A Game of Inches*, p. 29.

191 **The Industrial Revolution had transformed the leisure lives:** Kirsch, *The Creation of American Team Sports*, p. 67; Goldstein, *Playing for Keeps*, p. 24.

192 **"a class of players who are":** Cited in Paul Dickson, *The New Baseball Dictionary*, p. 333.

193 **"a German immigrant who was the possessor":** Morris, *A Game of Inches*, p. 44.

193 **baseballs were reputedly made from sturgeon eyes:** Ibid., p. 396.

193 **"We had a great deal of trouble":** Daniel "Doc" Adams, *The Sporting News*, February 29, 1896.

194 **Doc Adams's solution:** 19cbaseball.com.

194 **"escorted in carriages":** Goldstein, *Playing for Keeps*, p. 19.

195 **As Warren Goldstein points out:** Goldstein, *Playing for Keeps*, pp. 17–31.

198 **"Baseball clubs . . . are now enlisted":** Kirsch, *The Creation of American Team Sports*, p. 79.

201 **"What . . . can any club do?":** Goldstein, *Playing for Keeps*, p. 32.

202 **"The *boys* have a say"**: Kirsch, *The Creation of American Team Sports*, p. 65.

204 **Albert G. Spalding, a rising pitching star**: Peter Levine, *A. G. Spalding and the Rise of Baseball*.

212 **"For creation myths"**: Stephen Jay Gould, *The Creation Myths of Cooperstown*.

7: Played in America

216 **"Baseball . . . is what America aspires to be"**: Cited in Michael MacCambridge, *America's Game*, p. 454.

219 **"breaches of peaces, and pieces of britches"**: Mark Bernstein, *Football: The Ivy League Origins of an American Obsession*, p. 5.

220 **"the jerky little 'dummy' engine"**: Parke Davis, *Football: The American Intercollegiate Game*, pp. 42–50.

222 **"At one time it was banned"**: Marples, *A History of Football*, p. 95.

223 **an all-out attack on traditional mob football**: Ibid., pp. 98–100.

223 **"ludic zoos of the age"**: Goldblatt, *The Ball Is Round*, pp. 24–26.

225 **"The two sides close"**: Thomas Hughes, *Tom Brown's Schooldays*, p. 103.

225 **"do away with the courage and pluck"**: Cited in Goldblatt, *The Ball Is Round*, p. 31.

226 **"I will not permit thirty men"**: Bernstein, *Football: The Ivy League Origins of an American Obsession*, p. 9.

226 **the "Boston Game"**: Davis, *Football: The American Intercollegiate Game*, p. 53.

227 **"Football will be a popular game"**: Ibid., p. 65.

229 **"Kicking it. That's what the rest of the world does."** Sal Paolantonio, *How Football Explains America*, p. xxii.

230 **England looked to spread its newly sanctioned game:** Goldblatt, *The Ball Is Round*, pp. 87–98.

233 **Richard Lindon of Rugby:** Historical details to be found on www.richardlindon.com.

234 **Fourteen managers from 10 professional teams:** Robert Peterson, *Pigskin*, p. 69.

238 **70 percent of the world's stitched soccer balls:** From laborrights.org.

241 **Frederick Winslow Taylor:** Taylor, *The Principles of Scientific Management*.

241 **"managerial and technocratic perspective":** Michael Oriard, *Reading Football*, p. 37.

242 **When his teammates twice bucked his strategy:** John Sayle Watterson, *College Football*, p. 19.

243 **"A scrimmage takes place":** *Football: The American Intercollegiate Game*, p. 468.

243 **"What is, therefore, in the English game":** Walter Camp, *American Football*, pp. 9–10.

245 **"so disgusted spectators":** Camp, cited in Bernstein, *Football: The Ivy League Origins of an American Obsession*, pp. 19–20.

245 **"If on three consecutive fairs and downs":** Davis, *Football: The American Intercollegiate Game*, p. 470.

246 **"Division of labor . . . has been so thoroughly":** Walter Camp, "The Game and Laws of American Football," cited in Guttmann, *Sports: The First Five Millennia*.

248 **In 1884, Wyllys Terry of Yale:** Bernstein, *Football: The Ivy League Origins of an American Obsession*, p. 22.

249 **his take-no-prisoners play:** McQuilkin and Smith, "The Rise and Fall of the Flying Wedge."

250 **"No sticky or greasy substance":** Davis, *Football: The American Intercollegiate Game*, pp. 96–97.

251 **"is no longer a solemn festival":** Cited in Oriard, *Reading Football*, p. 93.

252 **"Captain Frank Ranken of the Montauk football team":** Cited in Marc S. Maltby, *The Origins and Early Development of Professional Football*, p. 26.

253 **Charles Eliot, Harvard's president:** Watterson, *College Football*, p. 30.

255 **"playing baby on the field":** Maltby, *The Origins and Early Development of Professional Football*, p. 28.

255 **Roosevelt was a fan of rough sports:** Watterson, *College Football*, pp. 64–65.

256 **"Out of heroism grows faith":** Bernstein, *Football: The Ivy League Origins of an American Obsession*, p. 38.

256 **"not soft but honest":** Maltby, *The Origins and Early Development of Professional Football*, p. 33.

257 **"I believe that the human body":** *New York Times*, Dec. 11, 1905, cited in Watterson, *College Football*, p. 76.

257 **As early as 1894:** Guttmann, *Sports*, p. 145.

257 **The purpose of the rules that emerged:** "The New Game of Football," *New York Times*, Sept. 30, 1906.

258 **Passes could only be thrown from five yards:** Bernstein, *Football: The Ivy League Origins of an American Obsession*, p. 85.

259 **Amos Alonzo Stagg claimed:** Allison Danzig, *The History of American Football*, p. 37.

259 **"It shall be tightly inflated":** Oriard, *King Football*, p. 132.

259 **"throwing laterals is an attempt":** Ibid., p. 331.

260 **"In the past it was a style of ball":** Ben McGrath, "Does Football Have a Future?," p. 47.

260 **According to Timothy Gay:** "Football Physics: Anatomy of a Hit," *Popular Mechanics*, Dec. 18, 2009.

262 **at a turning point in the safety debate:** "Game Changers," *Bostonia*, Fall 2010.

263 **"lay a pillow down":** *New York Times*, February 3, 2011.

264 **"competing desires for danger and safety":** Oriard, *King Football*, p. 335.

264   **perhaps even its "special glory":** Guttmann, *From Ritual to Record*, p. 118.

8: Nothing New Under the Sun

267   **"When it's played the way":** John Edgar Wideman, "Michael Jordan Leaps the Great Divide," *Esquire*, Nov. 1990.

268   **Naismith felt their pain:** Unless otherwise indicated, all quotes from James Naismith are from his book, *Basketball: Its Origin and Development*.

269   **"a competitive game, like football":** Rob Rains, James Naismith, p. 32.

272   **"The fewer players down to three":** James Naismith, *The Triangle*, Jan. 15, 1892.

274   **The first players to "post up":** Robert W. Peterson, *Cages to Jump Shots*, p. 41.

274   **"The ball was four pieces of leather":** Ibid., p. 49.

276   **"the game must remain":** Ibid., p. 37.

281   **"People see [the Square]" and other Aaron Williams quotes:** *The Republican*, July 18, 2010.

283   **"all that I know most surely":** Mandelbaum, *The Meaning of Sports*, p. 210.

284   **"These young guys were staying":** Phone interview with Harry Rock, director of YMCA Relations, Springfield College, May 11, 2011.

285   **"To win men for the Master":** James Naismith, from his original application to the YMCA Training School, Springfield College Archives.

286   **"Many business men at forty are fat and flabby":** YMCA source materials provided by Harry Rock.

290   **"Ruck," as he was known:** Nelson George, *Elevating the Game*, pp. 72–78.

301 **"cleared the lane"**: Ron Thomas, *They Cleared the Lane.*

302 **"She was smart and attractive"**: Ralph Melnick, *Senda Berenson*, p. 33.

302 **"Many of our young women"**: Pamela Grundy and Susan Shackleford, Shattering the Glass, p. 10.

303 **the idea that girls and women could withstand**: Grundy and Shackleford.

304 **"the so-called ideal woman"**: Melnick, p. 23.

304 **"Now that the woman's sphere"**: Senda Berenson, "The Significance of Basket Ball for Women."

304 **she posted a note on the outer door**: Melnick, p. 1

306 **Early teams captured this feeling**: Grundy and Shackleford, p. 19.

307 **"Gentlemen, if you attempt to do away"**: Ibid., p. 47.

307 **The SPHAs . . . got their start**: Peterson, *Cages to Jump Shots.*

309 **"Everywhere you looked, all you saw was concrete"**: Mandelbaum, *The Meaning of Sports*, p. 241.

309 **New York Renaissance Big Five**: Kareem Abdul-Jabbar, *On the Shoulders of Giants*, pp. 137–176.

310 **During those Jim Crow days**: Peterson, *Cages to Jump Shots*, p. 96.

311 **Douglas later estimated**: Thomas, *They Cleared the Lane*, p. 9.

311 **"slept in jails because they wouldn't put us up"**: Abdul-Jabbar, p. 162.

311 **When their manager protested an unfair call**: Ibid., p. 160.

312 **The two all-black barnstorming teams**: Abdul-Jabbar.

313 **"Naismith believed you can do"**: George, *Elevating the Game*, p. 86.

316 **In his recorded remarks, President Obama**: "Obama Hosts Dinner for Islamic Holy Month," Associated Press, Sept. 2, 2009.

Epilogue: Back to Basics

323 **United is, after all:** "More than Manchester," *Time*, May 28, 2011.

326 **I knew several Amazonian tribes had once played games:** Theodore Stern, *The Rubber-Ball Games of the Americas*, pp. 8–9.

327 **and two soccer balls:** www.lossoberanos.com/evidencia.

Selected Bibliography

Abdul-Jabbar, Kareem, with Raymond Obstfeld. *On the Shoulders of Giants: My Journey Through the Harlem Renaissance*. New York: Simon & Schuster, 2007.

Ackerman, Diane. *Deep Play*. New York: Vintage Books, 1999.

Azoy, G. Whitney. *Buzkashi: Game and Power in Afghanistan*. Long Grove, IL: Waveland Press, 2003.

Baker, William J. *Sports in the Western World*. Urbana and Chicago: University of Illinois Press, 1988.

Beals, Ralph L. *The Acaxee: A Mountain Tribe of Durango and Sinaloa*. Berkeley: University of California Press, 1933.

Beers, George W. *Lacrosse: The National Game of Canada*. Montreal: Dawson, 1869.

Bekoff, Marc. "Social Play and Social Morality." In *Encyclopedia of Animal Behavior*. Westport, CT: Greenwood Press, 2004.

Benavente, Toribio de. *Historia de los Indios de la Nueva Espana*. Mexico City: Editorial Porrúa, 1956.

Berenson, Senda. "The Significance of Basket Ball for Women." In *Women and Sports in the United States: A Documentary Reader*. Jean O'Reilly and Susan K. Cahn, eds. Boston: Northeastern University Press, 2007.

Bernstein, Mark F. *Football: The Ivy League Origins of an American Obsession*. Philadelphia: University of Pennsylvania Press, 2001.

Blanchard, Kendall. *The Anthropology of Sport: An Introduction.* Westport, CT: Greenwood Press. 1995.

Block, David. *Baseball Before We Knew It: A Search for the Roots of the Game.* Lincoln: University of Nebraska Press, 2005.

Brown, Stuart. *Play: How It Shapes the Brain, Opens the Imagination, and Invigorates the Soul.* New York: Avery, 2009.

Caillois, Roger. *Man, Play and Games.* Urbana and Chicago: University of Illinois Press, 2001.

Calvin, William H. *The Throwing Madonna: Essays on the Brain.* New York: McGraw-Hill, 1983.

Camp, Walter. *American Football.* New York: Harper & Brothers, 1891.

_____. *Football Facts and Figures: A Symposium of Expert Opinions on the Game's Place in American Athletics.* New York: Harper & Brothers, 1894.

Carlier, Yves, and Thierry Bernard-Tambour. *Jeu des Rois, Roi des Jeux: Le Jeu de Paume en France.* Musée National du Château de Fontainebleau, 2001.

Cooper, Jerold S. "Buddies in Babylonia: Gilgamesh, Enkidu, and Mesopotamian Homosexuality." In *Riches Hidden in Secret Places: Ancient Near Eastern Studies in Memory of Thorkild Jacobsen,* ed. by Tzvi Abusch. Winona Lake, IN: Eisenbrauns, 2002.

Culin, Stewart. *Games of the North American Indians.* New York: Dover, 1975.

Danzig, Allison. *The History of American Football: Its Great Teams, Players, and Coaches.* New York: Prentice-Hall, 1956.

Davis, Parke H. *Football: The American Intercollegiate Game.* New York: Charles Scribner's Sons, 1911.

Decker, Wolfgang. *Sports and Games of Ancient Egypt.* New Haven, CT: Yale University Press, 1992.

Dewey, Donald. "The Danish Professor and Baseball." *Scandinavian Review,* Summer 2006.

Díaz del Castillo, Bernal. *The Discovery and Conquest of Mexico, 1517–1521.* Edited by Genaro Garcia. London: Routledge, 1928.

Dickson, Paul. *The New Dickson Baseball Dictionary.* New York: Harcourt Brace, 1999.

Dohrmann, George. *Play Their Hearts Out: A Coach, His Star Recruit, and the Youth Basketball Machine.* New York: Ballantine Books, 2010.

Duran, Fray Diego. *Book of the Gods and Rites and the Ancient Calendar.* Translated by Fernando Horcasitas and Doris Heyden. Norman: University of Oklahoma Press, 1971.

Feldman, David. *When Do Fish Sleep? And Other Imponderables of Everyday Life.* New York: Harper & Row, 1989.

Fischer, Anthony L. *The Game of Pallone From Its Origin to the Present Day, Historically Considered.* London: Bell and Daldy, 1865.

Fisher, Donald M. *Lacrosse: A History of the Game.* Baltimore, MD: Johns Hopkins University Press, 2002.

Fox, John. "Playing with Power: Ballcourts and Political Ritual in Southern Mesoamerica." *Current Anthropology* 37, no. 3 (1996): 483–509.

_____. "Students of the Game: Archaeologists Are Researching Ulama—Oldest Sport in the Americas." *Smithsonian*, April 2006.

Gardner, Percy. *Catalogue of the Greek Vases in the Ashmolean Museum.* Oxford: Clarendon Press, 1893.

Garsault, François-Alexandre de. L'art du paumier-raquetier et de la paume. Descriptions des arts et métiers, faites ou approuvées par messieurs de l'Académie royale des sciences. Paris, 1767.

George, Nelson. *Elevating the Game: Black Men and Basketball.* New York: HarperCollins, 1992.

Gillmeister, Heiner. *Tennis: A Cultural History.* New York: New York University Press, 1998.

Goldblatt, David. *The Ball Is Round: A Global History of Soccer*. New York: Riverhead Books, 2008.

Goldstein, Warren. *Playing for Keeps: A History of Early Baseball*. Ithaca, NY: Cornell University Press, 1989.

Gould, Stephen Jay. "The Creation Myths of Cooperstown." *Natural History*, November 1989.

Gould, Todd. *Pioneers of the Hardwood: Indiana and the Birth of Professional Basketball*. Bloomington and Indianapolis: Indiana University Press, 1998.

Grundy, Pamela, and Susan Shackleford. *Shattering the Glass: The Remarkable History of Women's Basketball*. New York and London: The New Press, 2005.

Guttmann, Allen. *From Ritual to Record: The Nature of Modern Sports*. New York: Columbia University Press, 1978.

_____. *Sports: The First Five Millennia*. Amherst: University of Massachusetts Press, 2004.

Harris, H. A. *Sport in Greece and Rome*. Ithaca, NY: Cornell University Press, 1972.

Henderson, Robert W. *Ball, Bat and Bishop: The Origin of Ball Games*. Urbana and Chicago: University of Illinois Press, 1947.

Hill, Dean. *Football Thru the Years*. New York: Gridiron Publishing, 1940.

Hughes, Thomas. *Tom Brown's Schooldays*. London: MacMillan and Co., 1882.

Huizinga, Johan. *Homo Ludens: A Study of the Play Element in Modern Culture*. New York: Routledge, 2007.

James, William. *The Principles of Psychology*, vol. 2. New York: Henry Holt & Co., 1890.

Juster, F. Thomas, Frank Stafford, and Hiromi Ono. "Changing Times of American Youth: 1981–2003." Institute of Social Research, University of Michigan, 2004.

Kirsch, George B. *The Creation of American Team Sports: Baseball and Cricket, 1838–72*. Urbana: University of Illinois Press, 1989.

Krznaric, Roman. *The First Beautiful Game: Stories of Obsession in Real Tennis*. Oxford, UK: Ronaldson Publications, 2006.

Lee, Richard. "What Hunters Do for a Living, or, How to Make Out on Scarce Resources." In *Man the Hunter*, eds. Richard Lee and Irven Devore. New York: Aldine, 1968.

Levine, Peter. *A. G. Spalding and the Rise of Baseball*. New York: Oxford University Press, 1985.

Leyenaar, Ted. "The Modern Ballgames of Sinaloa: A Survival of the Aztec Ullamaliztli." In *The Sport of Life and Death: The Mesoamerican Ballgame*, ed. E. Michael Whittington. London: Thames & Hudson, 2001.

MacCambridge, Michael. *America's Game: The Epic Story of How Pro Football Captured a Nation*. New York: Random House, 2004.

Magoun, Francis Peabody, Jr. *History of Football from the Beginnings to 1871*. Bochum, Germany: H. Pöppinghaus, 1938.

Maltby, Marc S. *The Origins and Early Development of Professional Football*. New York and London: Garland Publishing, 1997.

Mandelbaum, Michael. *The Meaning of Sports: Why Americans Watch Baseball, Football, and Basketball and What They See When They Do*. New York: Public Affairs, 2004.

Marino, Lori. "Convergence of Complex Cognitive Abilities in Cetaceans and Primates." *Brain, Behavior and Evolution* 59, 2002.

Marples, Morris. *A History of Football*. London: Secker & Warburg, 1954.

Marshall, Julian. *The Annals of Tennis*. London: Strand, 1878.

Mártir de Anglería, Pedro. *Décadas del Nuevo Mundo. Colección de Fuentes para la Historia de América*. Buenos Aires: Editorial Bajel, 1944.

McGrath, Ben. "Does Football Have a Future? The NFL and the Concussion Crisis." *The New Yorker*, January 31, 2011.

McLean, Teresa. *The English at Play in the Middle Ages.* New York: HarperCollins, 1985.

McQuilikin, Scott A., and Ronald A. Smith. "The Rise and Fall of the Flying Wedge: Football's Most Controversial Play." *Journal of Sport History* 20, no. 1 (Spring 1993).

Melnick, Ralph. *Senda Berenson: The Unlikely Founder of Women's Basketball.* Amherst: University of Massachusetts Press, 2007.

Miller, Mary Ellen. "The Maya Ballgame: Rebirth in the Court of Life and Death." In *The Sport of Life and Death: The Mesoamerican Ballgame,* ed. E. Michael Whittington. London: Thames & Hudson, 2001.

Miller, Stephen J. *Arete: Greek Sports from Ancient Sources.* Berkeley: University of California Press, 2004.

Mills, Dorothy Seymour. *Chasing Baseball: Our Obsession with Its History, Numbers, People and Places.* Jefferson, NC: McFarland & Co., 2010.

Morris, Peter. *A Game of Inches: The Stories Behind the Innovations That Shaped Baseball.* Chicago: Ivan R. Dee, 2006.

Nadal, Laura F. "Rubber and Rubber Balls in Mesoamerica." In *The Sport of Life and Death: The Mesoamerican Ballgame,* ed. E. Michael Whittington. London: Thames & Hudson, 2001.

Naismith, James. *Basketball: Its Origin and Development.* New York: Association Press, 1941.

Neils, Jennifer, et al. *Coming of Age in Ancient Greece: Images of Childhood from the Classical Past.* New Haven, CT: Yale University Press, 2003.

Newsome, Elizabeth A. *Trees of Paradise and Pillars of the World: The Serial Stela Cycle of 18 Rabbit-God K, King of Copan.* Austin: University of Texas Press, 2001.

Oriard, Michael. *Reading Football: How the Popular Press Created an American Spectacle.* Chapel Hill: University of North Carolina Press, 1993.

————. *King Football: Sport and Spectacle in the Golden Age of*

Newsreels, Movies and Magazine, the Weekly and the Daily Press. Chapel Hill and London: University of North Carolina Press, 2001.

Paolantonio, Sal. *How Football Explains America*. Chicago: Triumph, 2008.

Peterson, Robert W. *Cages to Jump Shots: Pro Basketball's Early Years*. New York and Oxford: Oxford University Press, 1990.

————. *Pigskin: The Early Years of Pro Football*. New York and Oxford: Oxford University Press, 1997.

Rains, Rob. *James Naismith: The Man Who Invented Basketball*. Philadelphia: Temple University Press, 2009.

Robertson, John D. M. *The Kirkwall Ba': Between the Water and the Wall*. Edinburgh, UK: Dunedin Academic Press, 2005.

Sahagún, Bernardino de. *Primeros Memoriales*. Paleography of Nahuatl Text and English Translation by Thelma D. Sullivan; Completed and Revised, with Additions, by H. B. Nicholson. Norman: University of Oklahoma Press, 1997.

Sahlins, Marshall. *Stone Age Economics*. New York: Aldine, 1972.

Stern, Theodore. *The Rubber-Ball Games of the Americas*. Monographs of the American Ethnological Society 17. New York: J. J. Augustin, 1950.

Tarkanian, Michael J., and Dorothy Hosler. "An Ancient Tradition Continued: Modern Rubber Processing in Mexico." In *The Sport of Life and Death: The Mesoamerican Ballgame*, ed. E. Michael Whittington. London: Thames & Hudson, 2001.

Taylor, Frederick Winslow. *The Principles of Scientific Management*. New York: Harper & Bros., 1911.

Tedlock, Dennis. *Popol Vuh: The Mayan Book of the Dawn of Life*. Translated by Dennis Tedlock, with commentary based on the ancient knowledge of the modern Quiché Maya. New York: Simon and Schuster, 1985.

Thomas, Ron. *They Cleared the Lane: The NBA's Black Pioneers*. Lincoln and Nebraska: University of Nebraska Press, 2002.

Tordesillas, Antonio de Herrera. *Historia General de los Hechos de los Castellanos en Las Islas y Tierra Firme del Mar Océano.* Madrid: Tipografía de Archivos, 1934.

Traubel, Horace. *With Walt Whitman in Camden.* New York: Rowman and Littlefield, 1961.

Vennum, Thomas, Jr. *American Indian Lacrosse: Little Brother of War.* Washington, DC: Smithsonian Institution Press, 1994.

Watterson, John Sayle. *College Football: History, Spectacle, Controversy.* Baltimore, MD, and London: Johns Hopkins University Press, 2000.

Whitman, Malcolm D. *Tennis Origins and Mysteries.* New York: Derrydale Press, 1932.

Wideman, John Edgar. "Michael Jordan Leaps the Great Divide." *Esquire,* November 1990, 21.

Illustration Credits

119   The ancient Maya ball court at Cobá, Mexico. Wikimedia Commons 27527.

123   Ulama player holding ball. Copyright © Janet Jarman (www .janetjarman.com).

125   Ulama player striking ball. Copyright © Janet Jarman (www .janetjarman.com).

130-1 Late Classic Maya polychrome vase, St. Louis Art Museum (K5435). Copyright © Justin Kerr.

147   "Ball Play of the Choctaw—Ball Up, 1846-50," George Catlin (1796–1872). Courtesy of Smithsonian American Art Museum/Art Resource, NY.

153   Onondaga Lacrosse Team, ca. 1902. Courtesy of Onondaga Historical Association, NY.

165   Photograph of Alf Jacques. Courtesy of *The Post Standard*/ John Berry.

181   Leaves from *The Ghistelles Calendar*, Flemish, ca. 1301, parchment with ink and paint. Copyright © The Walters Art Museum, Baltimore.

183   "A Little Pretty Pocket-Book—The little k Play." Courtesy of Lilly Library, Indiana University, Bloomington, Indiana.

198   Vintage baseball in Washington, D.C. Courtesy of John Fox.

235   Ada, Ohio, high school football stadium. Courtesy of John Fox.

239   Footballs ready to be "turned" at the Wilson Football Factory in Ada, Ohio. Courtesy of John Fox.

252   "Out of the Game," Harper's Weekly, 1891. From Dean Hill, *Football Thru the Years*. New York: Gridiron Publishing.

258   "Football of the Future," Harper's Weekly, November, 1889. From Dean Hill, *Football Thru the Years*. New York: Gridiron Publishing.

273   Spalding basketball advertisement, 1894. Courtesy of Springfield College, Babson Library, Archives and Special Collections.

276 Early basketball action, ca. 1910. Courtesy of Springfield College, Babson Library, Archives and Special Collections.

297 Photograph of Bilqis Abdul-Qaadir. Copyright © Getty Images.

305 "Ball about to be tossed up at centre," with Senda Berenson officiating at a Smith College basketball game, 1903. From the 1903 edition of *Basket Ball for Women*. Courtesy of Smith College Archives.

Index

Page numbers in *italics* refer to illustrations.

About the author

About the book

Read on

Insights,
Interviews
& More . . .

Meet John Fox

JOHN FOX WAS BORN AND RAISED in the Inwood section of New York City. The apartment building where he grew up was built on the site of a 500-year old Lenape Indian village. Seventy years before he was born, when the rolling farmland of Manhattan's northern shores first gave way to paved streets on a grid, ceremonially interred dog carcasses had been uncovered on his corner, just a few paces from where home base was traced in chalk for neighborhood stickball games.

When he wasn't playing sports, John could often be found with a pack of friends exploring the Indian rock shelters tucked just above the Gaelic football field in Inwood Hill Park. The occasional pottery shard or arrowhead fragment lay just beneath the artifacts left by partying teens: mostly beer bottles and cigarette butts.

© Darlene DeVita

John left for college in Boston, where he received a B.A. in archaeology from Boston University. As an undergrad, he did fieldwork at a Roman village in the south of England, a 5,000-year-old cave in New Mexico, and a 19th-century millhouse in Massachusetts. Hooked on the past, he went on to pursue his Ph.D. in anthropology at Harvard University, where he specialized in the ancient Maya civilization. Over multiple seasons, he conducted field research in the wilds of Honduras, excavating ancient ball courts in an attempt to better understand the meaning and symbolism of the rubber ball game of *ulama* played by the Maya and neighboring civilizations. His articles interpreting this game were published in peer-reviewed journals and remain required reading for students of the subject.

After receiving his Ph.D. and teaching at both of his alma maters, John left academia to join a groundbreaking online adventure learning program called the Quests. From 1998 to 2003, he co-led a team of explorers, biologists, photographers, videographers, and multimedia artists on 10 educational expeditions across six continents. An online audience of about a million students and teachers, in 120 countries, logged on daily to set the course of the expedition.

Traveling by bicycle, canoe, and the occasional camel, he and his team explored some of the world's most extraordinary places along with some of its greatest historical and scientific mysteries—human origins in the Rift Valley, the collapse of the ancient Maya civilization, Marco Polo's fabled route across China, and the threatened tribes and wildlife of the Amazon rainforest, to name just a few.

The Quests won multiple educational awards and were cited by a congressional committee led by Senator John Glenn as a premier example of quality online learning. John appeared live on *Good Morning America* with Diane Sawyer from the top of a Maya temple. His field reports, many of which were syndicated at the time on CNN.com, were published in 2008 in his collection, *Around the World with a Million Kids: Adventures of an Online Explorer.*

He has written articles for *Outside, Smithsonian, Salon,* and other publications, and has been a regular commentator on sports and culture for Vermont Public Radio. In 2010, John was awarded a fellowship to the MacDowell Colony.

John lives just outside Boston with his wife, Stephanie; their children, Amelia and Aidan; and their half retriever, Eliot, who only half retrieves balls. ∾

A Conversation with John Fox

What made you decide to focus the book on the ball?

Aside from the fact that the ball is the most fascinating and least written about object ever invented? Well, my research on the ancient Maya ball game really got me hooked on the cultural dimensions of sport and play—this area of human behavior that, on the one hand, is totally frivolous and, on the other, is an essential part of the human experience. Looking at the Maya, it seemed crazy that a rubber ball game, of all things, could have been so important over thousands of years—important enough for it to be part of their genesis story and written about by kings. But then I thought of our present civilization, and it struck me that, really, it's the same story a thousand years later in a completely different place and culture. And at the center of it all is the ball.

As I write in the prologue, it was my son's innocent question that really sparked in me the desire to write this book. I knew then that I needed to go out and explore his question, firsthand, with the same playful spirit of curiosity and wonder in which it was asked. As an archaeologist by training, it made sense to me to focus on the *thing* at the center of it all, the object of play. When you're excavating an ancient site, the artifacts and other physical remains you uncover are often all that's left, and it's your job to piece them together until they tell a story about the past. Once I dug into the topic, however, I realized there was actually a treasure trove of history just waiting to be uncovered.

Having traveled the world in order to examine mankind's elemental attraction to the ball, did you return home with a favorite ball game?

Well, I came home with the same favorite game I left with: basketball. One of the things I learned in my research and travels is that sports work on us on many deep levels—from the neurological to the patriotic to the nostalgic. So a favorite ballgame is a personal thing, and I bet if you ask anyone that question you'll learn a lot about them from the answer. For me, it's basketball. It was the sport I played the most as a kid, so it still reminds me of hot summer days hanging out with my friends at my neighborhood park in New York City. Now it's my son's favorite game, so naturally his newfound passion for it has rekindled my own—there's a generational connection there.

One of the things I love about basketball is its simplicity: a round bouncing ball, a hoop to throw it in. That's all you need to play. I love that it's a team sport and a passing game, but it also has that element of flash and individual style, showmanship and buzzer-beating heroics. Studying the history of basketball's invention and spread only deepened my appreciation for the game. As the most recent major ball game to appear, and the only one invented wholesale, it drew from every game that came before it. Naismith and Gulick really put a lot of thought and craft into shaping the game and making it accessible and universal. It's no surprise that, unlike the other big American sports—football and baseball—basketball has in record time become a truly global game.

How did you choose which sports—and which balls—to write about?

Even though there's a lot of history in this book, it was never my goal to write a global history of sports or ball games. That's a much bigger and very different undertaking than what I set out to do. First and foremost, I wanted to explore the question of why we play the games we play today, to get to the heart of those games and examine their roots. To do that, I knew I needed to look at the evolution of balls and ball play through time and provide the broadest view possible. So I chose sports that I felt best defined and reflected particular moments in history and at the same time revealed universal aspects of play.

Take tennis, for example. In a sense, tennis reached its peak of cultural relevance around the year 1600 and lost steam after that. It was *the* sport of the Renaissance and really elevated sport to a new level of importance in European society. You can see that just in the number of references to tennis that appear in Shakespeare's writings and other literature of the age. On a more universal level, the story of tennis reflects the way the games we play can signal our position in ▶

society. Tennis was branded an elite sport early on and, despite efforts to rebrand it, has never been embraced, like soccer, as a sport of the people.

Similarly, *ulama* exposes the symbolic and religious dimension of sport—that in ancient times, and to some extent still today, games were ceremonial rites. The *ulama* and lacrosse stories remind us that the ball was not invented in one place and spread from there but rather was invented in parallel by many different civilizations. I love the image of tennis-playing Frenchmen arriving in the wilds of North America to encounter Indians playing their own game with a racket and ball—lacrosse! The story of baseball gets at the link between sports and national identity, while American football offers a window into the role of violence in sports. And so on.

Aside from* ulama, *did you come across other games—even ones that didn't make it into the book—that are on the brink of extinction?

Yes, I came across several traditions in Mexico alone in fact. At the time of the Spanish conquest, *ulama* was just one of hundreds of ball games being played by indigenous groups there. Some of them died off or were killed off early, but quite a few still hang on. One of the most unusual, *pelota purépecha*, is still played by around 800 people in the state of Michoacán. Two teams armed with oak sticks attempt to score goals with a ball made of twine and cotton rags that's been doused in fuel and lit on fire. I've seen it described as a kind of field hockey for pyromaniacs! They often play at night, and all you can see is this blazing orb streaking across the night sky. So cool.

Another pre-Columbian game, *pelota mixteca*, is a kind of handball played in Oaxaca with a small rubber ball covered with a suede lining. Players in teams of five pound the solid ball back and forth with an elaborately decorated 10-pound leather glove. Although the number of players has dwindled over time, the game is still played in Mexico as well as by immigrants in U.S. communities such as Fresno, Fort Worth, and East Los Angeles.

What's great is that the Mexican Sports Federation has actually focused a lot of attention and money recently on preserving these games. They're building a pre-Hispanic sports center in Mexico City, printing rule books for ancient games, and offering seminars in schools to try to get young people interested. The jury's still out on whether they'll be successful, but most kids I know would leap at the chance to play hockey with a flaming ball!

The ancient ball games you write about, and even games like ulama that are still played, are heavy in symbolism. Do our contemporary ball games—baseball, basketball, and American football (all of which you address)—reflect any latent cultural symbolism that some anthropologist hundreds of years from now might be interested in?

Certainly in our secular age sports no longer have the overt religious symbolism and ceremony of earlier times. We don't tend to offer sacrifices before or after important games, for example, or regard the outcome of a game as determining future weather patterns or harvests. But there's still a lot of symbolism wrapped up in our modern games. Baseball, for example, is steeped in superstition. There's the Curse of the Bambino, of course, which I'm almost certain is back with a vengeance after the Red Sox's inexplicable and catastrophic collapse at the end of the 2011 season. Also, batters and pitchers have any number of bizarre rites they perform on the plate or mound to ensure success, such as tugging sleeves, clapping hands, tapping bats on the ground a set number of times. Lots of players won't step on the foul lines coming on or off the field. Some players, reinforcing an ancient male superstition, will even abstain from sex on game days.

One of my favorite stories is of the construction worker who in 2008, hoping to curse the Yankees for years to come, buried a David Ortiz shirt under the new Yankees Stadium as it was being built. When the Yankees got a tip about it, they brought in a crew to jackhammer through three feet of concrete and the Yankees president presided over what he called an "excavation ceremony" to remove the shirt and any black magic it might have unleashed. The story reminds me of the Aztec who buried caches of jade and other symbolic offerings inside ball courts when they were built to imbue them with magical powers.

Then there's American football. I'll never forget a game I attended in 2009 at Buckeyes Stadium between Ohio State and Navy. Navy hadn't played in the stadium since 1931, so it was a big deal. Following "The Star-Spangled Banner," there was an F-18 flyover and recorded greetings on the scoreboard from military personnel stationed in Afghanistan. For the grand finale, the marching band performed their "script Ohio" ceremony, and former astronaut and U.S. senator John Glenn showed up as the honorary guest to dot the *i*. The entire experience was a kind of nationalistic spectacle affirming U.S. military strength in a time of war. No one seemed to question why such a rite would precede a ball game. It seemed entirely natural—like part of the game. ▶

A Conversation with John Fox *(continued)*

What do you think the future of the ball might be? Will we still be bouncing and kicking them thousands of years from now?

I'm no futurist and am way more comfortable in the past, but I'm pretty confident that the ball will still be kicking, or being kicked, around for a very long time. Obviously, there's been a trend toward the virtualization of play and there is definitely some cause for alarm as more and more kids spend their time plugged in and detached from the physical world. I'm no Luddite, and I believe the studies that indicate that kids playing *Madden NFL* or *NBA 2K12* are still playing, or at least their brains are playing. But we're physical beings who need to move our bodies now and then to maintain at least a modicum of mental and physical health. And there's really nothing like a plain old ball to engage our bodies and minds completely.

An interesting study was done recently looking at what happens to our brains while watching sports. The study showed that about one-fifth of the neurons in our pre-motor cortex that fire when we perform an action, say kicking a ball, also fire when we watch someone else do it. So in a very real way, our brains are *in* the game even when we're just watching. But that's still an 80 percent gap in brain activity—not to mention the 100 percent gap in physical activity—between actually playing a sport and just watching it.

In terms of the ball itself, I do think we'll continue to see it evolve in interesting ways. Some researchers at Carnegie Mellon University have been developing a "smart football" which contains a tiny GPS and accelerometer to continuously measure the location and speed of the ball. Aside from potentially taking some of the guesswork out of refereeing plays, the developers see applications for training players. With smart balls and gloves, for example, a quarterback can get real-time data on how he's throwing and make adjustments to improve precision. But even the most high-tech balls will still be subject to the quirks of physics and human error. The Adidas "jabulani" soccer ball used during the 2010 World Cup was a thing to behold with only eight (down from 14 in the previous World Cup) spherically molded panels and a "Grip 'n' Groove" surface technology designed to make the ball more aerodynamic. Despite such advances, the ball was widely criticized by players and was even blamed for low-scoring games in the first round of competition. Brazilian striker Luis Fabiano decried the ball as having supernatural powers because it changed direction in midair. Portugal, which beat North Korea 7-0 with it, thought it was just perfect. ∾

What About Bocce?
An Outtake from
The Ball

WHEN I WAS RESEARCHING the murky origins of ball games, I wanted to find a truly primitive game, still being played, that in an earlier form might conceivably have killed our ancestor's boredom between hunts. So naturally I thought of bocce, a Paleolithic game if ever there was one. For the deprived and uninitiated, bocce is played by two teams of three to six players on a narrow 60-foot-long alley. At the start, a round yellow stone ball called the *pallino* is thrown toward the other end of the court to start the game. Each team then takes turns rolling larger stone balls down the alley in an attempt to get them as close to the *pallino* as possible, displacing the competitor's balls to secure the best position.

An Italian game that became popular in the early days of the Roman Empire, bocce was then spread by Roman soldiers to France, where it is became *boules* (and the popular contemporary game of *pétanque*), and to England, where it developed into "bowls," or lawn bowling. The game in its many manifestations became hugely popular in villages across Europe through the Middle Ages—so popular that, like football, it was repeatedly banned for distracting the peasantry from archery practice.

Armed with this admittedly thin historical background, I decided to explore the game in all of its primitive glory and find out what's kept it popular for all these centuries. Although I could have just dropped in on one of the regular Saturday matches on the waterfront in Boston's Italian North End, that seemed ▶

What About Bocce? *(continued)*

far too easy. In my research, I encountered an "extreme bocce" movement that was attempting to bust the game loose from the confines of the traditional alley. I corresponded with a guy in Oregon who organized weekend matches on open mountain trails in the Cascades. And I talked to some hipsters who played an urban version on the streets, skate parks, and empty lots of Brooklyn.

Intrigued as I was by the extreme bocce angle, I decided to follow a more traditional course and cover the World Series of Bocce, held each July in Rome—Rome, New York.

Rome is a gritty, industrial city that straddles the Erie Canal 90 miles west of Albany. The Toccolana Club, located just down the street from an olive oil bottling plant and a steel plate factory, is a dedicated bocce facility with 15 indoor and outdoor courts that has hosted the World Series for more than 30 years. Started by Rome's mayor back in 1973 as a way to promote the city's Italian heritage and bring in tourists, the World Series has never quite lived up to its international name. But neither has baseball's World Series, locals happily point out.

"Hey, we've got Canadians here," said Pete Corigliano, 78, one of the event's organizers. "Last time I checked that was another country."

When I arrived at the facility, Pete's team, Corigliano Insurance, was battling Anger Management in an early round of competition. Even in the shade of corrugated metal shed roofs, players mopped their brows with handkerchiefs, trying to stay cool in the 90-degree heat.

"Good ball, Frankie!" yelled Pete as his teammate, an expert point man, gently curved his ball through a warren until it hugged the *pallino*.

"Kiss it!" shrieked an elderly lady with a bouffant hairdo from her folding chair.

Pete's father came from Calabria, Italy, where the family had a bocce court in the backyard. "My father and his friends would play all day in the shade of grapevines, drinking wine, arguing politics," he said. "It was a social thing. Still is."

Beer seems to be the choice of bocce players these days. The Toccolana Club goes through 20 to 25 kegs each year, the club owner told me—and a similarly impressive volume of sausage and pepper hoagies.

In search of shade, I made my way to the club's indoor courts, where Donna Ciotta and her Liquor Express team were on their usual winning streak. Donna and team, her son boasted, are the proud holders of the Guinness World Record for "Most Wins of the World Series of Bocce (Female Team)," having taken home the tournament's prize money nine times over a 20-year stretch. On the next court over, Barton's

Place Quality Assisted Living was living up to their team motto, emblazoned on their T-shirts: "I Don't Sweat You!"

To be honest, I'd never taken bocce seriously as a sport. Like croquet and horseshoes, it always seemed like a social activity designed to keep your other hand occupied while drinking beer. That was until I met Dr. Angel Cordano, a pediatrician with an elegantly trimmed beard who has teamed up with his son and grandson. Angel was born in Genoa, Italy, but immigrated to Peru as a young man, playing for years on that country's national bocce team. He then came to the United States and joined the national federation team. For Angel, bocce, when it's played well, is a demanding sport.

"If you are not in shape, forget it," he cautioned, patting his trim stomach. He and his family team practice 12 hours a week on a court behind their home in Naples, Florida. Although he makes the long trek to Rome every year, and enjoys the field of competitors the tournament draws, he's less than impressed with both the conditions and the quality of play.

"This court is for pasture, not for bocce!" he complained after a carefully placed ball veered suspiciously into the back corner. "Play this side, add five yards; play that side, take away five yards!"

His team having lost position, Angel directed his son to rearrange the field with a well-placed "spock." He wound up and whipped a fastball down court, blasting his opponent's well-placed ball away from the *pallino*.

Angel wistfully recalled the level of professionalism and competition of his Federation days, mocking the casual style of play that passes for bocce here in the wrong Rome.

"There's no finesse here," he said, shaking his head and gesturing to the courts around him. "It's like the difference between checkers and chess."

But everyone—young and old, family and old friends—seemed to be having a great time. The beer was flowing, clouds of sausage smoke wafted through the air. In the beer line, I ran into Al Cerra, who's been coming every year for nearly 25 years. Al offered a different philosophy on the game.

"The beauty of bocce is anyone can play. All you have to be able to do is roll a ball. That's why it's universally loved."

He paused and corrected himself: "Actually, my wife hates it. But you can't please everyone." ෴

Recommended Reading

MY TASTES IN SPORTSWRITING skew, predictably, toward the anthropological and sociological. I like books that purport to be about sports but are actually about something else, something bigger than the game. Of course, I love everything Roger Angell has ever written for *The New Yorker* and genuflect to Frank Deford, John Feinstein, Michael Lewis, and the other giants of the genre. But rather than retread such hallowed ground, I thought I'd offer up some titles that readers might be less likely to stumble upon. To me, each of these books exposes something deeply fascinating, or deeply disturbing, about the sports we play (or once played) and the power they wield over us.

Games of the North American Indians by Stewart Culin

This 846-page, 1,000-illustration tome, published in 1907, captured a vast array of American Indian sports and games before they were silenced by conquest and assimilation. Culin got hooked on games after curating an exhibition on the world's diversions at Chicago's 1893 Columbian Exposition. Inspired, he spent the years from 1900 to 1905 traveling from one Indian reservation to the next, meticulously documenting the fast-vanishing games and sporting traditions of American Indians. In this time-traveling book (now available in part via Google Books), you can read about *chunkey*, a game played by the Creek and other southeastern tribes that involved throwing spears at a rolling stone disc, as well as shinny, double ball, foot-cast ball, and hot ball. And, of course, lacrosse—one of the few survivors.

Levels of the Game by John McPhee

Speaking of lacrosse, no author has written about that sport as lovingly and precisely as honorary "Lax Bro" John McPhee. But this is a guy who has written with equal insight and eloquence about basketball, nuclear science, the geology of the American West, and . . . tennis. *Levels of the Game* opens with the ball tossed for the serve and ends with the scoring of the winning point. In between, he probes and prods the backgrounds and psyches of opponents Arthur Ashe and Clark Graebner—black vs. white, liberal Democrat vs. conservative Republican, disenfranchised vs. enfranchised—as they battle it out at the 1968 U.S. Open semifinals. "Physical equipment being about equal," he writes, "the role of psychology becomes paramount, and each will play out his game within the fabric of his nature and his background."

Amen: Grassroots Football by Jessica Hilltout

If, after reading my book, you have any lingering doubt that the ball is central to the human experience, I urge you to view this collection of photographs. On the eve of the 2010 World Cup in South Africa, Hilltout traveled 15,000 kilometers across Africa, exchanging new soccer balls for homemade balls made of rags, plastic bags tied with twine, clay, and whatever else was lying around. One photo shows a ball from old rags stitched by some mother's loving hands—complete with hexagonal and pentagonal patterns. The caption reads, "Am I kicked, beaten, used, crushed and trampled? Or am I strong, resilient, determined, unbeaten, proud? I am both. I am proof that with so little we can do so much. I am proof that simple pleasures are enduring. I am a ball. I am an African ball." ▶

Recommended Reading *(continued)*

Among the Thugs by Bill Buford

On the other extreme—actually, on the extreme of the other extreme—I felt bruised and beaten when I finished Buford's gutsy, from-the-trenches account of England's soccer hooliganism in the 1980s. To me, at least, this is as much a book about soccer as any other written, though balls barely factor in and most of the action takes place in the dark alleys of England's working-class cities rather than on its stadium pitches. Buford's account of the lager-soaked Red soldiers of the Inter-City Jibbers is as riveting as it is hard to read. His confessions to the allure of mob violence are stunning. My favorite chapter is his description of tensions rising on the terraces of Cambridge's Abbey Stadium as the mob waits for a goal, hopes for catharsis, but gets only another scoreless draw: "Five shots. . . . And again, each time, the sheer physical sensation: I could feel everyone round me tightening up, like a spring, triggered for release. Except there was no release. There was no goal."

Paper Lion by George Plimpton

I once had the unlikely honor of shooting late-night pool with George Plimpton at his Upper East Side apartment. He was the consummate gentleman and not only let me win but refreshed my gin and tonic halfway through the game. I'd long been a devoted fan of his journalistic stints (or stunts, more like it) with various professional sports teams, my favorite being *Paper Lion*. Here, Plimpton recounts his experience in 1963 as a wannabe, third-string quarterback (number zero) with the Detroit Lions. As with his other ethnographic sporting forays—tennis with Pancho Gonzalez, sparring with Archie Moore, a month on the PGA Tour—he was way, way out of his league. But that was the point. With his unique, self-effacing wit, he broke through that soon-to-be-impenetrable barrier between hapless amateur and seasoned pro, spectator and player, and captured a sort-of-insider view of America's national game.

Buzkashi: Game and Power in Afghanistan
by G. Whitney Azoy

Admittedly, this is a totally obscure, academic read that will attract only the bravest of readers. But you've got to love a book that explores the cultural meaning of a sport involving bareback horsemen scoring goals with *headless, disemboweled, sand-filled goat carcasses*! Aside from being a fascinating analysis of the political importance of this bizarre sport, Azoy's account of his time among the herding tribes of Afghanistan in the 1970s inadvertently describes the cultural backdrop of the current conditions there as well as anything I've read. As one Afghan friend told Azoy back then, "If you want to know what we're really like, go to a buzkashi game."

Play Their Hearts Out
by George Dohrmann

This is one of the absolute best, absolute saddest sports books I've ever read. Dohrmann, a *Sports Illustrated* investigative reporter, made a deal with Amateur Athletic Union coach Joe Keller. The author would get full access to Keller's star middle-school players, which included Demetrius Walker, a kid glowingly described by the basketball press as "14 going on LeBron." Dohrmann, in return, promised not to publish anything until the boys were in college. The result is a disturbing but incredibly poignant exposé ▶

Recommended Reading *(continued)*

of everything that's wrong with the big-time youth sports machine. As extreme as this story is, shades of this same wrongness unfold on local fields and courts every week. Read this book and help stop the madness. ∽

Don't miss the next book by your favorite author. Sign up now for AuthorTracker by visiting www.AuthorTracker.com.